EXPLORATIONS

3

EXPLORATIONS

3

L. C. KNIGHTS

UNIVERSITY OF PITTSBURGH PRESS

First published in Great Britain 1976
by Chatto & Windus Ltd

Published in the U.S.A. 1976
by the University of Pittsburgh Press

Library of Congress Catalog Card Number 75–29654
ISBN 0–8229–1125–6

Printed in Great Britain by
Cox & Wyman Ltd,
London, Fakenham and Reading

ACKNOWLEDGEMENTS

These essays were prepared for a variety of purposes and are collected here from a number of books and journals. 'Literature and the Teaching of Literature' was my contribution to *I. A. Richards: Essays in his Honour*, edited by Reuben Brower, Helen Vendler and John Hollander (Copyright © 1973 by Oxford University Press, Inc., N.Y.). The essays on Henry James and on Blake appeared in the *Sewanee Review* (University of the South, Tennessee), 83 (Winter 1975) and 79 (Summer 1971). 'Coleridge as Critic' was written for *Coleridge's Variety: Bicentenary Studies*, edited by John Beer (Macmillan, 1974); the second piece on Coleridge appeared as a review in the *New York Review of Books*, XVI, 7, April 22, 1971 (Copyright © 1971, Nyrev, Inc.). 'Ben Jonson, Public Attitudes and Social Poetry' was given as a paper at an uncommonly rewarding conference at the University of Toronto to mark the 400th anniversary of Jonson's birth, and was published in *A Celebration of Ben Jonson*, edited by William Blissett, R. W. Van Fossen and Julian Patrick (University of Toronto Press, 1973), to which Jonas Barish, George Hibbard, Clifford Leech, D. F. McKenzie and Hugh Maclean also contributed: Professor Maclean's paper on 'The Wit of Jonson's Poetry' was a more comprehensive appraisal of the poems than my own, though in some ways complementary to it. 'All or Nothing: A Theme in John Donne' was my contribution to *William Empson: the Man and his Work*, edited by Roma Gill (Routledge and Kegan Paul, 1974). The essay on George Herbert appeared in my *Explorations* (Chatto & Windus, 1946). 'Shakespeare's Tragedies and the Question of Moral Judgment' is reprinted from *Shenandoah: The Washington and Lee University Review*, XIX, 3, Spring, 1968. 'The Thought of Shakespeare' was published in *The Hidden Harmony: Essays in Honour of Philip Wheelwright* (The Odyssey Press Inc., N.Y., 1966). *Timon of Athens* was one of the essays presented to G. Wilson Knight in *The Morality of Art*, edited by D. W. Jefferson (Routledge and Kegan Paul, 1969). The essay on *The Tempest* was written for *Shakespeare's Last Plays: Essays in Honour of Charles Crow*, edited by

229236

Richard Tobias (Ohio University Press, 1975). 'Shakespeare: Four Histories' is the oldest of the Shakespearian pieces collected here. Under the somewhat misleading title of *Shakespeare: The Histories* it was published in 1962 as No. 151 in the 'Writers and their Work' series, published for the British Council and the National Book League by Longman, Green & Co. Because of its antiquity, and because it handles ideas that I have publicly pondered in two essays in *Further Explorations* and in one chapter of *Public Voices* (Chatto & Windus, 1964 and 1971 respectively), I hesitated to include it here. But it does, I trust, stand by itself, besides supplementing what I have written elsewhere. I am glad to make acknowledgment to all concerned for permission to reprint these pieces.

L.C.K.
January 1975

CONTENTS

Literature
and the Teaching of Literature

(i)

IT IS DIFFICULT to say simply and sincerely why one 'teaches literature,' if only because this involves trying to say what literature is 'for.'* Literature does many different things; and on the whole, criticism and teaching are most fruitful and rewarding when they engage with a particular work, or group of works, leaving the sense of why engagement with this poem—or these novels and plays—is worth while to emerge in insights that are directly related to the works in hand.

There are times, however, when one needs to stand back from what one enjoys doing and attempt some answer to the question, Why? There are special reasons in these days for attempting a periodic stock-taking. Our awareness of 'the state of the world'—wars and the threat of wars, the squandering of natural resources, the struggle for mere subsistence and survival in so many countries, the steady drift towards bureaucratization in the 'developed' countries—can sometimes make any particular job in hand seem very small beer, tempting us to look for some panacea, some simple saving formula. And when we turn from the universal to, so to speak, the domestic—the job in hand of students of English literature—we can't hide from ourselves the existence, not far below the surface, of a particular kind of worry: the sense that there is just too much in English literature alone that we are expected to be knowledgeable about; the sense that the study of literature necessarily opens up towards a wide range of other intellectual interests—psychology, philosophy, social anthropology . . . Indeed I have the impression that some students—the more active-minded or

* This paper was originally prepared for a series on 'The Nature of Literature' in the English Faculty of the University of Cambridge. The series itself was in response to the prompting of the Joint (Staff/Student) Academic Committee where it was (rightly) pointed out that although there were many lectures on authors, aspects, etc., we—the staff—rarely said exactly why we thought our job worth while. It is in short the apologia of one teacher of English and is offered here as a tribute to a great teacher. I have kept the spoken form of a lecture.

more worried—want to push 'English' rather strongly in the direction of other kinds of enquiry simply because these seem (at a distance) to offer more widely embracing answers to the enormous questions of which we are inescapably aware. Even if I am wrong in supposing this, the fact that the study of literature is linked in many ways with other, non-literary, interests, sharpens the question I began by asking about the nature of literature and literary studies.

Answers to that question are necessarily personal. If I were forced to make a short summary statement of the function of literature—say in answer to an enquiring scientist who could honestly see no difference between poetry and push-pin (different pleasures for different people)— I should claim that literature is a form of knowledge, an irreplaceable way of arriving at truths that are of the highest importance to us if we are to remain, or try to become, adequately human. But why 'irreplaceable?' There are two answers. One is that the truths in question are difficult to come at, not only because of 'the veil of familiarity' that gets between us and the actuality of our world, but because they have to penetrate our subtle defences. As Camus said of Dostoevsky, 'he teaches us only what we know, but what we refuse to recognize'; and as Melville said of Shakespeare, 'All that we seek *and shun* is there.' The other is that truth, in this context, is not something that we receive or acquire by logical demonstration, but something that we live our way into through a complex, varying activity when we engage with formal verbal structures of a particular kind.

All this, however, is far too general. It is merely the staking of a claim for literature as a form of knowledge, and in order to validate that claim—even to make sense of it—we must start with something much simpler. What, if anything, is common to all our experience of what we intuitively recognize as significant in literature—in literature not as acquired culture, but as 'meaning something' to us? It is, surely, a spurt of intellectual energy that does not dissipate itself in momentary pleasure (though it is accompanied by pleasure), but that is both sign and function of an organizing power that holds in one focus a segment of experience or potential experience (maybe fairly simple, as in a short lyric; maybe panoramic, as in a great tragedy). And the consciousness thus energized, although it starts from and will return to *this* particular work, is not simply a consciousness of this work or of that, but— even for the sake of the particular work itself—will continually make connexions with other works and with our experience as a whole.

I have, I know, raised some very large questions and left them unanswered (there is that word, 'intellectual,' for example, which is intended to cover far more than the usual processes of intellection), and I shall consider some of them later. For the moment all I want to insist on is the energies of art—energies that can display themselves in the smallest of ways as well as in the depth and scope of the great master-pieces. I am in a quandary here because my statement demands demon-stration, and demonstration would take far too long. Fortunately I can fall back on reminding you of what you already know. Consider your experience of reading poems—poems, I mean, that immediately or after some time seem to you 'worth while.' You may begin with an undifferentiated feeling of pleasure (or, for that matter of bafflement); but as you get to know a particular poem in depth you are likely to find there is something that prevents the mind skating easily over the sur-face, that insists on it doing some work for itself. It may be a latent conflict between two words brought into conjunction, as in Wordsworth's description of London as 'a sight so *touching* in its *majesty*,' where you have a microcosm of the paradoxes so unobtrusively built into the poem. It may be a not easily assimilable phrase:

My thoughts are all a case of knives,
    Wounding my heart
    With scatter'd smart,
As watring pots give flowers their lives.

George Herbert's mental wounds are felt as a scattering (not a single isolated impact), like the many tiny streams from the rose of a watering-can: that is simple enough. But they don't 'give life' to the poet's heart: far from it. Behind the phrase, however, lurks the so far unexpressed idea that they *ought* to, that perhaps 'those powers, which work for grief' *can* 'enter God's pay.' To turn over in one's mind the rather com-plicated simile within a metaphor is to reach a new level of under-standing of the movement from disintegration to integration that Herbert's *Affliction*, (*iv*) so powerfully expresses. The demands made on us may of course be of a different kind—to let filaments of sugges-tion play across from one part of the poem to another, to see if they do in fact cohere and, if so, why the whole is so much greater than the sum of its parts. I could demonstrate my point here by giving a lecture on Shakespeare's Sonnets. I will content myself with a quotation or two from Stephen Booth's recent book, *An Essay on Shakespeare's Sonnets*. Booth makes a detailed—and helpful—analysis of the different patterns of structure—formal, logical, syntactical, rhetorical, phonetic—to be found in the Sonnets. It is through these, and the complex ways in which they interact, he says, that 'the mind of the reader is kept in constant motion.' 'The shifting of the contexts in which the reader takes the meaning of a given word is like (other) sonnet characteristics . . . in that, in making the shift from one context to another, the reader's mind is required constantly to act.' Of the justly famous Sonnet 60 ('Like as the waves make towards the pebbled shore . . .'), where meanings from the world of ineluctable natural law at large, the daily and seasonal movement of heavenly bodies, and the life of man, overlap and fuse, Booth says: 'He (the reader) is not conscious of all the fleeting connections his mind makes, but his mind presumably makes them all the same. The nature of the substance before him is never fixed until the last lines, and the energy expended by the reader in moving from one pattern to another transmits urgency to the poem itself.' I don't want to give the impression, however, that the appeal to the reader to wake up and keep his wits about him is confined to obviously complex and 'difficult' poems, like Shakespeare's Sonnets and Donne's 'Songs and Sonets.' Simple-seeming poems can make similar demands. You have only to consider two short, much-anthologized poems—Wordsworth's 'A slumber did my spirit seal' and Frost's 'The Pasture'—to see what a formidable weight of meaning 'simplicity' can bear—when the reader is prepared to collaborate. As Charles Olson puts it,—'A poem is energy transferred from where the poet got it . . ., by way of the poem itself to, all the way over to, the reader. Okay. Then the poem itself must, at all points, be a high energy-construct and, at all points, an energy discharge.'[1] (This, incidentally, applies *mutatis mutandis* to all the arts: Francis Bacon, for example, refers to pictorial art as 'an energy system.')

The first purpose of all the devices of poetry,* then, is to activate the reader's mind in particular ways. This is obviously true of metaphor and imagery, whose powers of suggestion we often have to explore a very long way (taking care indeed not to overstep the bounds determined by the context of the work as a whole, not to explore in modes that the context declares inappropriate). It is true of rhythm, which Theodore Roethke once called 'the chief clue to the energy of the psyche.' It is true of the very sound of verse (or prose), when this is what Frost called 'the sound of sense,' determining tone, and therefore meaning, in ways that it would be impossible to determine otherwise: that is one reason why it is so important to read poetry aloud.

What is true of the parts is true of the larger structural devices of the long poem, the play or the novel. The writer puts this episode into relation with that, he puts this character into relation with that, he keeps alive a particular series of connotations in description or imagery; and in doing so he invites the reader to think about the possible significance of those connexions, contrasts, comparisons, and so on. There's no need here to take up the well-known (perhaps overworked) question of interlocking patterns of imagery in, say, Shakespeare's plays. And perhaps two simple examples will serve as a reminder of the way in which the mere placing of particular episodes or passages by the dramatist invites us to use our wits to discover what the connexion is intended

* If 'devices' is the word, for it suggests something more deliberate and contrived than is always the case.

to be. In *Henry V*, why—we ask ourselves—are there two sharply contrasting accounts of the battle of Crecy, one from the English and one from the French point of view? And why is Henry's martial rhetoric in the earlier parts of the play balanced and contrasted later by the Duke of Burgundy's noble eulogy of peace? Is it merely that his country has been defeated, and he has to negotiate what terms he can? Examples of episodes that demand to be connected in our minds once we attend to what lies behind both 'plot' and 'character' could be endlessly multiplied.

In the novel—that large loose term—the modes of appeal to the active intelligence are as many and various as they are in poetic drama. They range from the disposition of fictive events and persons round whatever it is that most engages the author's interest (a disposition we usually call the plot, and may carelessly dismiss as 'mere' narrative) to unobtrusive promptings in setting and circumstance which, when we notice them, we usually dignify with some such description as 'symbolic.' Here again there is an enormous range of possible effects, from the description of the female whales with their young in *Moby Dick* to the attention given to the various houses in which the destiny of Isabel Archer is worked out in *The Portrait of a Lady*. Everything in a good novel calls on us to make connexions, especially to the overriding interest or theme that dawns on us when the forward linear movement of our attention turns back on itself to ask what it is all *about*.[2] But we only do that—as in play or poem—when the writing, here and here, demands the fullness of our attention and rewards it with a quickened consciousness.

Very obviously, 'close analysis' won't tell us all we need to know about, say, long prose fictions. But consider a simple example. Read carefully the opening paragraph of Chapter 74 of *Middlemarch* ('In Middlemarch a wife could not long remain ignorant that the town held a bad opinion of her husband . . .'), and ask yourself whether the analysis of what can sometimes lurk behind the big words of moral approval, 'candour,' 'love of truth,' 'ardent charity,' could have been undertaken without the author's power of vivid dramatic enactment in a prose where every shift of the rhythm is an invitation to see something you hadn't seen. Certainly George Eliot could not have expressed one of her major preoccupations—the sense that there is no private life that is not intimately bound up with 'a wider public life'—unless she were capable of the vivacity of the passage I have referred to. Without that she must inevitably (in her own words) have lapsed 'from the picture to the diagram.' 'Vivacity'—under that large umbrella I include the effect of *all* animating elements in an author's style, down to minutiae that may well work on us without our full conscious awareness but that it sometimes pays off to look at rather closely. A recent fairly detailed study of linguistic forms in the later work of Henry James[3] amply justifies the praise of Vernon Lee fifty years ago. 'With what definiteness this man sees his way through the vagueness of personal motives and opinions, and with what directness and vigour he forces our thought along with him!' Our extended psychological perception is the result of 'this strong, varied, co-ordinated activity forced on to our mind.' This, I may add, follows an account of 'the splendid variety, co-ordination, and activity of the verbal tenses' in a passage from *The Ambassadors*.[4] But of course nothing like this would be worth our while unless we had already *felt* that the writer had something important to say.

You see I am following, however clumsily, in the steps of Coleridge. Almost always, when he has occasion to touch on the primary distinguishing marks of literature, he comes back to the energy and activity of mind that it demands from, and excites in, the reader. And the imagination—we can no longer avoid the word—is not only a form of energy, it is an ordering and unifying power. This, I am afraid, must remain unsupported by anything beyond an appeal to your own experience: we are all familiar—if only through our failures—with 'the great instinct of the human mind, the striving towards unity,' the need to bring different parts of our experience, different parts of our personalities, into relationship. (I. A. Richards' chapter on 'The Imagination' in *Principles* stays in the mind, even if he has now rejected the psychological terminology he then used.) The refreshment that we feel after reading a good poem comes partly from a kind of clarification—more, perhaps, than 'a momentary stay against confusion'—in which we see, and feel, hitherto-unperceived relationships. And this applies equally to the shortest lyric ('The Pasture,' 'A slumber did my spirit seal'), and to a great novel or a great tragedy (*The Portrait of a Lady, King Lear*). We are again coming close to the question of literary form, for it is through a particular form that we are enabled to see—we are, as it were, drawn into—a particular kind of order. (To quote Vernon Lee again: 'FORM is not merely something we perceive; it is something which determines our mode of perception and reaction.'[5]) That, however, is too big a question to be dealt with here. All I would say is that in talking about the ordering process which—as well as being an energizing process—any work of literature *is*, I want to avoid the suggestion of a static order, of something settled once and for all: questioning, reaching out for possible further meanings, the yielding of provisional assent and readiness to qualify our assent—these are all part of our 'appreciation' of literature. A sense of order, coherence, comes early in our understanding of any poem; but it is not an order we rest on: rather it is a sense of growth, of a *direction* of consciousness that is still capable of new assimilation, either on a fresh reading or when fresh experience (literary

or non-literary) alters the mutual interaction of the poem and the rest of
our known world.

(ii)

The end of that last sentence contained some large assumptions which
it is time to make explicit. How *does* poetry, literature, affect that large
part of our experience which is not the reading of literature? In a review
of the recent reissue of Coleridge's *The Friend*,[6] I. A. Richards quoted
with disapproval from a twentieth-century writer: 'Literature is an
individual matter and should be valued, not for its moral or intellectual
influences, but simply for what it is.' As Richards went on to say, this
is merely putting up No Trespass boards. Coleridge—with his life-long
attempt to bring all sides of human life, all aspects of the mind, into
relation—was the last man to set up a special isolated province
of 'aesthetic appreciation.' And yet there is a sense in which the
remark could be interpreted in a proper, a Coleridgean, sense. In
our dealings with literature there are no short cuts; moralistic, political
or pedagogic simplifications have to be repelled. All the same, it is
because we value literature for what it is essentially—and, I may
add, only when we value each work in its irreplaceable uniqueness—
that we can see what place it has in the life of the personality as a
whole, what, to put it crudely, its uses—moral, educational and even
political—are.

I said earlier that literature is a form of knowledge, and I have tried
to suggest that the knowledge it brings to being in the reader is a
complex, ordering, *activity*: without that responsive activity there is no
knowledge. And surely it is obvious that if this is so, to define *how*
literature works is to indicate something of its uses, its value. It is, as
Rosalind said, not good to be a post; and although experience suggests
some caution here, it is at least possible to hope that to exercise new
modes of awareness in reading is to strengthen them for use elsewhere.
It was in discussing Wordsworth's poetry that Coleridge noted 'the
advantage which language . . . presents to the instructor of impressing
modes of intellectual energy . . . so as to secure in due time the formation of a second nature'; and among 'the beneficial after-effects of verbal
precision' he included 'the preclusion of fanaticism, which masters the
feelings more especially by indistinct watch-words.' Here, at one jump,
is a connexion between poetry and politics. As for the ordering or
relating that goes on when we read poetry, it is even more difficult to
define and illustrate a carry-over from habits acquired in reading to the
habits of everyday living: some of us are moderately successful readers
of poetry, but still have areas of confusion in the backyards of our emotional life! But from our acquaintance with literature we at least have
some idea of what it means to move towards completeness, some

15

standards against which to check the unruly and the out of kilter.* The idea of a carry-over of this kind needs looking at in some detail by someone equally familiar with psychology and literature. But surely it isn't merely fiction in the pejorative sense, when, at the end of *The Idea of Order at Key West*, the listener to the girl's song is able to see a more meaningful pattern in what might have been a mere jumble of lights. It is because of the song that

> the glassy lights,
> The lights in the fishing boats at anchor there,
> As the night descended, tilting in the air,
> Mastered the night and portioned out the sea,
> Fixing emblazoned zones and fiery poles,
> Arranging, deepening, enchanting night.

I have already referred to George Herbert's *Affliction* (*iv*)—the poem that begins, 'Broken in pieces all asunder.' In living through that poem we have at least recognized the possibility of achieving some kind of integrity, of putting chaos in its proper place by facing it with courage and resource.

So much for the mental activity, kindled in our reading of literature, that can (perhaps) enter into our everyday knowing. But what is it that literature gives us direct knowledge of? In a sense the question is foolish, and the only answer is—of all those things that authors have written about: go and read as much as you can! But I have offered to be simple, and must now take the risk of simplification—which means reminding you of a handful of platitudes that are not less true for being obvious. Literature offers a particular kind of knowledge of the self, of what is not self (whether nature or neighbour), and of the relations between self and not-self; not that these are distinct and water-tight categories.

The ways in which literature offers opportunities for self-knowledge are of course legion. They include the invitation by the novelist or dramatist to assess different attitudes, presented with a far higher degree of specific realization than is possible if we use only the descriptive terms of moral discussion.[7] Consider how many different shades of 'egotism,' of aggression overt or disguised, are to be found in English fiction alone. And in following the presented 'case,' always of course with an engaged and lively sense of the particular pressures that make it what it is, and obtaining fresh lights from the particular set of

* As Elinor Shaffer, summarizing Kant, remarks: 'Our destination (by which Kant means the spiritual end of the race, or in Christian terms, immortality) is pointed out through art, but cannot be accomplished through it. Its reality depends on moral action.'—'Coleridge's Theory of Aesthetic Interest,' *Journal of Aesthetics and Art Criticism*, 27, Summer 1969, p. 4.

relations in which it is presented, we not only realize 'what human beings can be like,' but what we ourselves are capable of being and most want to be, or not to be. I have of course made the whole process sound too cut and dried. In reading literature a good deal seems to go on outside the area of clearly focused consciousness, in what Coleridge called the 'region of unconscious thoughts, oftentimes the more working the more indistinct they are.'*

As for the role of literature in relation to society; this is a topic for a series of discussions rather than a mere paragraph. Obviously literature 'extends our sympathies,' as Shelley pointed out in a notable passage of *A Defence of Poetry*. It can also help in a unique way in our understanding of different social forms and relationships. I don't mean that literature, unchecked by other sources, can often—or ever—be taken as straight documentation in the interests of social or cultural history. What it can do is to offer specific instances of social pressures and inter-relationships that have a 'spread' of implication outside the particular historical situations into which they are projected (e.g. Jane Austen's novels). And it can offer insights into social modes of which we may have no direct experience—the independence of the Lakeland 'statesmen' that we sense in *The Prelude*, the strange blend of squalor, brutality, and the thrusting up of new life and kindness in unexpected places that we are vividly made aware of (even in translation) in the first volume of Gorky's Autobiography. In *Villette* Charlotte Brontë is strong when she renders the feel of psychological undernourishment, of what it means—as we say so glibly—to be lonely; and because of this she can throw light on a whole social class—that of the unmarried woman of the nineteenth century, with inadequate means of support and a cruelly limited choice of careers. The point, of course, is that the artist does not deal with 'society' in the abstract, or with what can be documented, counted and assessed from the outside. With his 'passion for the special case,' he gives us the feel of social pressures; it is his ability to render with 'the freshness, raciness and energy of immediate observation' (to borrow Johnson's phrase) that compels us to live through the presented experience: he adds a dimension to our social understanding. Not of course (and this could equally well have been

---

* *Biographia Literaria* II, 250. No one who knows Coleridge will read this as a plea for vagueness where precision is necessary; it is simply a reminder that although knowledge demands thought, thought itself can have an antecedent phase in feeling, which in turn is related both to the sub-conscious and to the organic processes of the body: the poetry of self-discovery has reverberations along the whole range. See D. W. Harding, 'The Hinterland of Thought' (in *Experience into Words*); and, for thought and feeling as different 'phases' of a continuous process, Susanne K. Langer, *Mind: an Essay on Human Feeling* (1967), Vol. I.

said earlier) that he comes up with any 'solutions.' In October 1888, Chekhov wrote to a friend:

> You are right to require a conscious attitude from the artist to-wards his work, but you mix up two ideas: *the solution of the problem and a correct presentation of the problem.* Only the latter is obligatory for the artist. In *Anna Karenina* and *Onegin* not a single problem is solved, but they satisfy you completely just because all their problems are correctly presented. The court is obliged to submit the case fairly, but let the jury do the deciding, each according to its own judgment. . . .[8]

The social function of literature has further reaches to which I can only give a few sentences. The artist is often a radical questioner of his society. But literature and the study of literature are not only disturbing (they won't let us settle down on the assumptions of the majority, or even on those of the enlightened group to which we may happen to belong), they are also conservative and traditional. The paradox is more apparent than real. It is often by being confronted with ways of thought and feeling very different from our own (in medieval literature, for example) that we gain a new perspective on the present. We all know by now that the demand for 'relevance'—for what is immediately and on the short view relevant—can be misleading.[9]

The artist is a radical questioner of states of affairs for the same reason that, in writing, he hates clichés.[10] The language of the imagination and the language of the stereotype in which we do so much of our thinking are polar opposites. 'Poetry is the renewal of words for ever and ever.' That sentence—which comes from Robert Frost, but other poets have told us the same—points clearly enough to the connexion between 'imaginative literature' and the conduct of public affairs, something which still—in spite of the computers—needs the medium of language, as I recently tried to suggest in *Public Voices.* The case was forcibly put by Ezra Pound forty years ago (in *How to Read*), and there is no need to repeat it here. It isn't, I think, invalidated by what is rather loosely referred to as the current 'retreat from the word.' In 1905 Henry James, addressing the students of Bryn Mawr on 'The Question of Our Speech,' remarked:

> We may not be said to be able to study—and *a fortiori* do any of the things we study *for*—unless we are able to speak. All life therefore comes back to the question of our speech, the medium through which we communicate with each other; for all life comes back to the question of our relations with each other. These relations are made possible, are registered, are verily constituted, by our speech.

In public as in personal affairs we need to remember Whitehead's dictum: 'Style is the ultimate morality of mind.'[11]

(iii)

In trying to define some of the things that literature does and that we value it for, I have at least partially indicated my view of how it should be 'taught.' Literature does many things. The teaching of literature must be correspondingly varied and flexible. If literature only works by calling on a particular kind of intellectual energy in each reader, then the main business of those who offer to talk about literature is to help others, each in his own way, to direct and sharpen attention, and, I would add, to make relevant connexions. Attention is an active process, constantly reaching out and assimilating, first and foremost within this particular work, then within the work, the *œuvre,* of a writer as a whole, then within a body of work—a 'kind' or a tradition, and then within the developing life of individual minds that are likely to have many other intellectual interests besides purely literary ones: say history or psychology or the study of contemporary society.

What this means is that the teaching of literature calls for a variety of approaches. It is enough, but it is essential, that the ones we use should be directed towards the common aim of awakening the mind and suggesting to it the possibilities of self-direction and of self-discipline. Here I shall only touch briefly on two matters—the question of scholarship and the question of practical criticism—that, as a teacher, I have had to think about.

What has to be said about scholarship, if we confine our attention to the undergraduate level, is obvious enough. The student needs to acquire in an orderly and methodical way such knowledge, linguistic, historical, and so on—and it may be pretty considerable—as will enable him to make more fully his own the works that are the main objects of his attention. The only knowledge worth having is of the actively assimilative kind. The acquiring of information is *for* something, and in literary studies it is for the finer understanding and enjoyment of literature.

It is at the 'higher' levels that the problems become acute. Literary scholarship—indispensable as it is, and much as we owe to the great scholars—has its dangers. I am not now referring to the kind of scholarly industry that Edmund Wilson savaged in the later years of his life; though I am concerned when I read of a centennial edition of *Moby Dick* that its 315 pages of notes and apparatus—more than half as long as the novel itself—was made a matter of congratulation: 'No other American novel has ever received such liberal annotation.'* This sort

* I have lost my reference to the setting of this jewel. I think it was pointed out to me by my friend, the late Stanley Edgar Hyman.

of thing is of course related to the whole system of graduate training in research which, in some parts of the world, is effectively obscuring what a future university teacher of English ought to be doing to equip himself. It is of 'scholarly' training of this kind—'training in the administration of a vast body . . . of facts, comments, opinions, and mere phrases'—that I. A. Richards has said:

> It may fit (a man) to continue as a specialized researcher—within areas or on 'points' with no known relevance to any side of the world crisis. It quite evidently does not give him what he needs as a teacher of the humanities—reasonably rich and considered views of a person's relations to other persons. . . . It is preventing us from supplying our greatest need—teachers able to help humanity to remain humane.[12]

As long ago as 1903 William James—referring, it is true, to conditions somewhat different from our own—delivered a lecture at Harvard on what he called 'The Ph.D Octopus.'[13] The brute has grown since then, and has developed global ambitions. I am not for a moment belittling the work that very many graduate students in English are now doing. Nor am I saying anything so foolishly simple as, 'Abolish the Ph.D.' What I am saying is that among graduate students as I have known them over thirty-five years, there have been some with a coiled spring inside them, something that urged them towards a book they *wanted* to write. There have been others, equally intelligent and of equal potential, not yet ready to begin on a substantial 'contribution to knowledge'—however widely we may define that phrase. The result is a groping around for 'subjects' and the direction of young energies into channels which—whatever incidental benefits accrue—are not, for them, at this stage, the real right thing. To find the real right thing for those who show the necessary aptitude, and who need two or three more years after the B.A. in which to equip themselves to teach in universities, colleges of education, polytechnics etc., seems to me one of the most important tasks that Faculties in the Humanities have to face, if only because we are not only training scholars, we are (we hope) educating the educators of the future. William James said that what *made* a university was the presence of 'a few men, at least, who are real geniuses,' what he called 'the untameables.'[14] I agree about that need. But most of us are not geniuses; and in the context of what I have just said, it seems to me evident that among other necessary attributes of a university is a concern for the whole spectrum of education. An exclusive preoccupation with advancing this or that particular specialism (and again I exclude the few 'real geniuses,' who will go their way regardless) does nothing to foster that outward-looking concern; it merely strengthens professionalism.

As for the question of Practical Criticism: active engagement with particular works without too much fumbling and irrelevance still seems to me the basis of all literary study. All the same, here too there are some dangers. Anton Ehrenzweig, in *The Hidden Order of Art*, speaks of the importance for the painter of periods of relaxed and almost unconscious 'scanning'; Maritain, in *Creative Intuition in Art and Poetry*, has a chapter on the genesis of a poem in 'a kind of (wordless) musical stir' in the depths of the mind; Osip Mandelstam (according to his widow Nadezhda Mandelstam, in *Hope Against Hope*) insisted that 'a poem begins with a musical phrase ringing insistently in the ears';[15] other poets have told us much the same. Readers, like artists and poets, need the capacity for relaxed and attentive *listening*. Practical Criticism, explication, *can* become an externalizing routine, inhibiting that listening, even without the aid of all those books and articles that offer to do' your explication for you. The wrong kind of insistence on this necessary activity can in fact prevent what it sets out to do. It can inhibit the intuitive response to literature, which can't always easily be verbalized; it can produce unnecessary feelings of inferiority in the student who is afraid of making mistakes (mistakes are part of our growth), or who is over-anxious to produce something obviously clever and acceptable; and in—rightly—directing attention to *this* poem or *this* passage, it can have the effect of unduly narrowing the range of reading which is an essential part of an education in English. As Wordsworth said in his 'Reply to Mathetes' (in Coleridge's *The Friend*), speaking of the dangers of relying too exclusively on an admired and forceful teacher:

> In spite of his (the teacher's) caution, remarks may drop insensibly from him which shall wither in the mind of his pupil a generous sympathy, destroy a sentiment of approbation or dislike, not merely innocent but salutary; and for the inexperienced disciple how many pleasures may be thus cut off . . . whilst in their stead are introduced into the ingenuous mind misgivings, a mistrust of its own evidence, disposition to affect to feel where there can be no real feeling, indecisive judgments, a superstructure of opinions that has no base to support it. . . .

The appropriate calling of Youth (Wordsworth went on) 'is not to distinguish in fear of being deceived or degraded, not to analyse with scrupulous minuteness, but to accumulate in genial confidence.' We may disagree with some of this, but the tenor is sound. The problem is how to combine—how to encourage the combining—of analysis in (sometimes) scrupulous minuteness with an outgoing, exploratory 'accumulation in genial confidence.' With which we are back to the very obvious truth that where Practical Criticism is concerned—the education of basic skills in interpretation and response—everything depends on the tact of the teacher—his awareness of and respect for his pupils as persons, with different gifts and different rates of growth, and almost all of them with something to teach *him*.

There are many other problems in the teaching of English at university level and the arrangement of university courses in English: notably the relation of literary study to other disciplines, other fields of intellectual interest and enquiry. The question is a large one, and no universally applicable solution is in sight. Perhaps all we can do for the moment is to recognize that there *is* a problem. Whitehead was right when in 1938 he said, 'The increasing departmentalization of Universities during the last hundred years, however necessary for administrative purposes, tends to trivialize the mentality of the teaching profession.'[16] No 'subject' can be entirely isolated from other 'subjects': cross-fertilization is necessary, and something that a university exists to promote. How, when there is so much to be read in English literature alone, when English students—like their teachers—have to protect themselves from a morbid and paralysing sense of all they have *not* read, how can real cross-fertilization take place in a mere three or four years? Different universities are trying to tackle this problem in different ways. My own conviction is expressed by another remark of Whitehead's to the effect that 'rightness of limitation is essential for the growth of reality,' though he also said elsewhere, 'We must be systematic, but we should keep our systems open.'[17] An education in English has its own discipline: when a man is aware of *that*, when he knows when something is being said effectively and not merely gestured towards, then the more lively interests he has, the better for his literary studies. Insights can play across from one's reading in, say, history or psychology; but one must be careful not to force connexions, and the fact remains that there are no short cuts to the kind of knowledge that literature offers. Formal interdisciplinary work can, and I think ought to, be encouraged at the post-graduate level, where it would inevitably have an effect on other levels. Before that (assuming that premature specialization has not got a complete stranglehold in the schools), it seems best to start from a centre—the study of literature—and to open what perspectives one can as opportunity offers.

I return briefly to the large question of what literature is *for*. I hope it won't be assumed, because the word 'enjoyment' has appeared so rarely in this paper, that I regard the study of literature as a grimly solemn strengthening of the moral fibres. I take it for granted that much of what we value in literature is a celebration of the richness and variety of life. Not all literature—I would say, very little—is a simple celebration, a simple act of praise. But in all literature we value what Yeats named when he spoke of Blake's 'joyous intellectual energy.' We are shy of speaking of joy, but we need to use the word, even when speaking of tragedy; for it is through literature—even, and perhaps above all, through great tragedy—that the mind comes to know—to know by exercising—its own powers. Power and imaginative energy, however, are—there is no escaping it—correlatives of discipline. Only artists can speak with full authority of the discipline of their art. Those of us whose function it is to teach, to transmit, and to prompt to see, can however properly speak of the discipline of literary study. It is of course discipline for the sake of freedom—what Coleridge, in an early poem, called 'a livelier impulse and a dance of thought.' But freedom in this context —the ability to use creatively what has been acquired as knowledge or imaginative insight—is only possible for the mind that knows at first hand the discipline of concentration. Whitehead, in a telling phrase, speaks of 'the rhythmic claims of freedom and discipline.'[18] What that means each of us—teacher and pupil, teacher *with* pupil—has to discover for himself. What perhaps we may all agree on—even those of us who don't like to wave our banners too violently or too often—is that the final aim of literary study is nothing less than to set free and to foster the energies of the imagination, without which not only will our individual consciousness be less full and active than it might have been, but our collective life will be the mere 'efficient' mechanism—structured over vast areas of violent unreason—that it is in danger of becoming today.

Henry James and Human Liberty

(i)

HENRY JAMES'S reaction to the start of the First World War is well known. On August 5, 1914, he continued a letter to Howard Sturgis that he had begun the day before:

> The taper went out last night, and I am afraid I now kindle it again to a very feeble ray—for it's vain to try to talk as if one weren't living in a nightmare of the deepest dye. How can what is going on not be to one as a huge horror of blackness? . . . The plunge of civilization into this abyss of blood and darkness by the wanton feat of two infamous autocrats is a thing that so gives away the whole long age during which we have supposed the world to be, with whatever abatement, gradually bettering, that to have to take it all now for what the treacherous years were all the while really making for and *meaning* is too tragic for any words.

A few days later, to another correspondent, he referred again to 'the awful tide of the Great Interruption':

> This last (he said) is as mild a name for the hideous matter as one can consent to give—and I confess I live under the blackness of it as under a funeral pall of our murdered civilization . . . I find it such a mistake on my own part to have lived on—when, like other saner and safer persons, I might perfectly have not—into this unspeakable give-away of the whole fool's paradise of our past. It throws back so livid a light—*this* was what we were so fondly working for![1]

Even in the face of such horrors James could summon up courage and resource ('I hold we can still . . . *make* a little civilization, the inkpot aiding, even when vast chunks of it, around us, go down into the abyss . . . the preservation of it depends upon our going on making it in spite of everything and sitting tight and not chucking up'); but the man of 1914 seems more than a mere three or four decades removed from the young American who had so eagerly embraced the experience of 'Europe', who had indeed regarded 'a position in society' as 'a legitimate object of ambition'.[2] In the intervening years James, it is true, having achieved that position, had become more and more sharply critical of 'society': in 1886 the condition of the English upper class had seemed to him 'to be in many ways very much the same rotten and *collapsible* one as that of the French aristocracy before the revolution— minus cleverness and conversation; or perhaps it's more like the heavy, congested and depraved Roman world upon which the barbarians came down'.[3] But even to those who constantly return to his work—as to James himself in 1914—there may seem to be a gap between the novels and stories and the great public events that 'the treacherous years were all the while really making for'; they may fail to see the fundamental relation between his work and what we fondly call the larger issues,—the massive pressures that produce, now as then, the major crises and catastrophes.

James is indeed, as Conrad called him, 'the historian of fine consciences'. But the phrase (supported though it is by so much that can be extracted from the Prefaces, and applied to the fiction) will mislead unless we keep in mind other important truths: that, as James well knew, 'consciences' only exist in relationships ('all life', he told the students of Bryn Mawr, 'comes back to the question of our relations with each other'); that, as T. S. Eliot put it, 'the real hero, in any of James's stories, is a social entity'; and that the depiction of these social entities—even though these are far from being microcosms of the world at large—returns again and again to something that violently distorts the texture of our collective life, to corrosions of relationship and misdirections of human energies that make 'civilization' the precarious thing it is. It was in the course of World War II that D. W. Harding (in *The Impulse to Dominate*) reminded us that war itself is not something that simply *happens* to a society: it is a cultural product, deeply rooted in the patterns of domination and submission in our everyday life: 'For social relationships within the family provide the paradigm for every adult social relationship, including war'. More recently Erik Erikson has remarked:

> Families in which each member is separated from the others by asbestos walls of verbal propriety, overt sweetness, cheap frankness, and rectitude tell one another off and talk back to each other with minute and unconscious displays of affect—not to mention physical complaints and bodily ailments—with which they worry, accuse, undermine, and murder one another.[4]

If this is so, if the troubles and horrors that make the headlines are in fact related to the minutiae of daily life—and I do not see that we can avoid the truth of it—we do well to give our keenest attention to what a great writer can tell us about the ways in which members of small social groups do their—not necessarily conspicuous—undermining and murdering. In an essay on James published three years after the novelist's death, Ezra Pound, with his usual acuteness, went to the heart of the matter.

> I am tired of hearing pettiness talked about Henry James's style. The subject has been discussed enough in all conscience, along with the minor James. Yet I have heard no word of the major James, of the hater of tyranny; book after early book against oppression, against all the sordid petty personal crushing oppression, the domination of modern life . . . The outbursts in *The Tragic Muse*, the whole of *The Turn of the Screw*, human liberty, personal liberty, the rights of the individual against all sorts of intangible bondage! The passion of it, the continual passion of it in this man who, fools said, didn't 'feel' . . . This holds (Pound added in a footnote), despite anything that may be said of his fuss about social order, social tone. I naturally do not drag in political connotations, from which H. J. was, we believe, wholly exempt. What he fights is 'influence', the impinging of family pressure, the impinging of one personality on another; all of them in highest degree damn'd, loathsome and detestable.[5]

Domination is a major—though of course far from exclusive—theme in James; and although he is certainly not the only English novelist to treat intimate and damaging inter-personal pressures (one has only to think of Jane Austen, George Eliot and Ivy Compton-Burnett), his handling of the theme has not yet, it seems to me, had the explicit recognition that it demands. To suggest the variety and subtlety of that handling is the purpose of this paper.

This is not—to anticipate a possible objection—a moralistic approach. James's own phrase, 'the imagination of the moralist'—the 'greater imagination' which he said his admired Daudet lacked—serves to remind us that we are not dealing with any kind of didactic morality, but with something much more profound, that shows itself in the life—the livingness—of a work of art; we are concerned with what Pound called 'the amount of perceptive energy' concentrated in the major works. And since perceptive energy shows itself in the handling of the language, our pursuit of a particular theme demands a lively concern with particular words in particular arrangements. When we are attending to James's moral concerns we are—or ought to be—well out of the world of moral generalities; the question is always one of the degree of realization of the situations that James chose to study. And the effective presentation of each case—the extent indeed to which it ceases to be a mere 'case' and reaches out into life at large—depends on a particular kind of presentation in which the author does not simply tell, but prompts to see.

Seymour Chatman, in *The Later Style of Henry James*, remarks that 'it is difficult to understand why critics insist so frequently that James is always and only an author who *shows*, not *tells*'; and of course it is true, as Chatman demonstrates, that even when James is deliberately avoiding 'the platitude of statement' and reflecting his story indirectly through the mind of a particular character, his very choice of word and sentence structure reveals the author's system of values. My point is simply that, very emphatically, the medium is the message, and that our only way of getting at the kind and quality of the presented experience is through the wonderfully varying medium through which James chooses to present it. A very simple example is Count Vogelstein's account of America and Americans in *Pandora*—a short story which belongs to the 'international' series, and is very funny—where the Count's way of speaking, of thinking, reveals a mind bent on imposing a pattern and marshalling his 'observed' facts to suit it. A slightly more subtle example is the language of the narrator in *The Aspern Papers*—the predatory literary man hell-bent on prying loose from a very old woman the love letters that she had from a famous poet in the early years of the century, who finds it 'odious . . . to stand chaffering with Aspern's Juliana' (i.e.—about the price of rooms he wants to hire in her house), and who, as he sniffs and calculates, feels 'even a mystic companionship, a moral fraternity with all those who in the past had been in the service of art.' James doesn't tell us that the 'literary' atmosphere is sometimes very oppressive; it is enough that the language of his narrator has a very fish-like smell. Even when the theme is most clear and direct (as in, say, *Washington Square*, to which I shall return) we get at it—only, indeed, know what it is—through *style*, through a particular tone and manner, either of the presented character or of the author in presenting. As James develops, the elements demanding attention multiply—tone, metaphor, the calling up of a particular setting, the description of slight, almost unnoticed, actions; there's virtually nothing that isn't used, compellingly used, in the interests of a shaping idea. Even when, after the unsuccessful attempt at play-writing, James is most insistent in advising himself to 'dramatise, dramatise', when he follows as closely as possible the method of 'scenic' presentation in order to achieve something of the compression of drama, it is still in the *forms* of speech in dialogue (as well, of course, as in the 'substance' of the thing said) or in the particular cast of a character's self-communings, that we have to seek our clues. It is in fact the development of an unusually complex manner of presentation that makes us face the question whether we have to deal with some obscurity in the author's own mind or with something very different—namely, a human situation represented so fully in particular aspects that we can only recognize the theme as embedded in the ambiguities and the final 'unknowableness' of other lives: whether James is allowing himself an excessive preoccupation with 'style', or whether the style is not, as Chatman puts it, 'an attempt to catch the mind at work, in all its uncertainty, indeed assuming uncertainty to be its normal lot'. The first words of *Louisa Pallant* are, 'Never say you know the last word about any human heart'. I am not suggesting that we should accept with a dazzled awe all James's obliquities and indirections, or that in the end we shan't be left with very different individual valuations of some important novels. I am merely saying that in these novels and stories the theme of domination is an intricate one—part of what James, in *The Spoils of Poynton*, calls 'the tangle of life', which the simplifying Mrs Gereth slashes into 'with a great pair of shears'.

(ii)

I have called our theme—our guiding thread of interest—domination; and as I have indicated James is not alone among the English novelists in portraying that. But in his work as a whole 'domination' covers a very wide range indeed. One extreme is killing people: as in the unpleasant and melodramatic *The Other House*, where Rose Armiger drowns the child who stands in the way of her marriage; or in *The Author of Beltraffio*, where the wife of the novelist virtually lets her child die so that he shall not grow up to read her husband's 'immoral' novels; or, less melodramatically, in *The Pupil*, where the small boy is sacrificed to the shabby and second-rate social pretensions of his parents;* or in *Owen Wingrave*, where the young man is sacrificed to the unbending military traditions of his family. *The Turn of the Screw* should be included in this group, even though its powerful probing of unconscious pressures takes it into regions very remote from the other stories named.

Usually, however, James is concerned with the subtler forms of pressure, manipulation or victimization, whether by one person acting on another, more or less consciously, or by a social group whose assumptions and attitudes, without much deliberate intention, crush life and spontaneity, as in *The Awkward Age*.

That this preoccupation began early is—or should be—plain from James's first novel, *Roderick Hudson*. Roderick is a young, untaught, talented sculptor, discovered languishing in New England obscurity by the well-to-do Rowland Mallet, who takes him to Rome so that his genius can have full opportunity to flower in a more stimulating environment. In Rome he does a few good things, but gives himself up to dissipation and then to a tremendous passion. Feeling that his genius

* Seymour Lainoff, in a Note in *Nineteenth-Century Fiction*, 14 (1959–60), pp. 75–77, plausibly suggests that some lack of moral fibre in the boy's tutor —the narrator of the story—is a contributory cause of the catastrophe.

has deserted him and that he has harmed both his sweetheart and his benefactor (who has fallen in live with the girl), he goes to his death in a storm in the Alps. The story can be seen as illustrating the incompatibility of a passion for 'life' and a passion for 'art', or (with Leon Edel) as dramatizing two sides of James's own nature: 'In this novel the *feeling* self has to die. It was too great a threat to the rational self'.[6] The novel can of course be seen in some such way, but the conflict, as embodied in Roderick, doesn't engage us very deeply. In the Preface, James speaks of Rowland Mallet's consciousness as his real subject; and even without this suggestion we should be able to see that behind the question of Life and Art is another question, that doesn't lend itself to abstractions. It is, to what extent has one the right to take another's life in one's own hands? to be a sculptor (a 'mallet': James chose his names with care) of another life. Mallet to be sure is in no sense a villain; there's no doubt of his decency and disinterestedness; and what he does for Roderick is done with the best of intentions. But early in the book Rowland's shrewd cousin, Cecilia, tells him that 'for a man who's generally averse to meddling, you were suddenly rather officious', an opinion endorsed later by Mallet when he writes to his cousin, 'You were a shrewd observer and I was a meddlesome donkey'—a self-description which is hardly adequate to the tragic climax. What is missing in his genuinely caring attitude towards his friend is suggested by a metaphor when he is thinking about Roderick: 'He wished that for their common comfort the paste of Roderick's composition had had a certain softer ductility. It was like something that had dried to colour, to brilliancy; but hadn't it also dried to brittleness?' There is at least a suggestion there that Rowland is the artist shaping the paste of another man's life, and that the experiment has been carried out too precipitately. The question raised is not resolved in the novel; but it is, more than is commonly recognized, presented in all its prickly awkwardness.*

James made a number of studies of predators; and the spectrum of his analysis ranges from the psychological probings of *The Turn of the Screw* to the brilliant presentation of the social *mores* of Mrs Brookenham's set in *The Awkward Age*,—those 'votaries' of the 'temple of analysis' (that is, of endless gossip), whose sham sophistication goes with a shrewd perception of the value of hard cash, who almost succeed in destroying all that is genuine in the life of Nanda Brookenham. But there are only a few novels where the interest is centred exclusively on the forms of domination: James is equally interested in what it is in the 'victims' that lays them open to the fate

* D. W. Jefferson has some perceptive comments on Rowland, as a man capable of 'some act of sublime interference in another person's life', *Henry James*, pp. 24–6.

determined for them by others. It may seem absurd to bring together a minor novel, *The American*, and an assured masterpiece, *The Portrait of a Lady*; but the masterpiece will not suffer if we notice a thread of connexion. *The American* is the story of the defeat of the 'innocently' shrewd American businessman, seeking a wife in the European aristocracy, at the hands of the Bellegardes; and as a portrayal of two different modes of life—the new American and the old European 'aristocratic' mode—it is a failure because of James's inability to portray one side with what he called 'a high probity of observation': as he was to say years later, he simply had no direct knowledge of the world of the Bellegardes—'They would positively have jumped then, the Bellegardes, at my rich and easy American, and not have "minded" in the least any drawback'. But there is also Newman himself. James cheats a bit in the Preface when he speaks of him as 'a generous nature engaged with forces, with difficulties and dangers that it but half understands'; 'great and gilded the whole trap set . . . for his wary freshness and into which it would blunder upon its fate'. On the contrary—and whatever the novelist says, the novel shows us—if Newman is a victim it is partly because he embodies qualities that are almost as egotistically assertive as those of the Bellegardes,—and embodies them in a way that rewards a much fuller attention than the ways in which the pasteboard French aristocrats embody theirs. It's not merely that he has shown his powers in a highly competitive business world—'transcendent operations in ferocious markets'—even though there were meannesses he wouldn't descend to, and he is finally disgusted by the rat-race. But in spite of what James calls his 'unfathomable good nature', he brings into his personal life attitudes formed in the world where money is king. In marrying, he wants 'to make a great hit'; and when he is, so to speak, on view at the Bellegardes' party, he would have liked a detached view of the presented spectacle: 'It would have spoken to him of his energy and prosperity and deepened that view of his effective "handling" of life to which, sooner or later, he made all experience contribute'. Even when, we are told, he is genuinely in love, 'he had already begun to value the world's view of his possible prize as adding to the prospective glory of possession'. Here, and elsewhere, there is too much that smells of 'business'. *The American*, in short, shows something different from the crude assertion of power in one set of characters, stonily lodged in their unquestioned 'superiority', over the innocent representative ('Newman') of a fresher world. What we have is a clash of different kinds of assertion, so that even though there is no doubt of where our sympathies are intended to lie, there is a pretty obvious sense in which Newman asked for what he got.

I feel uncomfortable in giving only a few words to *The Portrait of a Lady*. But its greatness is sufficiently recognized, as is the nature of its central theme. Isabel Archer *is* a free spirit, trapped by a calculating worldling with a veneer of taste and sophistication; and the dramatic focus is sharp and clear in the famous passage of Isabel's self-communing (Chapter xlii), which has behind it all the fully realized pressures built up in the novel. My simple point is that the book is more than a moving account of the way in which one person can be used by another—'an applied handled hung-up tool, as senseless and convenient as mere wood and iron'—that the study of victim and predator includes some clear indications of the qualities in the victim that betray her.

> She had taken all the first steps in the purest confidence, and then she had suddenly found the infinite vista of a multiplied life to be a dark, narrow alley with a dead wall at the end. Instead of leading to the high places of happiness, from which the world would seem to lie below one, so that one could look down with a sense of exaltation and advantage, and judge and choose and pity, it led rather downward and earthward, into realms of restriction and depression where the sound of other lives, easier and freer, was heard as from above. . . .

'To look down . . . and judge and choose and pity': the temptation expressed there is common enough, but it *is*, surely, temptation. To be sure, the reader is too much engaged with the fate of Isabel Archer, too much aware of the life-potential she embodies, to lurch aside into irrelevant moralizing. But James pays us the compliment of expecting us to notice everything he has put in. When Isabel's aunt first discovers her in the family house at Albany she is in her favourite room, a disused 'office', which would have given her a view of the street if the sidelights of the bolted door had not been covered with green paper, and Isabel 'had no wish to look out . . . she had never assured herself that the vulgar street lay beyond'. In fact what lies across the way is a primary school: 'the little girl had been offered the opportunity of laying a foundation of knowledge in this establishment; but having spent a single day in it, she had protested against its laws and had been allowed to stay at home'. As a young woman, 'her thoughts were a tangle of vague outlines which had never been corrected by the judgement of people speaking with authority'. There is wilfulness as well as vulnerability in the attitudes she brings to bear on experience. I'm not trying to say something paradoxical about *The Portrait*, something that would lead us to Lawrence's, 'It takes two to make a murder, a murderer and a murderee'. The spectrum of attitudes presented with great liveliness is too wide, and the colours, so to speak, too finely shaded, running from Ralph's free and open nature, through—for example— Mrs Touchett (the edges of whose conduct 'were so very clear-cut that for susceptible persons it sometimes had a knife-like effect'), to Gilbert

Osmond, whom Ralph so well describes: 'under the guise of caring
only for intrinsic values Osmond lived exclusively for the world . . .
His ambition was not to please the world, but to please himself by
exciting the world's curiosity and then declining to satisfy it'. Isabel
sums up the difference between the two men: 'It was simply that
Ralph was generous and that her husband was not'. As for Isabel, we
are genuinely made to feel that 'she carried within herself a great fund
of life': her tragedy is that she is taken in by someone so far from free.
But the novel gives us enough material to show what it is in her that
makes her a victim. James laid his foundations thoroughly, and in the
retrospective Chapter VI he invites us to see Isabel as, in some respects,
'the American girl'. 'Like the mass of American girls Isabel had been
encouraged to express herself; her remarks had been attended to; she
had been expected to have emotions and opinions'. Later we are told
that 'the idea of a diminished liberty was particularly disagreeable to
her', just as we are told of her 'self-sufficiency', 'her habit of judging
quickly and freely'—something that is borne out by her conversation.
It is Ralph, who admires and loves her, besides only too fatally wanting
'to put some wind in her sails', who says to her, 'You think nothing in
the world too perfect for you', and 'You're extremely interesting to
yourself'. In short, some of our judgments—in terms of awakened
sympathy and that alert consciousness that the book demands from its
readers—are bound to be far from simple ones. The *Spectator* reviewer
found the presentation of Isabel in her relation with Osmond 'a
laborious riddle'; and another contemporary reviewer, having referred
to Lord Warburton, Caspar Goodwood and Ralph Touchett, says:

> The trains of feeling and association which lead a good and clever
> woman to prefer to types like these a person of Osmond's stamp,
> and the illusions she must create for herself before she can do so,
> are precisely the subjects on which a skilful analyst of human
> nature should be able to throw some light; but it is just here that
> Mr James leaves us most in the dark.[7]

But 'the illusions she must create for herself' *are* there: at all events
there is enough built into the novel—often in small but significant
ways—to allow us to say that it raises with some force the question of
what it is in the tragic victim that makes her one, even when she is
presented sympathetically as welcoming life, and indeed as capable of
heroism. James knew that life is a complicated business.

(iii)

It must be obvious by now that the pursuit of our theme could go on
almost indefinitely—to take in, all events, *The Princess Casamassima*, *The
Spoils of Poynton*, *The Ambassadors* and *The Wings of the Dove*, each in its

own individual way concerned with pressures applied, endured, or rejected. But I shall use the remainder of my space on the small master-piece, *Washington Square* (1881). It was with reference to that novel that a perceptive reviewer wrote: 'that which fulfils its function most com-pletely in the world is the power, inherent in most of us, to spoil or hamper the life of other people, an agency the conspicuous success of which almost all Mr. James's writings commemorate'.[8]

On the surface the story is a simple little tragedy of a rather simple girl for whom no 'happy ending' is possible: Morris Townsend is a fortune-hunter, and Dr. Sloper is right to be suspicious of the young man's attentions to his daughter. But James takes us further than that— to what lies behind the situation and has allowed it to develop. Catherine, we are told towards the end,

> became an admirable old maid. She formed habits, regulated her days upon a system of her own, interested herself in charitable institutions, asylums, hospitals, and aid societies; and went generally, with an even and noiseless step, about the rigid business of her life. This life had, however, a secret history as well as a public one—if I may talk of the public history of a mature and diffi-dent spinster for whom publicity had always a combination of terrors. From her own point of view the great facts of her career were that Morris Townsend had trifled with her affection, and that her father had broken its spring.

It is the 'secret history' that gives the story its depth. It is all so quietly done that a first reading may not bring out the full effect. There is only one scene that has some of the more obvious marks of tragedy: it is in Chapter xxiv, when the Doctor and Catherine, in the course of their prolonged holiday in Europe, are in the Alps. The pair have left their carriage and are following a mountain path.

> It was late in the afternoon, in the last of August; night was coming on, and, as they had reached a great elevation, the air was cold and sharp. In the west there was a great suffusion of cold, red light, which made the sides of the little valley look only the more rugged and dusky. During one of their pauses, her father left her and wandered away to some high place, at a distance, to get a view. He was out of sight; she sat there alone, in the stillness, which was just touched by the vague murmur, somewhere, of a mountain brook. She thought of Morris Townsend, and the place was so desolate and lonely that he seemed very far away. Her father remained absent a long time; she began to wonder what had become of him. But at last he reappeared, coming towards her in the clear twilight, and she got up, to go on. He made no motion to

proceed, however, but came close to her, as if he had something to say. He stopped in front of her and stood looking at her, with eyes that had kept the light of the flushing snow-summits on which they had just been fixed. Then, abruptly, in a low tone, he asked her an unexpected question:

'Have you given him up?'

The question was unexpected, but Catherine was only superficially unprepared.

'No, father!' she answered . . .

. . . He turned away, and she followed him; he went faster, and was presently much in advance. But from time to time he stopped, without turning round, to let her keep up with him, and she made her way forward with difficulty, her heart beating with the excitement of having for the first time spoken to him in violence. By this time it had grown almost dark, and she ended by losing sight of him. But she kept her course, and after a little, the valley making a sudden turn, she gained the road, where the carriage stood waiting. In it sat her father, rigid and silent; in silence, too, she took her place beside him.

It's not only that a good many of the descriptive phrases also define Catherine's personal plight, the situation is genuinely frightening. There is nothing else like it in the novel, which is mostly kept to a fairly low key. But when we reach the end, the father dead and Morris finally rejected—'Catherine, meanwhile, in the parlour, picking up her morsel of fancy work, had seated herself with it again—for life, as it were'——we know that the scene of desolate loneliness in the Alps has merely given heightened expression to the tragedy enacted in a quite 'commonplace' life, and all the time the novel has been exploring it.

It all goes back to Catherine's childhood,—the disappointment to her father, with his rigid ideas of what he wanted by way of an accomplished daughter, and the daughter's consequent retreat into substitutes for being loved. ('She never, that I know of, stole raisins out of the pantry; but she devoted her pocket-money to the purchase of cream cakes'.) You are clearly made to feel that she isn't stupid, only robbed of the affection that nourishes intelligence.*

* In Book II, Chapter ii of *The Ambassadors* James is explicit about the connexion, which hadn't the currency then that it has today. '[Strether] had again and again made out for himself that he might have kept his little boy, his little dull boy who had died at school of rapid diphtheria, if he had not in those years so insanely given himself to merely missing the mother. It was the soreness of his remorse that the child had in all likelihood not really been dull —had been dull, as he had been banished and neglected, mainly because his father had been unwittingly selfish.'

'He is not very fond of me', she says to her suitor, and a little later:

'You can tell when a person speaks to you as if—as if——' 'As if what?'—'as if they despised you', said Catherine passionately.

Cold exasperation is the tone of most of Dr. Sloper's remarks about his daughter: but it is not merely due to his justified suspicions of her young man: he is *never* shown treating her as a person,—she is virtually an object, 'a weak young woman with a large fortune', as he categorizes her at one point. An obvious example is the opening of Chapter xxi:

Dr. Sloper very soon imparted his conviction to Mrs. Almond, in the same terms in which he had announced it to himself. 'She's going to stick, by Jove! she's going to stick.'

'Do you mean that she is going to marry him?' Mrs. Almond inquired.

'I don't know that; but she is not going to break down. She is going to drag out the engagement, in the hope of making me relent.'

'And shall you not relent?'

'Shall a geometrical proposition relent? I am not so superficial.'

'Doesn't geometry treat of surfaces?' asked Mrs. Almond, who, as we know, was clever, smiling.

'Yes; but it treats of them profoundly. Catherine and her young man are my surfaces; I have taken their measure.'

'You speak as if it surprised you.'

'It is immense; there will be a great deal to observe.'

'You are shockingly cold-blooded!' said Mrs. Almond.

'I need to be with all this hot blood about me. Young Townsend indeed is cool; I must allow him that merit.'

'I can't judge him,' Mrs. Almond answered; 'but I am not at all surprised at Catherine.'

'I confess I am a little; she must have been so deucedly divided and bothered.'

'Say it amuses you outright! I don't see why it should be such a joke that your daughter adores you.'

'It is the point where the adoration stops that I find it interesting to fix.'

'It stops where the other sentiment begins.'

'Not at all—that would be simple enough. The two things are extremely mixed up, and the mixture is extremely odd. It will produce some third element, and that's what I am waiting to see. I wait with suspense—with positive excitement; and that is a sort of emotion that I didn't suppose Catherine would ever provide for me. I am really very much obliged to her.'

The tone is that of the distancing observer; and what Dr. Sloper doesn't say is as important as what he does. His manner is difficult to illustrate, since the evidence is scattered throughout, and one would have to quote too much. But very early in the novel James tells us of the Doctor, 'You would have surprised him if you had told him so; but it is a literal fact that he almost never addressed his daughter save in the ironical form'. Irony is a form of distancing, and when directed towards anyone in personal intercourse its use is to prevent communication. To quote Pound once more—'Peace comes of communication . . . All things that oppose this are evil, whether they be petty scoffing or obstructive tariffs.'* There's plenty in the novel to justify Catherine's sense that, as she says, her father 'is not very fond' of her. He never actually hits her, but brutality is the only word for his relations with his daughter. 'You would have had to know him well', James tells us— and he has taken care that we should know him well—'to discover that, on the whole, he rather enjoyed having to be so disagreeable'. In the scene at the end of Chapter xxxi, where Catherine has to let her father know of her broken engagement, there is not a shade in her father's tone to suggest that he is dealing with someone who is plainly suffering.

'It would be a convenience to me to know when I may expect to have an empty house,' he went on. 'When you go, your aunt marches.'

She looked at him at last, with a long silent gaze, which, in spite of her pride and her resolution, uttered part of the appeal she had tried not to make. Her father's cold grey eye sounded her own, and he insisted on his point.

'Is it tomorrow? Is it next week, or the week after?'

'I shall not go away!' said Catherine.

The Doctor raised his eyebrows. 'Has he backed out?'

'I have broken off my engagement.'

'Broken it off?'

'I have asked him to leave New York, and he has gone away for a long time.'

The Doctor was both puzzled and disappointed, but he solved his perplexity by saying to himself that his daughter simply misrepresented—justifiably, if one would, but nevertheless misrepresented—the facts; and he eased off his disappointment, which was that of a man losing a chance for a little triumph that he had rather counted on, by a few words he uttered aloud.

'How does he take his dismissal?'

* 'And this communication', Pound adds, 'is not a levelling, it is not an elimination of differences. It is a recognition of differences, of the right of difference to exist, of interest in finding things different.'

'I don't know!' said Catherine, less ingeniously than she had hitherto spoken.

'You mean you don't care? You are rather cruel, after encouraging him and playing with him for so long!'

The Doctor had his revenge after all.

After Dr. Sloper's death, when the contents of his will are made known—his daughter's share being much reduced, with reasons given—Catherine's aunt says to her that she supposes she will dispute the will. '"Oh no," Catherine answered, "I like it very much. Only I wish it has been expressed a little differently!"' It is 'expression' that we are invited to notice—especially Dr. Sloper's. His is a mode of speech that never varies with the person or the occasion; it is dry, ironical and wary: it is self-contained, with none of the flexibility of a genuinely responding mind. It is a form of speech designed to dominate; and in its very form—almost irrespective of what is being actually said—we can see what it is that has determined the small—that is to say the unspectacular—tragedy of Catherine Sloper.

I return to where I started. Henry James is not only an artist who offers a special enjoyment to the cultivated: together with all those other writers who make us use our imaginations in our relations with our fellows, he is what Wordsworth called the poet, 'a rock of defence for human nature'. The theme of *The Ambassadors* is the education of Lambert Strether, his emancipation from the rigidities of New England 'Woollett', as embodied in the felt presence of Mrs Newsome. In Paris, whilst sharpening his moral discriminations, Strether learns 'the lesson of a certain moral ease', whereas 'Mrs Newsome was essentially all moral pressure'. It is in Book Eleven, Chapter 1, where Strether is talking with Miss Gostrey, that James lets us have the straightest judgment on Mrs Newsome and all she stands for: 'She's all cold thought', 'she doesn't admit surprises'. Then, still more devastatingly from Strether—'There's nothing so magnificent—for making others feel you—as to have no imagination'; and from Miss Gostrey, 'Well, intensity with ignorance—what do you want worse?' The remarks reach rather far. What we learn from James is that judgment of people—since one must judge as well as sympathize—is not a matter of applying ready-made categories; it is a matter of using our imaginations, as James so splendidly makes us do: especially in an area of concern—the area of pressure and coercion—that is, quite literally, central to the future of our civilization.

Two Notes on Coleridge

(1) *Coleridge as Critic*[1]

THE LECTURES presented here were intended as an act of homage to a great man. But inevitably they deal only with selected aspects of a genius that is as multiform and various as it is commanding and, at times, enigmatic. It is not only that, as F. D. Maurice said, 'those who have most profited by what he has taught them, do not and cannot form a school', those who through a lifetime return to his works are likely to find that their understanding stops far short of anything they would care to call finality. Dr. Beer, who quotes Maurice's remark, concludes his second lecture by saying: 'Coleridge's career, in its intricate processes and riddling self-contradictions, continually beckons one . . . to further thought and investigation rather than to attempts at sweeping evaluation'. I think this is true; but it does not relieve us of the necessity of trying to clear up our minds about why we value Coleridge or to elicit the unifying principles that make his work as a whole so much more than a collection of false starts from which brilliant occasional insights emerge.

I have always thought that Coleridge's literary criticism—occupying, so to speak, a middle place between the poetry and the philosophy and general thought—offers the common reader the best purchase for further investigation. And since the essays collected here say very little about the criticism, it may be appropriate to give it some prominence in this Introduction.

When we try to define the value of Coleridge's literary criticism perhaps the observation to start from is that it is related to deep personal needs: it is not just 'literary criticism' as that phrase is only too often understood. Coleridge as critic is not simply the man of letters whose basic assumptions about life are more or less taken for granted, so that they can be kept outside his discussion of particular literary problems, as Dryden, for example, urbanely and intelligently but without moral resonance, discusses the problems of his craft. And I think it is in general true to say that the criticism that we most often go back to for insight and stimulus is either that of the creative writer urgently exploring the implications of some radically new way of writing that he practises (Eliot, Yeats, Lawrence), or that of a man whose feeling for life as a whole gets into and informs his criticism (Dr Johnson, Matthew Arnold). Coleridge, although he wrote some great poems, and would not have been the critic he was unless he had been capable of writing them, belongs to the second class. His criticism is immethodical, not always of the same high standard, and it can be sadly off the point. But at its best it is of great and permanent value because the question it asks is, How does *this* make for life? to what extent is *this* an expression of the imagination? And behind this, What *is* the imagination, and why is it so important that we should cultivate it? In other words, Coleridge's literary criticism springs from the same source as his thinking about education, psychology, religion, politics. It is part of his total confrontation of human experience, and is connected with the life of feeling and intuitive perception that it is the poet's special task to bring to expression. Coleridge's attempt to define the imagination began when he tried to make clear to himself the distinctive qualities of Wordsworth's poetry. But what invigorates and directs his criticism and, beyond that, his general thought, is not only the experience of an uncommonly sensitive reader of poetry, it is his own experience as a poet.

It is, then, helpful to preface even a brief account of the criticism with a reference to 'Dejection: An Ode'. That poem is, of course, about the loss of joy, the animating principle, 'my shaping spirit of Imagination'; but in the central stanzas, iv and v, there is the paradoxical recognition of joy as a principle of life. Paradoxical, because the poem records a defeat, but records it so faithfully and completely that Coleridge, at a deep level of engagement, *realizes* what is meant by the opposite of defeat. To put this in slightly different words, the intensity of the imaginative process—including an un-self-regarding steadiness of contemplation—has set free and established some of the fundamental insights of Coleridge's philosophy.* Professor Dorothy Emmet, in the brilliant paper that she wrote some twenty years ago,[2] says:

> I believe that Coleridge was concerned to explore not only a source of the creative power of imagination shown in genius but also more generally the liberation of the mind from deadness and dereliction, a liberation on which its growth depends . . . [His] philosophy was concerned with exploring the conditions which make possible, and the conditions which frustrate this joy which underlies the creative growth of the mind.

* I refer of course to the finished, the *worked at*, poem. The original verse letter to Sara Hutchinson is not only very much longer, with a different arrangement of parts, it is full of a self-pity that has been completely eliminated in the re-working.

And again:

> 'The Ancient Mariner', 'Christabel', 'Kubla Khan', give us above
> all symbols of dereliction and joy. Joy for Coleridge was not just
> an 'equipoise of the intellectual and emotional faculties', at any
> rate if this means the achievement of a balanced temperament,
> which he sorely lacked. It was a state in which it was possible
> to bless and be blessed; and to Coleridge there was no half-
> way house: its absence was like the misery of a curse. And
> what he learnt about joy came as much from his failure to achieve
> liberty of spirit as from the rare moments when he did achieve
> it.

Coleridge's central preoccupation was indeed with growth and
creativeness, and with the activity of consciousness, the energy and joy,
that are the conditions, the signs and the consequences of creativeness.
To grasp the implications of that takes us to the heart of his philosophy
and shows us the close connexion between his literary criticism and the
wider aspects of his thought. As Shawcross put it, in the Preface to his
edition of the *Biographia*, 'The search for a criterion of poetry involved
him in the wider search for a criterion of life'. The statement could
equally well be reversed. What is important is to realize that in
Coleridge's thinking the attempt to understand and to find a criterion
for poetry is inseparable from the attempt to understand and to find a
criterion for all other aspects of life. As he said of his projected book on
poetry (in a letter to Humphry Davy, 9 October, 1800). 'its Title would
be an Essay on the Elements of Poetry', but 'it would be in reality a disguised System of Morals and Politics', adding, a few months later (3
February, 1801), 'the Work would supersede all the Books of Metaphysics hitherto written, and all the Books of Morals too'. A rather
large claim, but not to be dismissed as the compensatory fantasy—
Carlyle's 'bottled moonshine'—of a man who was too indolent, or too
troubled, to carry to completion any work he planned.

'Life' of course is somewhat too big to talk about. Coleridge knew
as well as Blake that life only reveals itself in—sometimes minute—
particulars. If the guiding principles of Coleridge's thought are in fact
revealed or intimated in his literary criticism, this is because 'principles'
and 'practical criticism' are intimately and necessarily connected: one
recalls the significant collocation in the first sentence of Chapter xv of
the *Biographia Literaria*. Coleridge was a first-class practical critic. As
Professor William Walsh has said—referring to 'the tonic effect' of his
criticism—it has a 'fiercely individual and personal bite . . . It braces and
concentrates attention.'[3] Again and again a sure personal judgment—
disciplined and sustained, not dissipated, by a remarkable range of
reading—goes straight to the mark. He had a very clear perception of

Wordsworth's greatness as a poet, and—long before Wordsworth was an accepted classic—his praise was generous, sure and discriminating. He was a pioneer in the rehabilitation of Donne and 'our elder poets' of the early seventeenth century, noting their 'pure and genuine mother English'[4] even in the expression of difficult thoughts. Of George Herbert he wrote,

> the scholar and the poet supplies the material, but the perfect well-bred gentleman the expressions and the arrangement;
>
> (BL II 73)

and (ahead even of cultivated taste by a century) of the lively expressiveness of Donne's rhythms:

> Read even Donne's Satires as he meant them to be read, and as the sense and passion demand, and you will find in the lines a manly harmony (Misc C 67)

His lectures and notes on Shakespeare and the Jacobean dramatists are uneven, but they are a quarry of perceptions that lead the mind further into particular plays. There is psychological acumen, as when he notes the contrast between Macbeth's and Banquo's response to the witches; there is a feeling for the relation between immediate dramatic effect and the unfolding whole of which it forms a part, as in the superb account of the contrasting opening scenes of *Hamlet*, *Macbeth* and *King Lear*,[5] and always attention is focused on the particular, and poetic, use of words, as when he comments on Lady Macbeth's welcome to Duncan, 'the very rhythm expresses the insincere overmuch in [her] answer to the king'.[6] Poetic, one should say, *and* dramatic: a casual remark on Shakespeare's versification anticipates what is sometimes thought of as a modern discovery:

> Shakespeare never introduces a catalectic line without intending an equivalent to the foot omitted, in the pauses, or the dwelling emphasis, or the diffused retardation. (ShC 1 24)

Almost everywhere, in short, we find evidence of Coleridge's feeling for 'the blessed machine of language'[7]—the way in which it carries within it a human history that can enter into new, subtle and precise expression. Many years ago I jotted on a fly-leaf of Owen Barfield's *Poetic Diction* (a book which, with its companion, *History in English Words*, Coleridge would have enjoyed) a sentence from *Aids to Reflection*:

> There are cases, in which more knowledge of more value may be conveyed by the history of *a word*, than by the history of a campaign. (AR 6n)

Coleridge's criticism, however, is valuable not only for the particular perceptions that show him coming to grips with and illuminating what is actually there in front of him, but because it constantly circles round and refers to certain *principles* or 'organising insights'.[8] Of these the most important are the conception of poetry as a form of energy—the 'vigour' with 'a substrate of profound feeling'[9] that he calls attention to in distinguishing Donne from Cowley—and the belief that in good poetry 'the poet's ever active mind' is answered by a corresponding 'activity of attention required on the part of the reader'.[10] I know very well that literary criticism cannot be conducted in these general terms: when we want to define the excellence of a particular poem we don't rhapsodize about any access of energy it may give, we point to this or that in the structure and texture of the poem—its 'sound of sense', the choice and order of words, the imagery or the rhythm. But sometimes we need to see what all these things are *for*. Coleridge's principles not only emerge from his own direct experience of literature—both as maker and critic—they help us, once we have grasped them, to organize our thinking about literature, and much else besides; and it is worth noticing in what varied ways, in the *Biographia* and elsewhere, the principle of energy is put to work. The phrases that I have quoted about the activity of the poet's mind and the corresponding activity of the reader are parts of a remarkable account of what modern criticism calls 'realization', that sense of living actuality that comes about when the mind is called on to do several different things simultaneously, and finds that they cohere in one complex act of attention. We may note in passing that all that needs to be said about the nature of pornography is contained in the remark that 'a mind roused and awakened' cannot be 'brooded on by mean and indistinct emotion'. What is more important is that by associating energy with vividness and precision, and the unformed or indistinct with 'the merely passive of our nature', Coleridge makes explicit and intelligible a fundamental criterion not only for literature but for the general life of the mind. Fanaticism, we may recall—elsewhere associated with a 'debility and dimness of the imaginative power'—is said to 'master the feelings more especially by indistinct watchwords'.[11] It is not simply as a *literary* critic that Coleridge recommends 'the advantage which language alone . . . presents to the instructor of impressing modes of intellectual energy'.[12]

In this wide context we should be able to focus more clearly on the famous passage on the imagination at the end of Chapter XIV of the *Biographia*, beginning, 'The poet, described in ideal perfection, brings the whole soul of man into activity . . .' Professor Wellek has said some hard things about this,[13] but even its 'random eclecticism' cannot obscure the fundamental insights that it contains. The imagination is a form of energy, but it is no undirected *élan vital*; it 'struggles to unify' not only thoughts and feelings that often war unnecessarily with each other, but the different modes of being through which the self, including the subliminal self, exercises its powers. It is a function of the whole person, a dynamic integrating force through which we not only come to know ourselves and the world, but experience that sense of creative freedom which in 'Dejection' is called joy. I do not know any more profound account, any account more suggestive and fertilizing, of why poetry matters, or of why 'the cultivation of the judgment is a positive command of the moral law'.[14]

For Coleridge, then, the imagination is not a special faculty cultivated by poets and readers of poetry, it is simply life coming to consciousness. R. J. White, referring to Coleridge's achievement in 'The Ancient Mariner', says that he 'spent the rest of his life translating his experience of the creative mind into terms of a philosophy of life, in showing to men that the way of creative genius is the way of ordinary humanity.'[15] In exploring the ways of poetry and the imagination he is also exploring the life of reason as a whole. Professor Emmet—in the paper to which I have referred and in her contribution to the present volume—brings out how, for Coleridge, thinking is not simply a clearly delimited *mental* activity. It is not merely that, as he puts it in *The Friend*,[16] 'in the moral being lies the source of the intellectual'; moral integrity is related to the sympathies and the feelings, which themselves relate closely to the organic life of the body. In matters of essential concern 'knowledge' is not simply deduction from experience or the end of a logical process, it is a function of being, including that 'unconscious activity' that is 'the genius in the man of genius'.*

Bishop Hort, in his 1856 essay, speaks of the influence of Plato and the New Testament in leading Coleridge 'to a region not unfamiliar to English travellers, the first step in which is the identification, in some sense or other, of knowledge and being'.[17] *Quantum sumus, scimus.* In Chapter XXIV of the *Biographia*, dealing with the question of religious faith, Coleridge speaks of 'what we can only *know* by the act of *becoming*'.

* There is no need to make a mystery of this; nor is anything that has been said at variance with Coleridge's known dislike of 'floating and obscure generalities' and his insistence on the virtues of vividness and precision. It is simply that the meaning of the word 'precision' varies with the context within which, or the level at which, it is used. In literary criticism precision refers to a clearly directed energy, springing from and supported by feelings that cannot be entirely brought to light. As Coleridge is reported as saying in the lectures on Shakespeare and Milton, 'the grandest efforts of poetry are where the imagination is called forth, not to produce a distinct form, but *a strong working of the mind*' (my italics). So too, in important regions of our thought, 'meaning' is inseparable from an energetic *reaching out* of the mind, and 'precise' definition may put a stop to that. None of which however relieves us of the need to think as clearly as we can.

Mutatis mutandis the same could be said of our knowledge of poetry: 'You feel Shakespeare to be a poet inasmuch as, for a time, he has made you one, an active creative being.'[18] As I have said, there is no compartmentalizing in Coleridge's thought. Whether he is dealing with poetry, with religion, with the art of thought, with education or with politics, the same principles are at work, and there is the same fundamental concern for zest of life, vitality, growth and creativeness: all of which he knew—knew in specific and detailed forms—from his direct experience as man, as poet and as critic—though he also knew them (as more than one contributor to this volume points out) from his failures. Some of those principles—'living Sparks' or 'Kindlefuel', as Coleridge called the Platonic Recollections[19]—will be found at work in the lectures that follow; though it is entirely in keeping that they should work in such different ways and in different fields of thought.

(ii) A Tract for the Times: Coleridge and *The Friend**

The periodical essays that make up this strange miscellany[1] belong to the most troubled period of Coleridge's life. 'Dejection,' the last of the great poems, was written in 1802; *Biographia Literaria*, the critical work by which he is still best known, came out in 1817. Between these dates, apart from the time spent in Malta (1804–5) as private secretary to Sir Alexander Ball, the British High Commissioner in Malta, Coleridge was almost continuously beset with troubles, domestic and financial. Occasional journalism, occasional lectures, and help from friends barely supplied his own needs and those of his family. Besides, there was the strong inner drive to get his own ideas—his thoughts about metaphysics, religion, and the world at large—into some sort of order. Periodical essays might keep the wolf from the door, and the sense of an audience would perhaps provide the incentive to regular work that he needed so badly. As early as 1804 he had thought of bringing out a series of essays with the resounding title of

> Consolations and Comforts from the exercise and right application of the Reason, the Imagination, and the Moral Feelings, addressed especially to those in Sickness, Adversity, or Distress of Mind, *from Speculative Gloom* etc.

It was not, however, until the summer of 1809—and then in spite of almost insuperable difficulties—that the first number of his paper *The*

---

* First of all gratitude to Kathleen Coburn, the editor, and the Bollingen Foundation, the sponsors, of the sorely needed Collected Works of Coleridge; then to Professor Barbara Rooke, the editor of *The Friend*, which is the first of the works to appear.

Friend finally appeared. Twenty-seven numbers were issued before the project had to be abandoned in March, 1810. The periodical was re-issued in book form in 1812, and, with major changes, in a three-volume edition in 1818.

The first of the two volumes now before us contains the definitive text, Coleridge's reworking of the original publication, with its tidying-up, omissions, and additions, of which the most important is the restored 'Treatise on Method,' so sadly mangled when it came out in the *Encyclopaedia Metropolitana* for which it had been commissioned. Volume II contains the text of *The Friend* as it first appeared in 1809 and 1810, together with notes on subscribers, collation tables, and other useful information. Lavish footnotes give printed and manuscript variants; quotations are traced to their sources and translated.

In a long Introduction Miss Rooke tells the heroical–tragical–comical story of Coleridge's attempt to keep his periodical going, traces the history of *The Friend* to the '*rifacimento*' of 1818, indicates its effect on such nineteenth-century figures as Frederick Denison Maurice, and adds—all too briefly—some comments of her own on Coleridge's 'toughness of mind' which went with his openness of imagination. In short, Miss Rooke has done a splendid piece of work. The price of these two handsome volumes is very high, however: in view of the standard of editorial care and of production it is hard to see how it could be otherwise. But Coleridge is not meant only for the well-to-do; he is meant for students, many of them poor, and *The Friend*, until now virtually unobtainable, is essential reading. Is it too much to hope that the publishers will consider a cheap reprint of Volume I, perhaps a paperback containing nothing but a shortened Introduction, the text, and a few essential footnotes?

That *The Friend* is essential reading is not self-evident to everyone who reads it. Even Professor McFarland, who rightly holds that Coleridge's work is 'unified by a group of organizing ideas,' admits that 'to enter upon the study of his mind is to wade into a morass. Coleridge is a writer almost unique in his special combination of allusiveness, fragmentariness of statement, complication of interests, and neurotic inability to attend to the demands of formal presentation.'[2] This certainly applies to *The Friend*, and the task of exposition is not made easier by the Coleridgean voice, earnestly preaching or exhorting in a tone not always easy to distinguish from the tone when his mind is really engaged. There are defects in abundance—unnecessary digressions, ejaculations, occasional obscurities. So the admirer must accept the challenge to say simply and clearly why this hodge-podge of a book —if you can call it a book—is important for others besides the professionals.

It seems best to attempt an answer to the doubters by first pointing to the essays on political philosophy. Since in the Coleridgean world everything is connected with everything else this can lead rather far. These essays, it is true, get off to a wobbly start, for although Reason in Coleridge is an honorific term and Understanding is often pejorative, Coleridge is here mainly intent on exposing the inadequacies of, and offering an alternative to, 'the politics of pure reason.' The difficulty disappears as soon as we see that he uses 'reason' in two different senses. Reason as the supreme activity of the mind—constantly veering towards the 'completing power' of the imagination—is the source of principles and ideas regarded as powers of growth in the integrated human being. The application of reason in this sense to social and political issues results in prudence—not 'the vulpine prudence of the understanding,' which is narrowly calculating and self-regarding, but the intellectual virtue that mediates between universal principles and the needs of particular times and circumstances.

Reason in the secondary sense is 'rationalized understanding'; it attempts to generalize from a selection of observed phenomena, producing 'laws' analogous to those of science. Coleridge is concerned to show what happens when reason in *this* sense is used as a tool of political analysis or as a guide to action. Hobbes had had his own rigid scheme, based on an inadequate conception of human nature, which Coleridge effectively exposes. But the real danger was (and is) nearer at hand, in the ruthless application of 'the politics of pure reason' or 'legislative geometry' by men who believed they had a blueprint for human happiness, and that 'whatever is not *everywhere* necessary, is *no where* right.' 'By this system the observation of Times, Places, relative Bearings, History, national Customs and Characters, is rendered superfluous . . . and by the magic oracles of certain axioms and definitions it is revealed how the world with all its concerns should be mechanized, and then let go on of itself.'

Coleridge's arguments against 'Jacobinism' demand to be read in full. They are the more effective because he was not a mere anti-Jacobin: his aim was not denunciation but understanding. He has some notable pages on the 'panic of property' and 'the errors of the Aristocratic party . . . full as gross, and far less excusable.' And he warned his readers that 'in recoiling with too incautious an abhorrence from the bugbears of innovation, they may sink all at once into the slough of slavishness and corruption. Let such persons recollect that the charms of hope and novelty furnish some palliatives for the idolatry to which *they* seduce the mind; but that the apotheosis of familiar abuses . . . is the vilest of superstition.'

But the warnings against what in a later century would be known as

'substitutism' are still valid: the triumph of a party claiming a mathe-
matical certainty for its own programme, and therefore representing the
will of the people if only the people knew their own minds, leads
inevitably to tyranny ('an ever-neighbouring tyranny' he called it in a
Courier essay, with an eye on the dictator's police state), in which the
true meaning of a State—a body politic composed of individual
members with their own personal and interpersonal needs—would be
sacrificed to an abstraction.

> Now this contains the sublime philosophy of the sect of Econom-
> ists (sc. physiocrats). They worship a kind of non-entity under the
> different words, the State, the Whole, the Society, &c. and to this
> idol they make bloodier sacrifices than ever the Mexicans did to
> Tescalipoca.

> The Jacobins spared no human hecatomb to build the pedestal for
> their Truth . . . The counterpart to their absolute faith in a meta-
> physical idea was their absolute distrust of living people.

The last quotation is from Trotsky.*

Not that Coleridge preached political inactivity or acquiescence in
the corruptions of society. It was simply that with reason restored to
its proper sphere—the working of the individual mind and conscience
—prudence, knowledge, and a feeling for man as man would show
what *particular* fields called for energetic action (e.g., child labour in
factories). But since politics would continue to be a welter of competing
interests, men of intellect—*les clercs*—would in the long run be most
politically effective if they devoted their energies to 'that most weighty
and concerning of all sciences, the science of EDUCATION.' 'Can we
wonder,' he said, contemplating the understandable outbreaks of
violence in the oppressed classes, 'that men should want humanity, who
want all the circumstances of life that humanize?'

Education, in fact, is what *The Friend* is all about: not education as
mere instruction, the filling of empty buckets, but education as the

---

* Quoted by Isaac Deutscher, *The Prophet Armed: Trotsky 1879–1921*
(Oxford University Press, 1954), p. 91. 'Substitutism' means the substitution
of a party for the working classes, of the party organization for the party, of
a central committee for the organization, and of a dictator for the committee;
see Deutscher *op. cit.* and *The Prophet Unarmed*. Deutscher also brings out the
fluctuations and inconsistencies in Trotsky's own views. For the dictatorial
tendencies inherent in Leninism see Rosa Luxemburg, *The Russian Revolution*
and *Leninism or Marxism* (Ann Arbor Paperbacks). I have used the substance
of the last two paragraphs in a wider context of political discussion in *Public
Voices: Literature and Policies with Special Reference to the Seventeenth Century*.

awakening of 'the principle and method of self-development.' His aim, as he said of Plato, was 'not to assist in storing the passive mind with the various sorts of knowledge most in request . . . but to place it in such relations of circumstance as should gradually excite the germinal power that craves no knowledge but what it can take up into itself, what it can appropriate, and re-produce in fruits of its own.'

Coleridge himself valued the restored 'Essay on Method' (the substance of Section the Second, which also lurches towards its true beginning) 'more than *all* [his] other prose writings.' I find this valuation hard to accept, although the philosophical sermon that he preaches is, in essentials, an admirable one. Method, or appropriate order, is necessary not only for the pursuit of truth but for creative living: fragmentariness in life is the equivalent of incoherence in expression, for both alike are destructive of meaning, which is a function of relationship.

But method does not mean formal arrangement ('confusion and formality are but the opposite poles of the same null-point'): the method that makes for life must proceed from an informing principle or power of growth, for what it seeks to clarify is 'a truth originating in the *mind*, and not abstracted or generalized from observation of the parts.' 'Mental initiative,' therefore, is necessary to all method: even in the humbler forms of classification, 'some *antecedent* must be contributed by the mind itself; some purpose must be in view; or some question at least must have been proposed to nature, grounded, as all questions are, upon *some* idea of the answer.'

Modern science would, I suppose, accept this view of the creative hunch. Where moral and metaphysical truth is concerned, Coleridge holds, we must go further. The 'laws' by which we live must be capable of progressive and ever-widening application: common to all men, they only reveal themselves in the individual consciousness with all its tensions and necessary polarities. How do we reach them? Negatively, by clearing away the 'idols,' distortions of prejudice, and so on; positively, by recognizing that perception of essential truth depends on the integration of the mind's diverse powers, including not only the intellect but sympathy, conscience, and will. In ultimate matters the truth, in Christian terms, is one with the way: truth and being are correlative.

Certainly we can't ignore the essays on method; but the reader who goes to them for the quintessence of Coleridge's thinking is likely to be irked or baffled. What Coleridge has to teach us is not neatly parcelled but scattered throughout *The Friend*. Miss Rooke quotes F. D. Maurice: 'Its merit is, that it is an enquiry, that it shews us what we have to seek for, and that it puts us into a way of seeking.' It is as important to get the truth of this recognized as it is difficult to substantiate it in a short review. Summarize these scattered but interlinked *aperçus* and you sound leadenly preceptorial. Ponder them—above all in the context of some compelling interest—and you go a very long way indeed in the practice of the difficult art of thinking.

Like his modern exponent I. A. Richards, Coleridge is especially concerned with the internal blockages to a genuinely free activity of the mind—ranging from arrogance (which has an important essay to itself) to the sloth that is content with indistinct and confused conceptions: these tyrannize over our feelings and substitute emotionally charged opinions for steady principles. The correlative to the 'habituation of the intellect to clear, distinct, and adequate conceptions concerning all things that are the possible objects of clear conception' is simply the willingness to *listen* to others:

> Our minds are in a state unsusceptible of Knowledge, when we feel an eagerness to detect the falsehood of an adversary's reasonings, not a sincere wish to discover if there be truth in them.

> Every speculative error which boasts a multitude of advocates has its *golden* as well as its dark side.

The two splendid essays on tolerance (Section the First, XI-XII) link the healthy functioning of mind and the healthy functioning of society. 'God has ordained us to live in society, and has made the progressive improvement of all and each of us depend on the reciprocal aids, which directly or indirectly each supplies to all, and all to each.' The imagination, we remember, is also a reconciling power, though only those who have a strong sense of unavoidable tensions and polarities are able to steer 'reconciling' away from any suggestion of mere compromise. Tolerance, which does not mean the absence of firm conviction, is as necessary for life and creativeness in society as it is in the internal economy of the individual.

What prevents these admirable guidelines from degenerating into moral–intellectual commonplace ('truths . . . considered as so true that they lose all the powers of truth, and lie bed-ridden in the dormitory of the soul') is Coleridge's power of engaging the reader's own mind. He invites you not only to examine the grounds of his principles but to test them by putting them to work in your own experience, for it is out of shrewdly observed experience—diverse, but all bearing on some central insight—that they have emerged.

He is often accused of wandering when he does not wander. Take as a characteristic example Essay V, in which he may perhaps seem to be freewheeling. The basic assumption is that 'Truth is self-restoration.'

Therefore, since 'the duties which we owe to our own moral being, are the ground and condition of all other duties,' pious frauds are as bad as the indistinct conceptions that prevent us from knowing ourselves. This leads into an account of the resentment we all feel when we are deceived. ('With whomsoever we play the deceiver or flatterer, him at bottom we despise.') Then—

> Every parent possesses the opportunity of observing how deeply children resent the injury of a delusion; and if men laugh at the falsehoods that were imposed on themselves during their child-hood, it is because they are not good and wise enough to contemplate the past in the present, and so to produce ... that continuity in their self-consciousness, which Nature has made the law of their animal life ... Men are ungrateful to others only when they have ceased to look back on their former selves with joy and tenderness. They exist in fragments. Annihilated as to the Past, they are dead to the Future, or seek for the proofs of it everywhere, only not (where alone they can be found) in themselves.

In short, the essay is bringing to light the relation between what Erikson calls 'basic trust' and the formation of a stable core of the personality which can *afford* to accept itself in all its stages of growth; and in its concern that the growing mind shall not be 'set at strife with itself' it anticipates a good deal of contemporary psychiatry and child psychology. Indeed whenever Coleridge touches on the education of the young he demands the attention of those whose professional concerns make them aware of the undue emphasis that our age puts on education as training or as adjustment to social norms.

With all this goes a wealth of aphorisms and asides that must strike any reader with a sense of their timeliness. Here is one for 'the ecological decade':

> Natural calamities that do indeed spread devastation wide ... are almost without exception, voices of Nature in her all-intelligible language—do this! or cease to do that! ... What need we deem unattainable, if all the time, the effort, the skill, which we waste in making ourselves miserable ... were embodied and marshalled to a systematic war against the existing evils of nature. ... *As Man, so the World he inhabits.*

And this for a world obsessed with 'productivity': Coleridge is speaking of the necessary balance between Trade and Literature, or, as we might say, between technology and the humanities:

> As is the rank assigned to each in the theory and practice of the governing classes, and, according to its prevalence in forming the

foundation of their public habits and opinions, so will be the outward and inward life of the people at large. . . . That under the
ascendancy of the mental and moral character the *commercial* relations may thrive to the utmost *desirable* point, while the reverse is
ruinous to both, and sooner or later effectuates the fall or debase-
ment of the country itself—this is the richest truth obtained for
mankind by historic Research: though unhappily it is the truth, to
which a rich and commercial nation listens with most reluctance
and receives with least faith.

That needs little translating for the 1970s. I don't happen to regard
topicality or immediate 'relevance' as the sole criterion for an intellectual work, but with all its faults *The Friend* is very much a tract for the
times—and, I suspect, for all times.

Early Blake

BLAKE'S POETICAL SKETCHES, privately printed in 1783, have an anonymous Advertisement, perhaps by the Rev. A. S. Matthews, who together with Flaxman seems to have paid for the printing:

> The following sketches were the production of untutored youth, commenced in his twelfth, and occasionally resumed by the author till his twentieth year; since which time, his talents having been wholly directed to the attainment of excellence in his profession, he has been deprived of the leisure requisite to such a revisal of these sheets, as might have rendered them less unfit to meet the public eye. Conscious of the irregularities and defects to be found in almost every page, his friends have still believed that they possessed a poetic originality, which merited some respite from oblivion. These their opinions remain, however, to be now reproved or confirmed by a less partial public.

We certainly owe a debt of gratitude to the friends; but no one would now dare, with Blake's formidable later achievement before him, to strike quite that patronizing note. Most accounts of Blake select a scattering of the Poetical Sketches for praise; Margoliouth has suggested some of the ways in which they point forward to later and more important things; and Margaret Lowery, in *Windows of the Morning* has shown at length, from echoes and 'imitations', how widely the young poet had read—not only in the Bible, Milton, Spenser and Shakespeare, but in a very considerable number of less canonical works, ranging from Jonson's *The Under-wood* and *Miscellanies* to Percy's *Reliques* and *Ossian*. 'There is, perhaps,' Miss Lowery rightly observes, 'no better way to understand how a true poet surmounts and becomes, to a remarkable degree, independent of his own direct environment than to see how far afield his mind reaches in the quest for congenial companionship'.[1]

My purpose is not to attempt a reassessment of the Sketches as a whole, but to call attention to the remarkable group of eight Songs that come midway in the collection of shorter poems preceding the dramatic fragment, *King Edward the Third*, and the prose pieces. These poems seem to me to be considerably more than dim premonitions—

'though well for a lad'—of what is still to come: taken together—and to see what they are doing it is necessary to take them together—they represent a positive achievement for which no apology is needed. They are not in any sense Shakespearian derivatives, but if we look for anything comparable before Blake we have to go back to Shakespeare.

The Songs can be read and enjoyed by themselves. Since, however, as I hope to show, they are also an intrinsic part of Blake's work as a whole, it is useful to take our bearings from a line in *Milton*:

Distinguish therefore States from Individuals in those States.[2]

A major part of Blake's achievement as a poet lies in his ability to define —to make fully and concretely present—those 'states' that are familiar to us all: some that may become more or less permanent dispositions; some temporary moods that we need to sort out and understand; some that we have to learn to live with, even though 'contrary' to what we feel as our main bent. In other words Blake's poetry is inseparable from his psychological insight. It is of course important to get clear what this means. The poetry isn't the description or embodiment of previously thought out 'views' of the nature of the mind; it is the way in which Blake *felt his way towards* his insights. The value of Blake's 'psychology' is dependent on his success as a poet, and we may apply here what Susanne Langer says of artistic conception in general: 'The facts which it makes conceivable are precisely those which literal statement distorts. Having once symbolized and perceived them, we may talk about them; but only artistic perception can find them and judge them in the first place.'[3]

We cannot be sure of the order that Blake intended for the eight Songs, though the arrangement of the Sketches as a whole suggests that the printed order is not haphazard. As they stand they form a series of contrasts, all, except 'Mad Song', explicitly dealing with sexual love, and all written in the first person. The imagined speaker however is not Blake; he (or she) is a persona representing one of the many ways in which experience, especially the experience of love, can be met.[4] Three of them—'Love and harmony combine', 'I love the jocund dance', and 'Fresh from the dewy hill, the merry year'—are songs of happy love; the other five define various 'states' in which individual fulfilment, as measured by the happy poems, is impossible. Of these, only one—'How sweet I roam'd'—presents the state from the outside; the others define by a form of dramatic embodiment. In all five the comment is entirely implicit; the reader is left to make his own assessment by responding to the poetry. Finally, in all the poems to be considered, as throughout the Sketches, there is a new and distinctive music. It is through the music—the way the poems demand to be read (or sung?)—that subtleties of tone are mediated. Perhaps to be alert to this is the best start for seeing what Blake is about. As Jack Lindsay said in his short appreciative study of Blake's metric, 'Vitality of rhythm is part of emotional clarity'.

J. T. Smith, who knew Blake, having referred to the printing of *Poetical Sketches*, says,

> Much about this time, Blake wrote many other songs, to which he also composed tunes. These he would occasionally sing to his friends; and though, according to his confession, he was entirely unacquainted with the science of music, his ear was so good, that his tunes were sometimes most singularly beautiful, and were noted down by musical professors.[6]

It is unlikely that we shall ever know more about the way in which some of Blake's lyrics were set to music; and certainly I am not competent to determine how the vitality of speech rhythm, which is so obviously there, could be conveyed in a musical setting. But one way of pointing to the distinctive quality of 'How sweet I roam'd' is to say that if it begins by sounding like a conventional love song, (though 'the summer's pride' and 'the prince of love' should alert us), it clearly ends as something very different indeed.

> How sweet I roam'd from field to field,
>   And tasted all the summer's pride,
> 'Till I the prince of love beheld,
>   Who in the sunny beams did glide!
>
> He shew'd me lilies for my hair,
>   And blushing roses for my brow;
> He led me through his gardens fair,
>   Where all his golden pleasures grow.
>
> With sweet May dews my wings were wet,
>   And Phoebus fir'd my vocal rage;
> He caught me in his silken net,
>   And shut me in his golden cage.
>
> He loves to sit and hear me sing,
>   Then, laughing, sports and plays with me;
> Then stretches out my golden wing,
>   And mocks my loss of liberty.

Miss Mona Wilson, rightly protesting against 'a tendency among students of Blake's symbolic books . . . to impose too systematic and definite a meaning upon the lyrics in the light of their own interpretations of the details of his other works', takes this poem as an example.

After quoting some interpretations that she considers forced, she writes,

> Equally destructive of the picture is the suggestion that the fourteen-year-old Blake symbolized marriage by the golden cage in the *Song*, 'How sweet I roam'd'. This would mean the superfluous insertion of a second little bird sulking in a corner of the cage or trilling unheeded songs from an importunate throat.[7]

Surely it is Miss Wilson who is doing the 'too systematic and definite' reading here. For the speaker, the prince of love has become the all-too-human lover or husband who has devised a very pretty captivity for his wife; naturally he is not in the cage himself. If we dismiss from our minds all thoughts of the 'second little bird sulking in a corner', which Blake does not give us, and allow what he does give to take effect, what we hear, unmistakably, is the voice of a woman who does not quite understand anything except that the promise of fulfilment in love has inexplicably turned into a sense of constraint and non-fulfilment—a captivity no less sure (a golden cage) for the apparent gentleness (silken net) and 'loving' playfulness that compose it. There is no doubt that the speaker is 'placed': she is a conventionally poetically minded girl whose 'vocal rage' is 'fir'd' as in a good many eighteenth-century pieces. But we are certainly not invited to look down on the dawning feelings of young love: there is a tenderness and freshness in the opening stanzas that lifts them out of the merely conventional. And in the imagery, the rhythm and alliteration of the closing lines, Blake's protest against male dominance and possessiveness comes through very strongly indeed. But although the man's lazy and self-regarding pride in his possession ('He loves to sit and hear me sing') is the main target, there is at least the suggestion that this kind of young woman would indeed attract this kind of lover.*

In the next poem it is the woman speaker herself who is the main object of attention.

---

* We may agree with Miss Wilson about the dangers of 'reading in'; but in the work of a poet who so consistently developed his ideas through recurrent imagery, it is surely legitimate to confirm a reading of one poem—even to seek help in the reading—by reference to others. Miss Lowery refers to 'The Golden Net' in the Pickering MS (where it is a man who is the captive) and to Quid's song in *An Island in the Moon*—'Come and be cured of all your pains In Matrimony's Golden cage'; Blake may also have known John Davies' 'A Contention betwixt a Wife, a Widow, and a Maid', 'Wives are as birds in golden cages kept', and it would be like him to make a sardonic comment on that.—*Wings of the Morning*, p. 103; Plate 7 of *The Gates of Paradise* (*Complete Writings*, p. 765) is probably relevant too. In the end of course one comes back to success or failure in the particular instance.

My silks and fine array,
  My smiles and languish'd air,
By love are driv'n away;
  And mournful lean Despair
Brings me yew to deck my grave:
Such end true lovers have.

His face is fair as heav'n,
  When springing buds unfold;
O why to him was't giv'n,
  Whose heart is wintry cold?
His breast is love's all worship'd tomb,
Where all love's pilgrims come.

Bring me an axe and spade,
  Bring me a winding sheet;
When I my grave have made,
  Let winds and tempests beat:
Then down I'll lie, as cold as clay.
True love doth pass away!

If proof of poetic genius were wanted it could be found in the subtly changing rhythms of this poem. No account in terms of shifts from iambic to trochaic, reversed stresses, and so on, can do it justice; all one needs to do is to see how tone and rhythm define meanings that could not otherwise be put into words. The plangent tone that comes with the shift of rhythm in the fifth line of the first stanza has just that shade of self-conscious self-awareness that warns us against identifying with the speaker, who unconsciously reveals, as well as expresses, herself. Not that we are invited to put too sharp an edge on our criticism:* love has made the girl relinquish her conscious attractions—'My smiles and languish'd air'—and to my mind there is something honestly touching in the second stanza, as there is indeed throughout. But with the return of the falling rhythm—'Bring me an axe and spade'—we are back to what sounds like the *dressing* of a real emotion: it is not only Blake, we feel, but his imagined speaker who has read *Hamlet*. I do not know of anything in English lyric poetry before Blake that has achieved this kind of dramatic presentation—something that 'places' as it expresses, and simultaneously invites sympathy and detached understanding.

* * *

* As we are with Miss Gittipin in *An Island* (p. 61):
  Leave, O leave me to my sorrows,
  Here I'll sit & fade away: etc.

The next two songs are in marked contrast to the two that precede them, as they are to the two that follow, for they both deal with fulfilment in love, though in significantly different ways.

Love and harmony combine
And around our souls intwine,
While thy branches mix with mine
And our roots together join.

Joys upon our branches sit,
Chirping loud, and singing sweet;
Like gentle streams beneath our feet
Innocence and virtue meet.

Thou the golden fruit dost bear,
I am clad in flowers fair;
Thy sweet boughs perfume the air,
And the turtle buildeth there.

There she sits and feeds her young,
Sweet I hear her mournful song;
And thy lovely leaves among,
There is love: I hear his tongue.

There his charming nest doth lay,
There he sleeps the night away;
There he sports along the day,
And doth among our branches play.

I love the jocund dance,
    The softly breathing song,
Where innocent eyes do glance
    And where lisps the maiden's tongue.

I love the laughing vale,
    I love the echoing hill,
Where mirth does never fail,
    And the jolly swain laughs his fill.

I love the pleasant cot,
    I love the innocent bow'r,
Where white and brown is our lot,
    Or fruit in the mid-day hour.

I love the oaken seat,
    Beneath the oaken tree,
Where all the old villagers meet,
    And laugh our sports to see.

I love our neighbours all,
But, Kitty, I better love thee;
And love them I ever shall;
But thou art all to me.

In the handling of the verse there are perhaps some signs of the apprentice hand—in the occasional awkward inversion and a scattering of mildly obtrusive auxiliaries. But for the most part rhyme and rhythm are *used*—not only in isolated felicities ('Or fruit in the mid-day hour': the distribution of stresses beautifully suggests the noon pause), but in cumulative effects that distinguish each poem from its companion. In the first the rhyme sustained through each stanza suggests the desired concentration on the one relationship. In the second the shorter lines, the predominantly iambic rhythm and the alternate rhymes, help towards the impression of a shared jollity. Both poems contain rather remarkable anticipations of the later Blake. In both there is the celebration of a sturdy joy—joys are 'chirping loud', love 'sports along the day', and the poet 'loves the laughing vale': and in the first, images of natural growth and fruition are used, without any suggestion of artifice, to define the exultant personal love. But whereas the vigorous singing movement of that poem serves a private celebration, the simpler measure and the simple catalogue of loved objects in the second—like the straightforward and entirely non-symbolic references to an actual community—relate individual fulfilment to a social group. Taken together the poems indicate two constant preoccupations of Blake— with 'private' experience in its intenser moments, and with the 'social' world that supports (or frustrates) that experience, and can in turn be transformed by it. It is sufficient praise to say that they are clearly by the author of 'The Ecchoing Green'.

*   *   *

Memory, hither come,
And tune your merry notes;
And, while upon the wind
Your music floats,

I'll pore upon the stream,
Where sighing lovers dream,
And fish for fancies as they pass
Within the watery glass.

I'll drink of the clear stream,
And hear the linnet's song;
And there I'll lie and dream
The day along:

And, when night comes, I'll go
To places fit for woe,
Walking along the darken'd valley
With silent Melancholy.

This too is deceptively simple. The appeal to Memory's 'merry notes' and the limpid development of the first two stanzas, with their odd suggestion of a medieval miniature, seem like a straightforward invitation to share a pleasantly indulged mood. It is the second half of the poem that reveals the standpoint from which Blake is seeing the picture created by his speaker. In the vigorous 'Love and harmony combine', love 'sleeps the night away' and 'sports along the day'. Here the order is reversed; the speaker joins the other 'sighing lovers' in dreaming 'the day along', and spends the night that is meant for sleep seeking 'places fit for woe',

Walking along the darken'd valley
With silent Melancholy.

Sense and music combine to create, and so to define, a mood of self-cherishing and inactive love-melancholy. Blake, who was to celebrate energy, who was to define Vice as 'a Negative . . . the omission of act in self & the hindering of act in another'[8] and who was to invite the reader of *Jerusalem* to 'love me for this energetic exertion of my talent'[9], even at this early stage didn't much believe in languid dreaming. If the poem begins with song, it ends with silence and self-absorption. Memory, for Blake, was always connected not only with a fixed world of mechanical rules but with passivity: his poetry, he insisted, was the daughter, not of memory, but of inspiration. It seems impossible to doubt that an important aspect of Blake's philosophy is here taking shape, not as thought but as a sensitive feeling into a mood and its implications. On this reading we have in little an example of what is meant by poetic thought and of what I have referred to as the virtual identity of Blake's psychological insight and his power as a poet.

*   *   *

How conscious was the intention to create just the effect that 'Memory, hither come' does in fact achieve, is perhaps a question not worth asking. Poets, it seems, are not always fully conscious of what, looking back, we may properly see as their deeper intentions; and their poems, when they have made them, have to speak for themselves. But with the much-praised 'Mad Song' before us it is hard to deny that the youthful Blake was sometimes capable of the same subtle insight as he showed in his maturity.

The Wild winds weep,
   And the night is a-cold;
Come hither, Sleep,
   And my griefs infold;
But lo! the morning peeps
   Over the eastern steeps,
And the rustling birds of dawn
   The earth do scorn.

Lo! to the vault
   Of paved heaven
With sorrow fraught
   My notes are driven:
They strike the ear of night,
   Make weep the eyes of day;
They make mad the roaring winds,
   And with tempests play.

Like a fiend in a cloud,
   With howling woe,
After night I do croud,
   And with night will go;
I turn my back to the east,
From whence comforts have increas'd;
For light doth seize my brain
   With frantic pain.

Miss Lowery has pointed out that there are various analogues to this poem in Percy's *Reliques*.[10] I suspect that the relation is one of contrast rather than comparison. One can feel nothing but astonishment at the sheer technical ability displayed—the way in which marked and abrupt variations in the underlying pattern of rhyme and rhythm create the sense of mind and feelings disorganized, 'like sweet bells jangled, out of tune and harsh'. Blake of course doesn't tell us, but it does seem legitimate to see the poem as representing one possible result of the perversions and inadequacies demonstrated in the three earlier poems that dealt with various obstructions in the way of love. But even without that connexion the meaning is clear. The speaker invokes sleep, but the rigid consciousness refuses the relaxation of sleep,—Frost's

      interruption of the night,
   To ease attention off when overtight . . .
   And ask us if our premises are right;

and the new day only brings a renewal of misery—a keying-up of melancholy towards madness, curiously echoed in the broken rhyme of 'vault' and 'fraught' and the failure of rhyme in lines 5 and 7 of the second stanza, where rhyme might have been expected. The total effect is a half-pitying definition-by-expression of a particular kind of pain, — but only half-pitying: for with the return of the basic rhyme pattern and a more insistent, less broken rhythm in the final stanza, Blake brings out how much of this distressed and distressing consciousness is in fact willed. The speaker exults in his desperate attempt to keep ahead of the dawn, to prevent the flooding in of light, —

> I turn my back to the east,
> From whence comforts have increas'd . . .

The madness is not less poignantly expressed for containing this implicit criticism; it is as though the poet said, —this frantic pain, which is real and wounding, is one with the turning of the back on 'light' and 'comfort'; see how, in refusing life, human beings can so desperately maim themselves. It is not only the 'fiend in a cloud' that reminds us that what we have here is the future author of *Songs of Experience*.

* * *

I do not see how the first six poems of the sequence can be read otherwise than as deliberate inventions in which Blake uses a rapidly maturing poetic power in the service of psychological exploration. And the last two poems are clearly intended as a contrasting pair in which two of the 'contrary states of the human soul' are given dramatic expression.

> Fresh from the dewy hill, the merry year
> Smiles on my head, and mounts his flaming car;
> Round my young brows the laurel wreathes a shade,
> And rising glories beam around my head.
>
> My feet are wing'd, while o'er the dewy lawn
> I meet my maiden, risen like the morn:
> Oh bless those holy feet, like angels' feet;
> Oh bless those limbs, beaming with heav'nly light!
>
> Like as an angel glitt'ring in the sky
> In times of innocence and holy joy;
> The joyful shepherd stops his grateful song
> To hear the music of an angel's tongue.
>
> So when she speaks, the voice of Heaven I hear:
> So when we walk, nothing impure comes near;
> Each field seems Eden, and each calm retreat;
> Each village seems the haunt of holy feet.

But that sweet village, where my black-ey'd maid
Closes her eyes in sleep beneath night's shade,
When'er I enter, more than mortal fire
Burns in my soul, and does my song inspire.

When early morn walks forth in sober grey,
Then to my black ey'd maid I haste away;
When evening sits beneath her dusky bow'r,
And gently sighs away the silent hour,
The village bell alarms, away I go,
And the vale darkens at my pensive woe.

To that sweet village, where my black ey'd maid
Doth drop a tear beneath the silent shade,
I turn my eyes; and, pensive as I go,
Curse my black stars, and bless my pleasing woe.

Oft when the summer sleeps among the trees,
Whisp'ring faint murmurs to the scanty breeze,
I walk the village round; if at her side
A youth doth walk in stolen joy and pride,
I curse my stars in bitter grief and woe,
That made my love so high, and me so low.

O should she e'er prove false, his limbs I'd tear,
And throw all pity on the burning air;
I'd curse bright fortune for my mixed lot,
And then I'd die in peace, and be forgot.

In the first of these, a youthful song of affirmation and fulfilment, there is more than the pathetic fallacy in the merry year, the sun's flaming car and his rising glories. The scene is at least half created by what Coleridge was to call a 'strong music in the soul', a music that (to repeat it once more) is not something super-added but intrinsic to the power to see, to feel, and to realize.

So when she speaks, the voice of Heaven I hear:
So when we walk, nothing impure comes near;
Each field seems Eden, and each calm retreat;
Each village seems the haunt of holy feet.

The second song, which has affinities with 'Memory, hither come', reverses all this. In the first, the black-ey'd maid 'Closes her eyes in sleep beneath night's shade' and inspires the poet's song. In the second, she 'drops a tear beneath the silent shade' and the 'pensive' lover curses his black stars. The imagined situation is of course different: in the second poem the lover never has a chance to say 'we'. But Blake seems to be less interested in indicating the thwarting circumstances, 'That made my love so high, and me so low', than in defining a form of 'pensive' love-melancholy, cherishing itself and turning sour with fantasies of revenge. The poems indeed show less assured power than some of their predecessors, but there is no immaturity in the linking of a rather impotent aggressiveness and an inactive self-pity,—'And then I'd die in peace, and be forgot'. Here, surely, we are very close to Miss Gittipin.

*   *   *

I hope that this small demonstration has served its purpose. The poems, to be sure, may not appear to all readers as good as, on repeated readings, they seem to me. But they certainly deserve more attention than they have had. The dramatic poet of *Songs of Innocence and Experience* is there; so is the innocently shrewd psychologist; and so is the master of a subtle music. Of course there are immaturities. But this young poet, intuitively feeling his way towards the sure and sharp penetration of mood and feeling of the later poems was also working with some deliberation: the technical sureness proves it,—the control of very varied verse forms for discernible purposes; so too does the arrangement of the poems that virtually forces on the reader a criss-cross of mutually enlightening insights. The poems, I have said, need to be read together, not sampled in anthologies. And when they are so read they reveal through their contrasting voices a variety of contrasting 'states' which are defined for us once and for all. Perhaps it is only the fact that every reader who approaches the *Poetical Sketches* knows in advance that they were written by a young man not yet twenty that has prevented them from having their due recognition: a boy, we automatically assume, couldn't do the sort of thing I have claimed he was doing. To which the only answer is that the boy was William Blake; and if we are prepared to allow extreme precocity to, say, Rimbaud, I do not see why we should deny it to Blake.

V

George Herbert

(i)

THE POETRY of George Herbert is so intimately bound up with his beliefs as a Christian and his practice as a priest of the Church of England that those who enjoy the poetry without sharing the beliefs may well feel some presumption in attempting to define the human, as distinguished from the specifically Christian, value of his work. The excuse for such an attempt can only be the conviction that there is much more in Herbert's poetry for readers of *all* kinds than is recognized in the common estimate. That his appeal is a wide one is implicit in the accepted claim that he is a poet and not simply a writer of devotional verse; but I think I am right in saying that discussion of him tends to take for granted that admirers are likely to be drawn from a smaller circle than admirers of, say, Donne or Marvell. Even Dr. Hutchinson, whose superbly edited and annotated edition of the complete Works is not likely to be superseded[1]—it would be difficult to imagine a better-qualified editor and introducer—even Dr. Hutchinson remarks that, 'if today there is a less general sympathy with Herbert's religion, the beauty and sincerity of its expression are appreciated by those who do not share it'. True; but there is also much more than the 'expression' that we appreciate, as I shall try to show. Herbert's poetry is an integral part of the great English tradition.

It is, however, with expression, with form and manner, that appreciation must begin, and Dr. Hutchinson directs our attention to what are unquestionably the most important features of Herbert's style. 'His craftsmanship is conspicuous. Almost any poem of his has its object well defined', he says. And again:

> Few English poets have been able to use the plain words of ordinary speech with a greater effect of simple dignity than Herbert. From Donne he had learnt the use of the conversational tone, which establishes an intimacy between poet and reader; and when his poems are read aloud, the emphasis falls easily on the natural order of the speaking idiom.

In other words, Herbert, like Donne, is a realist in literature. The first *Jordan* poem ('Who says that fictions onely and false hair Become

a verse?') is not only an expression of personal dedication, it is
also, as the second poem of the same title is explicitly, a literary
manifesto:

> Is it no verse, except enchanted groves
> And sudden arbours shadow course-spunne lines?
> Must purling streams refresh a lovers loves?
> Must all be vail'd, while he that reades, divines,
>   Catching the sense at two removes?
>
> Shepherds are honest people; let them sing:
> Riddle who list, for me, and pull for Prime. . . .

The 'pure, manly and unaffected' diction that Coleridge noted, the
rhythm that, though musical, is close to the rhythm of living speech,
the construction that almost always follows the evolution of thought
and feeling, even in the most intricate of the stanza forms that he used
in such variety—these elements of Herbert's style show his determina-
tion to make his verse sincere and direct, to avoid even the slightest
degree of the distortion that occurs when a preconceived idea of 'the
poetical' takes charge of the matter. And the effort of craftsmanship
involved was one with the moral effort to know himself, to bring his
conflicts into the daylight and, so far as possible, to resolve them. It is
in the wide application of Herbert's self-discovery that the value of his
poetry lies; but before approaching the substance of his verse I should
like to examine some aspects of his style that have had less attention
than those so far glanced at. For the 'definition of the object' that Dr.
Hutchinson rightly puts in the forefront of Herbert's achievement as a
poet is not simply a matter of surface purity and naturalness; it has
depth and solidity, and we need to become conscious of the variety of
resources brought to bear in the process—simple only in appearance—
that the defining is.

It is here that literary criticism necessarily joins hands with 'the
sociology of literature', since what we are concerned with is the personal use of a more than personal idiom with its roots in tradition and the
general life. To the critic no less than to the student of English civilization in the first half of the seventeenth century it is of considerable
significance that Herbert, as man and artist, is not the product of
one social class alone. An aristocrat by birth, and related to some of
the more prominent figures at court, the protégé of James i, the friend
of Donne and Bacon, he has also that ingrained sense of 'common'
English life which in so many representative figures of the time blends
with and modifies the intellectual currents from the world of courtly
refinement, learning and public affairs. His poetry has plainly an upper-
class background. The Metaphysical subtlety and intellectual analysis

that he learnt from Donne,* the skill in music—so pleasantly attested by Walton—that one senses even in his handling of the spoken word, the easy and unostentatious references to science and learning, all imply a cultivated milieu.† And although the rightness of tone that keeps even his most intimate poetry free from sentimentality or over-insistence springs from deeply personal characteristics, it is also related to the well-bred ease of manner of 'the gentleman'.‡

Turn, however, to that poem with the characteristic title, *The Quip*, and a different aspect of Herbert's genius, implying a different source of strength, is at once apparent.

> The merrie world did on a day
> With his train-bands and mates agree
> To meet together, where I lay,
> And all in sport to geere at me.
>
> First, Beautie crept into a rose,
> Which when I pluckt not, Sir, said she,
> Tell me, I pray, Whose hands are those?
> *But thou shalt answer, Lord, for me.*
>
> Then Money came, and chinking still,
> What tune is this, poore man? said he:
> I heard in Musick you had skill.
> *But thou shalt answer, Lord, for me.*
>
> Then came brave Glorie puffing by
> In silks that whistled, who but he?
> He scarce allow'd me half an eie.
> *But thou shalt answer, Lord, for me . . .*

* Herbert's metaphysical wit has marked differences from Donne's as well as affinities with it. It tends in one direction towards humour, which is saved by its intellectual quality from anything like whimsicality. The following verse from *Vanitie* (i) shows his amused play of mind:

> The subtil Chymick can devest
> And strip the creature naked, till he finde
> The callow principles within their nest:
>   There he imparts to them his minde,
> Admitted to their bed-chamber, before
>   They appeare trim and drest
> To ordinarie suitours at the doore.

† See in this connexion his fine poem, *The Pearl*.

‡ That Herbert's invariable courtesy is based on a genuine responsiveness to other people—that it is not simply 'good manners'—is plain from the advice given in *The Church Porch*, e.g. stanzas 52–55. See also Letter XII in Dr. Hutchinson's edition, where Herbert discusses the needs of his orphan nieces.

The personifications here have nothing in common either with Spenser's allegorical figures or with the capitalized abstractions of the eighteenth century: 'Brave Glorie puffing by In silks that whistled' might have come straight from *The Pilgrim's Progress*. And Bunyan, as Dr. G. R. Owst has shown,[2] had behind him not only the rich folk-culture that produced the ballads, but also a long line of preachers in the vernacular. Again and again Herbert reminds us of the popular preacher addressing his audience—without a shade of condescension in doing so—in the homely manner that they themselves use. There is humour, mimicry and sarcasm, seen most clearly when the verses are read aloud with the inflexions they demand.

> He doth not like this vertue, no;
> Give him his dirt to wallow in all night:
> These Preachers make
> His head to shoot and ake. (*Miserie*)

> *Love God, and love your neighbour. Watch and pray.*
> *Do as ye would be done unto.*
> O dark instructions; ev'n as dark as day!
> Who can these Gordian knots undo? (*Divinitie*)

> To be in both worlds full
> Is more then God was, who was hungrie here.
> Wouldst thou his laws of fasting disanull?
> Enact good cheer?
> Lay out thy joy, yet hope to save it?
> Wouldst thou both eat thy cake, and have it? (*The Size*)

Herbert, we know, made a collection of 'Outlandish (*sc.* foreign) Proverbs' for the community at Little Gidding, and although he does not often, as in the last quotation, incorporate a popular saying, many of his terse sentences have a proverbial ring.

Herbert's 'popular' manner is, however, far more deeply grounded— and serves a more important purpose in his poetry—than these last examples might suggest.

> Let forrain nations of their language boast,
> What fine varietie each tongue affords:
> I like our language, as our men and coast:
> Who cannot dresse it well, want wit, not words.

This, from *The Sonne*, is explicit,—'I like our language': and one way of enforcing the judgment that he is in the great English tradition is to point out how surely he uses the native idiom to give the effect of something immediately present, something going on under one's eyes.

In the colloquial expostulation of *Conscience* an over-active scrupulous-
ness comes to life as it is rebuked:

> Peace pratler, do not lowre:
> Not a fair look, but thou dost call it foul:
> Not a sweet dish, but thou dost call it sowre:
> Musick to thee doth howl.
> By listning to thy chatting fears
> I have both lost mine eyes and eares.

The opening of *The Discharge* has a similar, almost dramatic, effect:

> Busie enquiring heart, what wouldst thou know?
> Why dost thou prie,
> And turn, and leer, and with a licorous eye
> Look high and low:
> And in thy lookings stretch and grow?

Even his simplest poems have a muscular force, an almost physical
impact, as in the description of 'the honest man' (in *Constancie*):

> Whom neither force nor fawning can
> Unpinne, or wrench from giving all their due.

He uses alliteration and assonance in the native Elizabethan way, not,
that is, as a poetic or musical device, but as a means of controlling
emphasis and movement so as to obtain the maximum immediacy.
To the examples already given may be added these lines from *The
Flower*:

> Many a spring I shoot up fair,
> Offring at heav'n, growing and groning thither,

where the effect is, in Shakespearian fashion, to assimilate the participles
to each other, so that the groans seem an intrinsic part of the growing.
It is the artist's feeling for *all* the resources of 'our language' that gives
to the greater poems of spiritual conflict their disturbing immediacy.

Herbert's style, then, is 'popular' as well as courtly and Metaphysical,
and his leaning towards the manner of common Elizabethan speech is
further emphasized by his well-known liking for homely illustrations,
analogies and metaphors. His poems contain plenty of learned allusions
(especially, as was natural in that age, to astronomy), but he certainly
'goes less far afield for his analogies than Donne and finds most that
will serve his purpose from common life',—from carpentry, gardening
and everyday domestic activity: Redemption 'spreads the plaister equal
to the crime', after the refreshment of sleep, day will 'give new wheels

to our disorder'd clocks', and so on. But although this feature of Herbert's style is so commonly recognized that further illustration is unnecessary, its function is sometimes misinterpreted, as though Herbert's experience were somehow *limited* by his interest in the commonplace. Even Professor Grierson, after listing some of Herbert's comparisons, remarks:

> These are the 'mean' similes which in Dr. Johnson's view were fatal to poetic effect even in Shakespeare. We have learned not to be so fastidious, yet when they are not purified by the passionate heat of the poet's dramatic imagination the effect is a little stuffy, for the analogies and symbols are more fanciful or traditional than natural and imaginative.

The last sentence, it is true, contains a qualifying clause, '*when* they are not purified by . . . imagination'; but since Professor Grierson goes on to describe Herbert as a 'sincere and sensitive' rather than a 'greatly imaginative' poet, some undue emphasis remains on the phrase 'a little stuffy'.*

The significance of Herbert's 'homely' imagery—pointing as it does to some of the central preoccupations of his poetry—is something that we need to get clear. But before taking up this question—or, rather, as a way of taking it up—I should like to bring into focus another aspect of his imagery. As well as metaphor and simile Herbert uses symbols and allegory. Now whereas metaphor conveys its meaning directly from common experience, in symbolism there is usually an element of the arbitrary. *The Church-floore* is an obvious example:

> Mark you the floore? that square & speckled stone,
> Which looks so firm and strong,
> Is *Patience*.

But this arbitrary use of symbols is not characteristic of Herbert. Much more often his verse (like Bunyan's prose) gives life to his symbolic figures and allegorical situations, so that they appear as something immediately experienced, and carry their meaning with them. Even the highly emblematic poem, *Love Unknown*, has a matter-of-fact quality that makes it something more than a monument to a bygone taste. In *The Pilgrimage* the allegory is completely realized in terms of the actual.

* 'But if not a greatly imaginative, Herbert is a sincere and sensitive poet, and an accomplished artist elaborating his argumentative strain or little allegories and conceits with felicitous completeness, and managing his variously patterned stanzas . . . with a finished and delicate harmony.'— *Metaphysical Lyrics and Poems of the Seventeenth Century*, pp. xlii–xliv.

I travell'd on, seeing the hill, where lay
    My expectation.
A long it was and weary way.
    The gloomy cave of Desperation
I left on th' one, and on the other side
    The rock of Pride.

And so I came to Fancies medow strow'd
    With many a flower:
Fain would I here have made abode,
    But I was quicken'd by my houre.
So to Cares cops I came, and there got through
    With much ado.

That led me to the wilde of Passion, which
    Some call the wold;
A wasted place, but sometimes rich.
    Here I was robb'd of all my gold,
Save one good Angell, which a friend had ti'd
    Close to my side.

Mr Empson, analysing the rich meaning of the third verse,[3] remarks that Herbert's manner is that of a traveller, 'long afterwards, mentioning where he has been and what happened to him, as if only to pass the time'. But the air of verisimilitude, the impression of a difficult journey actually undertaken, is not only an effect of the sober tone; it springs also from the sensitive and subtle movement. In reading the second verse we feel that we ourselves have been in 'Cares cops' and scrambled out

        —got through
        With much ado—

as best we might. The fourth verse, making skilful use of the varied lengths of line and of the slight end-of-line pauses, reproduces the sensations of the traveller, as expectation—rather out of breath but eager and confident—gives way abruptly to flat disappointment:

At length I got unto the gladsome hill,
    Where lay my hope,
Where lay my heart; and climbing still,
    When I had gain'd the brow and top,
A lake of brackish waters on the ground
    Was all I found.

The allegorical form is of course a reminder that what we are concerned with is a graph of more than one kind of experience, but at no point in the poem are we simply interpreting an allegory; the bitter poignancy of the conclusion springs from deeply personal feelings that we have been made to share.

> With that abash'd and struck with many a sting
>   Of swarming fears,
>   I fell, and cry'd, Alas my King!
>   Can both the way and end be tears?
> Yet taking heart I rose, and then perceiv'd
>   I was deceiv'd:
>
> My hill was further: so I flung away,
>   Yet heard a crie
>   Just as I went, *None goes that way*
>   *And lives*: If that be all, said I,
> After so foul a journey death is fair,
>   And but a chair.

This use of vivid allegory—tied down, as it were, to the actual and immediate—represents one aspect of Herbert's method. In poems such as *Vertue* and *Life* ('I made a posie, while the day ran by') we have the opposite and complementary process, where natural objects, without ceasing to be natural, have a rich symbolic meaning. In the lovely lines of *Vertue* the rose is no less a real rose, 'angrie and brave', for being at the same time a symbol of life rooted in death. It is here that we see something of the significance of Herbert's consistent use of homely and familiar imagery. We may recall Coleridge's account of the genesis of the *Lyrical Ballads*: 'Mr. Wordsworth was to propose to himself as his object to give the charm of novelty to things of every day, and to excite a feeling analogous to the supernatural, by awakening the mind's attention from the lethargy of custom, and directing it to the loveliness and wonder of the world before us.' It is 'the things of every day' that Herbert's poetry keeps consistently before us; but instead of invoking a rather adventitious 'charm of novelty' or exciting 'a feeling analogous to the supernatural' (one thinks of *Peter Bell*), he sees them in direct relation to a supernatural order in which he firmly believes. Thus in his poetry, just as the supernatural is apprehended in terms of the familiar, so common things—*whilst remaining common things*, clearly observed, and deeply felt—have a supernatural significance, and the familiar is perpetually new. 'This is the skill, and doubtless the Holy Scripture intends thus much', he says, 'when it condescends to the naming of a plough, a hatchett, a bushell, leaven, boyes piping and dancing; shewing that things of ordinary use are not only to serve in the way of drudgery, but to be washed and cleansed, and serve for lights even of Heavenly Truths.'[4] Once more we are reminded of Bunyan, in whose blend of Biblical language and native idiom the august events of the Bible seem

to be transacted in a familiar world, and the humble doings of every day
are placed in a context that reveals how momentous they are.

(ii)

Herbert's message to Nicholas Ferrar when, a few weeks before his
death, he sent him the manuscript of *The Temple*, is well known.

> Sir, I pray deliver this little book to my dear brother Ferrar, and
> tell him he shall find in it a picture of the many spiritual conflicts
> that have passed betwixt God and my soul, before I could subject
> mine to the will of Jesus my Master; in whose service I have now
> found perfect freedom; desire him to read it: and then, if he can
> think it may turn to the advantage of any dejected poor soul, let it
> be made public; if not let him burn it; for I and it are less than the
> least of God's mercies.

Herbert's poetry was for him very largely a way of working out his
conflicts. But it does not, like some religious poetry, simply *express*
conflict; it is consciously and steadily directed towards resolution and
integration. Dr. Hutchinson rightly describes the poems as 'colloquies
of the soul with God or self-communings which seek to bring order
into that complex personality of his which he analyses so unsparingly'.

This general account of conflict and resolution as the stuff of Herbert's
poetry is, I believe, commonly accepted. But the conflict that gets most
—indeed almost exclusive—attention is the struggle between the ambitious man of the world and the priest. Dr. Hutchinson rightly insists
that Herbert's conflict of mind was not simply about the priesthood,
that his spiritual struggle 'was over the more general issue of his submission to the Divine will' (p. lxviii); but he elsewhere records the
opinion that 'his principal temptation, the "one cunning bosome-sin"
which is apt to break through all his fences, is ambition'[5] Now it would
certainly be unwise to underestimate Herbert's worldly ambitions, or
the severity of the struggle that took place in one 'not exempt from
passion and choler', who liked fine clothes and good company, before
he could renounce his hopes of courtly preferment and, finally, become
a country parson. But it seems to me that if we focus all our attention
there, seeing the struggle simply as one between 'ambition' and 'renunci-
ation', we ignore some even more fundamental aspects of Herbert's
self-division and at the same time obscure the more general relevance
of his experience. Most criticism of the poet tends to suggest that we
are simply watching someone else's conflict—sympathetic, no doubt,
but not intimately involved ourselves.

Behind the more obvious temptation of 'success' was one more
deeply rooted—a dejection of spirit that tended to make him regard his
own life, the life he was actually leading, as worthless and unprofitable.

Part of the cause was undoubtedly persistent ill-health. 'For my self,' he said, 'I alwaies fear'd sickness more then death, because sickness hath made me unable to perform those Offices for which I came into the world, and must yet be kept in it' (p. 363); and this sense of the frustration of his best purposes through illness is expressed in *The Crosse* and other poems:

> And then when after much delay,
> Much wrastling, many a combate, this deare end,
> So much desir'd, is giv'n, to take away
> My power to serve thee; to unbend
> All my abilities, my designes confound,
> And lay my threatnings bleeding on the ground.

It is, however, difficult to resist the impression that his agues and consumption only intensified a more ingrained self-distrust. Commenting on some lines from *The Temper* (i),

> —O let me, when thy roof my soul hath hid,
> O let me roost and nestle there—

Dr. Hutchinson remarks that 'Herbert often shows a fear of unlimited space and loves the shelter of an enclosure'; and his shrinking from the kind of experience that was possible for him shows itself now in the frequently recorded moods of despondency, now in the desire for a simpler and apparently more desirable form of existence:

> My stock lies dead, and no increase
> Doth my dull husbandrie improve. (*Grace*)

> All things are busie; onely I
> Neither bring hony with the bees,
> Nor flowres to make that, nor the husbandrie
>   To water these.

> I am no link of thy great chain,
> But all my companie is a weed. . . . (*Employment* (i))

> Oh that I were an Orenge-tree,
>   That busie plant!
> Then should I ever laden be,
>   And never want
> Some fruit for him that dressed me. (*Employment* (ii))

Now this feeling of uselessness and self-distrust has two further consequences: one is a preoccupation with time and death,

> —So we freeze on,
> Untill the grave increase our cold; (*Employment* (ii))

the other is a sense that life, real life, is going on elsewhere, where he happens not to be himself. It was his weakness, as well as his more positive qualities of 'birth and spirit', that made a career at court seem so intensely desirable: 'the town' was where other people lived active and successful lives. Certainly, then, it was not a small achievement to 'behold the court with an impartial eye, and see plainly that it is made up of fraud, and titles, and flattery, and many other such empty, imaginary, painted pleasures; pleasures that are so empty, as not to satisfy when they are enjoyed'.* But it was an even greater achievement to rid himself of the torturing sense of frustration and impotence and to accept the validity of his own experience. His poems come home to us because they give new meanings to 'acceptance'.

The first condition of development was that the disturbing elements in experience should be honestly recognized; and here we see the significance of Herbert's technical achievement, of his realism, of his ability to make his feelings immediately present. In the masterly verse of *Affliction* (i) we have one of the most remarkable records in the language of the achievement of maturity and of the inevitable pains of the process. In the opening stanzas movement and imagery combine to evoke the enchanted world of early manhood, when to follow the immediate dictates of the soul seems both duty and pleasure.

> When first thou didst entice to thee my heart,
>   I thought the service brave:
> So many joyes I writ down for my part,
>   Besides what I might have
> Out of my stock of naturall delights,
> Augmented with thy gracious benefits.
>
> I looked on thy furniture so fine,
>   And made it fine to me:
> Thy glorious houshold-stuffe did me entwine,
>   And 'tice me unto thee.
> Such starres I counted mine: both heav'n and earth
> Payd me my wages in a world of mirth.
>
> What pleasures could I want, whose King I served,
>   Where joyes my fellows were?
> Thus argu'd into hopes, my thoughts reserved
>   No place for grief or fear.
> Therefore my sudden soul caught at the place,
> And made her youth and fierceness seek thy face.

* Herbert to Woodnot, on the night of his induction to Bemerton; recorded by Walton.

At first thou gav'st me milk and sweetnesses;
    I had my wish and way:
My dayes were straw'd with flow'rs and happinesse;
    There was no moneth but May.

But implicit in the description—as we see from 'entice' and 'entwine'* and the phrase, 'argu'd into hopes'—is the admission that there *is* enchantment, an element of illusion in the 'naturall delights', and we are not surprised when the triumphant fourth verse ends with the sudden bleak recognition of ills previously unperceived but inherent in the processes of life:

> But with my yeares sorrow did twist and grow,
> And made a partie unawares for wo.

The three central verses not merely describe the 'woes'—sickness, the death of friends, disappointed hopes—they evoke with painful immediacy the feelings of the sufferer.

> Sorrow was all my soul; I scarce beleeved,
> Till grief did tell me roundly, that I lived.

With characteristic honesty Herbert admits the palliative of 'Academick praise'—something that temporarily 'dissolves' the mounting 'rage'; but the current of feeling is now flowing in a direction completely opposite to that of the opening.

> Whereas my birth and spirit rather took
>   The way that takes the town;
> Thou didst betray me to a lingring book,
>   And wrap me in a gown.
> I was entangled in the world of strife,
> Before I had the power to change my life.

'Betray' and 'entangle' make explicit a sense already present but not openly acknowledged in 'entice' and 'entwine'; and instead of direct spontaneity—'I had my wish and way'—there is division and uncertainty:

> I took thy sweetned pill, till I came where
> I could not go away, nor persevere.

* The earlier reading, in the Williams MS., is more explicit:

> I looked on thy furniture so rich,
>   And made it rich to me
> Thy glorious houshold-stuffe did me bewitch
>   Into thy familie.

In the eighth stanza the potentialities of emphasis latent in the spoken language are used to evoke the full sense of frustration and conflict:

> Yet lest perchance I should too happie be
>   In my unhappinesse,
> Turning my purge to food, thou throwest me
>   Into more sicknesses.
> Thus doth thy power crosse-bias me, not making
> Thine own gift good, yet me from my wayes taking.

Stanza nine is quieter in tone, bringing into prominence an element in the whole complex attitude of the poet previously expressed only in the quiet control of the verse in which such turbulent feelings have been presented:

> Now I am here, what thou wilt do with me
>   None of my books will show:
> I reade, and sigh, and wish I were a tree;
>   For sure then I should grow
> To fruit or shade: at least some bird would trust
> Her household to me, and I should be just.

The opening lines of the last stanza can be read in two ways according as we bring into prominence the resigned or the rebellious tone:

> Yet, though thou troublest me, I must be meek;
>   In weaknesse must be stout . . .

But resignation and rebellion are alike half-measures, and it is here, where the feelings are so subtly poised, that the need for an absolute decision makes itself felt. Return for a moment to the eighth stanza. There the last line, with its strong alliterative emphasis, makes plain that the problem of the will ('*my* wayes') is the central theme of the poem. What we call happiness ('no moneth but May') is the result of events meeting our desires,—'I had my wish and way'; but the universe is not constructed on our plan, and when the will cannot bring itself to accept the cross-bias of existence frustration is inevitable. This commonplace is something that everyone admits in a general way; to accept it fully, in terms of our own personal experience, is another matter. It is because Herbert has faced the issues so honestly and completely that the first alternative that presents itself in the moment of decision has only to be brought into focus to be seen as no real solution at all; and it is because its rejection has behind it the whole weight of the poem that the sudden reversal of feeling is so unforced, the undivided acceptance of the ending so inevitable.

Yet, though thou troublest me, I must be meek;
   In weaknesse must be stout.
Well, I will change the service, and go seek
   Some other master out.
Ah my deare God! though I am clean forgot,
Let me not love thee, if I love thee not.

In *The Collar* the same problem is approached from a slightly different angle.

I struck the board, and cry'd, No more.
   I will abroad.
What? shall I ever sigh and pine?
My lines and life are free; free as the rode,
   Loose as the winde, as large as store. . . .

But as I rav'd and grew more fierce and wilde
   At every word,
Me thoughts I heard one calling, Child!
   And I reply'd, *My Lord.*

At one time I felt that in this well-known ending—a similar sudden 'return' to that of *Affliction* (i)—Herbert was evading the issue by simply throwing up the conflict and relapsing into the naïve simplicity of childhood. But of course I was wrong. The really childish behaviour, is the storm of rage in which the tempestuous desires—superbly evoked in the free movement of the verse—are directed towards an undefined 'freedom'. What the poem enforces is that to be 'loose as the wind' is to be as incoherent and purposeless; that freedom is to be found not in some undefined 'abroad', but, in Ben Jonson's phrase, 'here in my bosom, and at home'.

The mature 'acceptance' that one finds in Herbert's poetry has little in common with a mere disillusioned resignation. The effort towards it is positive in direction. Just as Herbert shows no fear of any imposed punishment for sin—of Hell—but only of the inevitable consequences of sin's 'venome',* so the recurring stress of his poetry is on life. That 'nothing performs the task of life' is the complaint of *Affliction* (iv);

O give me quicknesse, that I may with mirth
   Praise thee brim-full,

is his prayer when 'drooping and dull' (*Dulnesse*). And one reason why his religion appears so humane, in a century tending more and more to associate religion with fear and gloom, is that his God is a God of the living.

* See the second verse of the poem, *Nature*, in which it is not, I think, fanciful to see some resemblance to the far more searching analysis of evil in *Macbeth*.

Wherefore be cheer'd, and praise him to the full
Each day, each houre, each moment of the week,
Who fain would have you be new, tender, quick.
(*Love Unknown*)

It is because he actually did learn from experience to find life 'at hand',* life realized in the commonplace details of every day, that so many of his 'homely' metaphors have such freshness and are the opposite of 'stuffy'. But acceptance has a further, final meaning. It involves the recognition not only of one's limited sphere but (the paradox is only apparent) of one's own value. It is this that gives such wide significance to the poem, 'Love bade me welcome: yet my soul drew back', placed deliberately at the end of the poems in 'The Church':

You must sit down, sayes Love, and taste my meat:
So I did sit and eat.

The achieved attitude—accepted and accepting—marks the final release from anxiety.

With this release not only is significance restored to the present ('Onely the present is thy part and fee . . .'),[6] but death is robbed of its more extreme terrors.† The ending of the poem *Death* (which begins, 'Death, thou wast once an uncouth hideous thing') is entirely unforced:

Therefore we can go die as sleep, and trust
Half that we have
Unto an honest faithfull grave;
Making our pillows either down, or dust.

The integration of attitude thus achieved lies behind the poetry of *Life* ('I made a posie while the day ran by'), and of the well-known *Vertue*— a poem that shows in a quite personal way the characteristically Metaphysical 'reconciliation of opposites': the day has lost none of its freshness because its end is freely recognized as implicit in its beginning.

But it is in *The Flower* that the sense of new life springing from the resolution of conflict is most beautifully expressed.‡

*   Poore man, thou searchest round
    To finde out *death*, but missest *life* at hand. (*Vanitie* (i).)
† I should like to refer to D. W. Harding's review of *Little Gidding* in *Scrutiny* (Spring, 1943), reprinted in *Experience into Words*: 'For the man convinced of spiritual values life is a coherent pattern in which the ending has its due place and, because it is part of a pattern, itself leads into the beginning. An over-strong terror of death is often one expression of the fear of living, for death is one of the life-processes that seem too terrifying to be borne.'
‡ I think it should be noticed that in the original order, apparently Herbert's own, *The Flower* is immediately preceded by *The Crosse*, another poem on the theme of acceptance, ending, '*Thy will be done*'.

How fresh, O Lord, how sweet and clean
Are thy returns! ev'n as the flowers in spring;
　To which, besides their own demean,
The late-past frosts tributes of pleasure bring.
　　　Grief melts away
　　　Like snow in May,
　　As if there were no such cold thing.

Who would have thought my shrivel'd heart
Could have recover'd greenesse? It was gone
　Quite under ground; as flowers depart
To see their mother-root, when they have blown;
　　　Where they together
　　　All the hard weather,
　　Dead to the world, keep house unknown.

He still feels the need for security, for a guaranteed permanence:

　　O that I once past changing were,
　　Fast in thy Paradise, where no flower can wither.

But in the poem as a whole even the fact that the good hours do not last, that they are bound to alternate with 'frosts' and depression, is accepted without bitterness:

　　These are thy wonders, Lord of power,
　　Killing and quickning. . . .

As a result the renewed vitality, waited for without fret or fuss, has something of the naturalness and inevitability of the mounting sap. The sixth stanza takes up the spring imagery:

　　And now in age I bud again,
　　After so many deaths I live and write;
　　I once more smell the dew and rain,
　　And relish versing: O my onely light,
　　　　It cannot be
　　　　That I am he
　　　On whom thy tempests fell all night.

The sense of refreshment, conveyed in imagery of extraordinary sensuous delicacy, is as completely realized as the suffering expressed in the poems of conflict. And like the flower it comes from 'under ground', from the deeper levels of the personality.

　　The account I have given of the positive direction of Herbert's poetry is not meant to imply that anything like a continuous development can be traced in the poems, few of which can be dated with any precision.[7] In any case, development—when it is of the whole man, not simply of a line of thought—rarely shows the smooth curve that biographers like to imagine. We do know, however, that his life at Bemerton was one of uncommon sweetness and serenity, expressing what Dr. Hutchinson calls 'an achieved character of humility, tenderness, moral sensitiveness, and personal consecration, which he was very far from having attained or even envisaged when he was dazzled by the attractions of the great world'. The poems in which the fluctuating stages of this progress are recorded are important human documents because they handle with honesty and insight questions that, in one form or another, we all have to meet if we wish to come to terms with life.

VI

Ben Jonson: Public Attitudes
and Social Poetry

J OHN HOLLANDER, in the Introduction to his selection of Jonson's
poems in the Laurel Poetry Series, wrote:

> Considering that they are the work of a literary genius, Ben
> Jonson's poems have had a curious critical fate. The epoch that
> most intimately responded to their virtues never singled them out
> for special praise, while our own age, so acutely conscious of
> history, acknowledges their importance and success and at the
> same time retains a fundamentally unsympathetic view towards
> them, seldom praising without apologizing.

The useful little volume from which I am quoting appeared in 1961.
Since then a good deal has been published that explains and praises
without apologizing, notably Wesley Trimpi's *Ben Jonson's Poems: a
Study of the Plain Style* (1962), but also various articles, to some of which
I shall refer: and I have the impression that more of the intelligent
young have a genuine and unprompted interest in Jonson's poems than
was the case, say, twenty years ago, when the plays had long outgrown
the 'deadly' reputation that *they* had when T. S. Eliot wrote his well-
known essay. But it is doubtful whether even yet they have the reputation they deserve. It is true that not many of them are poems that one
returns to again and again, as one does to the poetry of Herbert, Blake
and Eliot. But the best of them—a larger number than is sometimes
supposed—ought to be a living part of the peopled landscape that
those who care at all for poetry carry in their minds: without them an
important individual voice, that speaks to us even when we are not
actually reading poetry, is missing. To define that voice, or—to change
the metaphor again—to say as simply as possible what there is in the
poems that is capable of nourishing our minds, not as scholars but
simply as men, is the purpose of this paper. This involves the attempt to
define a particular social mode of verse-writing; for although Jonson
wrote a few intimately personal poems, such as 'To Heaven' or the
epitaphs for two of his children, the bulk of his poems, as Hollander
and others have recognized, are 'public' in a sense in which, for
example, Donne's *Songs and Sonets* are not.

It is perhaps unfortunate that I used the term 'social poetry' in my title, for I am quite unable to define it. Certainly it is not a poetic category, even in the sense that love poetry, elegy or satire can be said to be different 'kinds'. A wide definition would include an enormous number of poems that are not intimately personal, but that have for subject the life of man in society, whether they are occasioned by particular events (e.g. 'An Horatian Ode', 'Easter 1916') or have a more general reference (e.g. 'Coriolan'). Here I use the term to mean poetry written for a particular, fairly limited, social group, or with that group in mind, which embodies or comments on the values of that group. J. B. Bamborough points out that Jonson's Epigrams belong to a literary 'kind' that he calls familiar and moral; that 'except in length there is little difference between them and his longer "Epistles"'; and that—as others have said too—in the bulk of his poetry Jonson aimed at providing 'an English equivalent of Horace's *sermones*—'conversational poems' or, literally, 'talks"'.[1] But unlike Coleridge's so-called conversation-pieces Jonson's poems do not tend towards meditation in the imagined presence of one or two intimates: they assume a fairly wide public (if not, like the plays, the public at large) whose shared concerns are reflected in the verse. And this public includes not only fellow professionals and scholars but men and women with an assured and often conspicuous place in the Jacobean–Caroline social order.

To say this is to point to the first of various obstacles in the way of appreciation that must at least be recognized. Both Donne and Jonson —to go no further—were dependent on patronage, Donne at all events until he was safely installed as Dean of St. Paul's, and Jonson all his life. And the word 'patronage' at once introduces us to a strange and unfamiliar world. It is a world that those of us who have never taken two steps in what are quaintly called the corridors of power are likely to find in many respects objectionable: not only because of the power-struggles centring on the Court, the ferocity of the greed, the courting of favourites, the conspicuous consumption,[2] but also because of the ways in which good and honourable men, as well as men of genius with a worldly streak, accepted an hierarchical system and found nothing dishonourable in seeking the favour of the great. To read, for example, Hacket's *Life* of Archbishop Williams (*Scrinia Reserata*) is to enter a world very remote from us,—one that Donne and Jonson took for granted, but that it costs some imaginative effort for us to reconstruct in our minds. Describing how Williams solicited Buckingham for the Deanery of Westminster, Hacket says, 'The Deanery to be vacated, had many that longed for it; a fortunate Seat, and near the Court: Like the Office over the King of Persia's Garden at Babylon, which was stored with the most delicious fruit'; and he quotes Pliny: 'He that was trusted with the Garden was the Lord of the Palace', It is obvious that Williams carefully cultivated the great; and in his attitude towards the common people he sometimes sounds like one of Shakespeare's Patricians in Coriolanus. Yet there seems no doubt of his probity and charity, especially to scholars, unfortunate gentlemen and pensioners— 'so great a Dealer', says Hacket, 'in the Golden Trade of Mercy'. He obtained an office for Selden and 'in sooth there was never a greater stickler than he to bring Afflicted Ones out of Durance and Misery when he could effect it by Power and Favour: none that lent their hand more readily to raise up those that were cast down. But if a Gentleman of Dr. Seldens merit went under the peril of Vindicative Justice, he would stretch his whole interest, and cast his own Robe, as it were to save him'.

It is indeed in some important respects a very remote world, and I cannot attempt to sketch it here. But before we make caustic democratic comments on, for example, Donne's flattery of noble ladies, we should at least reflect that the milieu for poets then, as now, was a very mixed affair. We may well be critical of the way in which men of power and their hangers-on grabbed for the richest pickings in the dish of state, just as we may laugh at the circumstances in which Court masques were performed. But we should also remember that some at least of the aristocracy, even quite close to the Court, had a genuine feeling for literature and a wish to promote it. There is reliable evidence to this effect in Clarendon; Heminge and Condell's dedication of the Shakespeare First Folio 'to the most noble and incomparable pair of brethren' the Earls of Pembroke and Montgomery—like Jonson's dedication of his *Epigrammes* to Pembroke—doesn't sound like mere flattery; and, as we shall see, although Jonson admitted that he might 'have praysed, unfortunately [some one] that doth not deserve it'[3], his poems do suggest a courtly and aristocratic circle that was far from unfavourable to learning and letters.[4] All the same, a hostile critic might say that Donne's and Jonson's verse letters to aristocratic patrons were, in effect if not in title, 'epistles mendicant'. This is a charge that can't be dealt with until we have looked a little further.

A second obstacle may be dealt with more briefly. John Donne's poetic output forms a unity,—by which I do not mean anything so simple as a straight progression or even full coherence of attitude. It is merely that all his poems are recognizably by the same person; to understand them we properly make connexions from one to the other, and his 'social' poems—such as the verse letters—are clearly part of one *œuvre*. Jonson's works are all 'recognizably by the same person', but even so there is a division within them. Putting it briefly, the plays express strong negative feelings; they are—often savagely—destructive; they do not merely attack abuses in the light of an accepted norm, they bring in question the ability of the society depicted to formulate and make effective any kind of norm that a decent man would find acceptable. As Jonas Barish puts it, 'Something in Jonson insists on probing until it has exposed a layer of folly in everyone, in everything.'[5] In the non-dramatic verse some of the Epigrams, to be sure, are destructive attacks. But the more 'biting' snippers of satire are not characteristic—as they are certainly not among the best—of the poems as a whole, where acceptance of shared codes in a given social order is integral to the poetry. Putting all this in another way, in reading Donne's social verses we are always looking for flashes of the author of *Songs and Sonets*; in reading Jonson's addresses to friends and patrons we are not disappointed when we fail to find the poet of *Volpone*. Or, rather, we ought not to be disappointed, for I suspect that it is the failure to find the comic and destructive dramatist in the author of *The Forrest* that partly explains a certain underrating of the poems, which form as it were a separate province in Ben Jonson's empire.

The province, I have already suggested, is a limited one; and, as a final stage in clearing the ground for appreciation, it may be helpful to say, at the risk of obviousness, what the poems do *not* do, what it is no use expecting of them. (It does no harm from time to time to remind ourselves how foolish it is to try to make poets conform to any Act of Uniformity.) Ted Hughes says that his writing poems was partly a continuation of his earlier pursuit of small animals and birds.

> The special kind of excitement, the slightly mesmerized and quite involuntary concentration with which you make out the stirrings of a new poem in your mind, then the outline, the mass and colour and clean final form of it, the unique living reality of it in the midst of the general lifelessness, all that is too familiar to mistake. This is hunting and the poem is a new species of creature, a new specimen of the life outside your own.[6]

I doubt whether that would have been intelligible to Jonson, who, he told Drummond, 'wrote all his first [drafts for poems] in prose, for so his master Camden had learned him'.[7] His poems do not read like the tracking-down of an unknown quarry; nor do they spring from 'a wordless musical stir', nor from 'a musical phrase ringing insistently in the ears', at first inchoate and only later taking a precise form.[8] There is, then, an obvious contrast between Jonson's poetry and the kind of poetry we are perhaps most attuned to today, and that our common critical methods are designed to deal with. I think here of Valéry's account of the genesis of '*Le Cimetière Marin*', of the evidence provided by the facsimile of T. S. Eliot's drafts for *The Waste Land*, and by the drafts of some of Yeats's most famous poems that show both poets in the process of finding—as opposed to simply expressing—their meanings.[9] With Jonson you can't use Eliot's distinction between 'poetic thought' and 'the thought of the poet'.[10] Wesley Trimpi—to pursue this point a little—speaks of Jonson's preference for couplets, as not racking the sense, and his dislike of elaborate rhyme schemes, quoting 'A Fit of Rime against Rime'[11]:

> Rime, the rack of finest wits,
> That expresseth but by fits,
>   True Conceipt,
> Spoyling senses of their Treasure,
> Cosening Judgment with a measure,
>   But false weight.
> Wresting words, from their true calling. . . .

Jonson, however, was wrong to generalize. George Herbert, for example, sometimes seems to have *discovered* what he wanted to say by wrestling with intricate stanza patterns; and in general I think it is true to say that many poets have found not easily conceptualized meanings in the process of overcoming 'technical' problems. But the best of Jonson's poems—even the more directly personal ones—seem to be the expression of something already formed: they do not explore the more obscure hinterland from which thought emerges.[12]

All this, however, is only helpful in a limited preparatory way. The important question is, What values do the poems embody and help to keep alive? Jonson of course often defines his values by negatives, not only in the satiric epigrams but in poems that are not predominantly satirical. The vices are mostly—as in the plays—some kind of lust, either lust in its ordinary sexual meaning or an inordinate itch to get money or power, or simply to be conspicuous and feel important.

> How blest art thou, canst love the countrey, Wroth,
>   Whether by choice, or fate, or both;
> And, though so neere the citie, and the court,
>   Art tane with neithers vice, nor sport:
> That at great times, art no ambitious guest
>   Of Sheriffes dinner, or Maiors feast.
> Nor com'st to view the better cloth of state;
>   The richer hangings, or crowne-plate;
> Nor throng'st (when masquing is) to have a sight
>   Of the short braverie of the night;
> To view the jewells, stuffes, the paines, the wit
>   There wasted, some not paid for yet!
> . . . .
> Let this man sweat, and wrangle at the barre,
>   For every price, in every jarre,

And change possessions, oftner with his breath,
    Then either money, warre, or death:
Let him, then hardest sires, more disinherit,
    And each where boast it as his merit,
To blow up orphanes, widdowes, and their states;
    And thinke his power doth equall Fates.
Let that goe heape a masse of wretched wealth,
    Purchas'd by rapine, worse then stealth,
And brooding o're it sit, with broadest eyes,
    Not doing good, scarce when he dyes.
Let thousands more goe flatter vice, and winne,
    By being organes to great sinne,
Get place, and honour, and be glad to keepe
    The secrets, that shall breake their sleepe:
And, so they ride in purple, eate in plate,
    Though poyson, thinke it a great fate.

In opposition to such deviations Jonson invokes an ideal of attitude and behaviour that is both humanist and Christian. Clearly he is not 'a religious poet', like Herbert or Hopkins, and of the specifically devotional poems perhaps only the sombrely powerful 'To Heaven' would demand inclusion in a short selection from his non-dramatic work. But there is Christian feeling in, for example, 'An Elegie on the Lady Jane Paulet', where his recurring sense of life as merely 'lent'

    —Goe now, her happy Parents, and be sad
      If you not understand, what Child you had,
      If you dare grudge at Heaven, and repent
      T'have paid againe a blessing was but lent—

joins with a vision of transience not unworthy to stand beside Prospero's.

    If you can cast about your either eye
    And see all dead here, or about to dye!
    The Starres, that are the Jewels of the Night,
    And Day, deceasing! with the Prince of light!
    The Sunne! great Kings! and mightiest Kingdomes fall!
    Whole Nations! nay, Mankind! the World, with all
    That ever had beginning there, to 'ave end!
    With what injustice should one soul pretend
    T'escape this common knowne necessitie . . .

The sense of *that*—the sense also that only Christian virtue can lift a man above the wretchedness of knowing it (ll.95–100) lies behind all Jonson's poems about man as a social being and implicitly places the worldly scene he writes about, as in the superb passage in *The Staple of News* (III, ii):

> What need hath nature
> Of silver dishes, or gold chamber-pots?
> . . . . poor, and wise, she requires
> Meat only; hunger is not ambitious . . . .

In the poems the sobering recognition of natural limits is not too much insisted on; it simply provides a background and a tone.

Often in Jonson it is the tone that largely determines the meaning. In a world not always amenable to our desires a man must be firmly centred in himself. But Jonson's way of putting this not very recondite truth is completely free from the touch of braggadocio that one finds in Chapman's Senecal heroes.

> He that is round within himselfe, and streight,
> Need seek no other strength, no other height . . .
>
> Be always to thy gather'd selfe the same. . . .

Thus to Sir Thomas Roe; and to Selden,—

> you that have beene
> Ever at home: yet, have all Countries seene:
> And like a Compass keeping one foot still
> Upon your Center, doe your Circle fill
> Of general knowledge . . . .

To another recipient ('An Epistle to Master Arth: Squib') he writes,

> looke, if he be
> Friend to himselfe, that would be friend to thee.
> For that is first requir'd, A man be his owne,

—though he adds, characteristically,

> But he that's too much that, is friend of none.

The same note is struck in the beautiful close of 'To the World', where Jonson clearly speaks through the persona of the 'gentle-woman, vertuous and noble' for whom it was written:

> No, I doe know, that I was borne
>   To age, misfortune, sicknesse, griefe:
> But I will beare these, with that scorne,
>   As shall not need thy false reliefe.
> Nor for my peace will I goe farre,
>   As wandrers doe, that still doe rome,
> But make my strengths, such as they are,
>   Here in my bosome, and at home.

And, for a last example, in 'An Epistle answering to one that asked to be Sealed of the Tribe of Ben':

> Live to that point I will, for which I am man,
> And dwell as in my Center, as I can,
> Still looking too, and ever loving heaven;
> With reverence using all the gifts thence given.
> 'Mongst which, if I have any friendships sent
> Such as are square, wel-tagde, and permanent,
> Not built with Canvasse, paper, and false lights
> As are the Glorious Scenes, at the great sights . . .
> But all so cleare, and led by reasons flame,
> As but to stumble in her sight were shame,
> These I will honour, love, embrace, and serve

With 'square' (stoutly and strongly built) and 'wel-tagde' (the parts firmly joined) a further aspect of the cluster of qualities that Jonson most valued comes into view. The good life doesn't simply grow ('like a tree', as he puts it in the Cary-Morison Ode); it is something made, the parts properly ordered. Vincent Corbet's was

> A life that knew nor noise, nor strife:
> But was by sweetning so his will,
> All order, and Disposure, still.

In this touching poem Corbet's life is compared to his well-kept gardens. In the Cary-Morison Ode the well-lived life, however short, is compared to a well-made poem,—

> for life doth her great actions spell,
> By what was done and wrought
> In season, and so brought
> To light: her measures are, how well
> Each syllab'e answer'd, and was form'd, how faire;
> These make the lines of life, and that's her ayre.*

* The analogy has of course been used by other poets, notably Eliot. To be 'free' (which, as Hugh Maclean notices, is a recurring word in the poems) is to accept order and discipline. In a poem to the Countess of Bedford (*Epigrammes*, LXXIX) Jonson writes of his ideal woman,

> Onely a learned, and a manly soule
> I purpos'd her; that should, with even powers,
> The rock [distaff], the spindle, and the sheeres controuled
> Of destinie, and spin her own free houres.

Naturally Jonson knew that no one could control the shears of Atropos. A man or woman is only 'free' in the sense that, within recognized and accepted limits, he acts in accordance with his own integrity, and does not leave his proper sphere of action 'to wracke on a strange shelf'. (This memorable

To *make* something, moreover, is to act:

> Yet we must more then move still, or goe on,
> We must accomplish, ('An Epistle to Sir Edward Sacvile')

and in the world of necessary action the poet has his rightful place. It is his awareness that the poet has a recognized social role

> —Although to write be lesser than to doo,
> It is the next deed, and a great one too—
> ('To Sir Henry Savile')

that allows Jonson his tone of manly independence. We all know that he told Drummond, 'he never esteemed of a man for the name of a lord'—'the cork of title' that keeps some men afloat—a claim that is borne out not only by explicit declarations in the poems

> —That some word
> Might be found out as good, and not *my Lord*.
> That Nature no such difference had imprest
> In men, but every bravest was the best:
> That blood not mindes, but mindes did blood adorne—
> ('To Sir William Jephson')

but above all by the tone of such things as the 'Epistle to Sir Edward Sacvile, Now Earle of Dorset' (*The Underwood*, XIII). Perhaps we may recall here the splendid collocation (and the order of reference to the two monarchs) when he praises Lord Lisle's hospitality in the famous address 'To Penshurst':

> . . . all is there;
> As if thou, then, wert mine, or I reign'd here:
> There's nothing I can wish, for which I stay.
> That found King James, when hunting late, this way . . .

It will be obvious from these references and quotations (and not unfamiliar to any reader of the poems) that the values Jonson most prized have a social reference. And most of his poems—there are exceptions—are directly or indirectly concerned with the expression of those values. The poems therefore are not simply a miscellaneous collection; they form a coherent body of work, unified by certain major themes. These have been so well described by Hugh Maclean that all I need do here by way of summary is to borrow from his excellent

---

image is from the poem, 'To Sir Robert Wroth': 'God wisheth, none should wracke on a strange shelf; To him, man's dearer, then t'himselfe'.—*The Forrest*, III.)

essay.[13] In the poems, he says, 'we find . . . not an explicit and detailed outline of the social order Jonson admired, but rather "notes" on particular elements that ought to mark a society properly ordered, as well as suggestions for conduct in the midst of a disordered one. The negative strictures of the comedies, accordingly, are supplemented and completed by positive advice in the poetry and *Discoveries*.' The three main themes are (i) 'the virtue of friendship between good men, who are receptive by nature to the free exchange of opinion and counsel, and on the strong resource such friendships constitute for the ordered society and the secure state'; (ii) the relations that ideally should obtain between prince—or aristocratic patron—and poet; and (iii) 'the social attitudes and actions befitting a "ruling class" which thoroughly understands the nature of its responsibilities and desires to make them effective'. Even in his panegyrics, of course, Jonson does not offer a map of 'upper-class' society in his day, only a map of what it might be and ought to be. He was, incidentally, a master of the device of advising by praising.* Perhaps all that needs to be added to Maclean's account is some recognition of the *extension* of Jonson's feeling for the necessary interrelationships between men of different parts and functions to include the dependence of all on a given 'Nature,' as in 'To Penshurst'. The less well-known Epithalamion for the marriage of Hierome Weston and Lady Frances Stuart embodies in its ingeniously woven verse an even more widely embracing sense of relationship—of days and seasons, of the generations, of court and country, king and subjects, man and nature.

It remains to ask why poems so firmly attached to a particular time and place should still be read today for other than historical reasons. A short answer is that Jonson does more than describe public or quasi-public qualities that are valuable in any social order, he does so *as a poet*: that is, there is an inherent perennial vitality in the poems that, as in all good poetry, calls out a corresponding energy of apprehension in the responsive reader. What this means in turn is that we are concerned with a particular *style*, which not only conveys the particular subject matter, but in its own individual way goes beyond the paraphrasable sense, beyond whatever it was that Jonson first wrote as a prose draft.

In our understanding of the poetry we all owe a particular debt to

---

* See the admission in 'An Epistle to Master John Selden' (*The Under-wood*, xiv),

> Though I confesse (as every Muse hath err'd,
> And mine not least) I have too oft preferr'd
> Men, past their termes, and prais'd some names too much,
> But 'twas with purpose to have made them such.

Wesley Trimpi, whose study of 'the plain style' has done so much to help us get the perspective right. What I have now to say can be regarded as a supplementary note to Trimpi's work, with—since I lack his classical learning—rather different emphases from his own. Whatever Jonson owed to the classical—or, to a lesser extent—the native plain style,[14] the individual accent, as Trimpi of course admits, is what makes any study of context or tradition worth while. In defining the peculiarly Jonsonian manner we do well to call to mind the combined delicacy and firmness in the verse movement of the songs in the masques and plays. In the more intimate of the poems—the epitaphs on his first daughter, on his first son, and on Salomon Pavy (*Epigrammes* XXII, XLV, CXX)—the studied lack of insistence makes the subtle rhythmic variations the more effective, as in the almost undefinably moving,

> This grave partakes the fleshly birth.
> Which cover lightly, gentle earth.

In another epitaph, on Vincent Corbet, 'classical' simplicity and restraint are similarly married to the tones and rhythms of personal feeling.

> No stubbornnesse so stiffe, nor folly
> To licence ever was so light,
> As twice to trespasse in his sight,
> His lookes would so correct it, when
> It chid the vice, yet not the Men.
> Much from him I professe I wonne,
> And more, and more, I should have done,
> But that I understood him scant;
> Now I conceive him by my want . . .

The plain style, then, is not neutral or colourless.* Jonson's verse (which demands to be read aloud, with a feeling for 'the *sound* of sense') has not the obvious richness of texture of Donne's, but it has its own quasi-dramatic way of rendering movements of mind and feeling.

> Though you sometimes proclaim me too severe,
> Rigid, and harsh, which is a Drug austere
> In friendship, I confesse: But deare friend, heare.
> ('An Epistle to a Friend', *The Under-wood*, XXXVII)

---

* 'That verses stood by sense, without either colours or accent, which yet other times he denied.' — *Conversations*, Herford and Simpson, I, p. 143.

Or, addressing Selden,

> Which Grace shall I make love too first? Your skill
> Or faith in things? or is't your wealth and will
> T'instruct and teach? or your unweary'd paine
> Of Gathering, Bountie in powring out againe?
> (*The Under-wood*, XIV)

—where in the last line quoted the syllables crowded into the rhythmic unit before the unexpectedly early caesura suggest something of Selden's close-packed labours, and the second part of the line, from the reversed stress of 'Bountie', seems to pour itself out with something of Selden's own abundance.

It is because Jonson's verse possesses resources such as these that the poems still capture the imagination when they speak to friends and patrons of different aspects of a shared social world. The epigram addressed to Sir Henry Nevil (*Epigrammes*, CIX) both sums up Jonson's ideal for a man with a part to play in his country's affairs and the poet's relation to such men, and finely exhibits the qualities that I have tried to indicate.

> Who now calls on thee, Nevil, is a Muse,
> That serves nor fame, nor titles; but doth chuse
> Where virtue makes them both, and that's in thee:
> Where all is faire, beside thy pedigree.
> Thou are not one, seek'st miseries with hope,
> Wrestlest with dignities, or fain'st a scope
> Of service to the publique, when the end
> Is private gaine, which hath long guilt to friend.
> Thou rather striv'st the matter to possesse,
> And elements of honour, then the dresse;
> To make thy lent life, good against the Fates:
> And first to know thine owne state, then the States.
> To be the same in roote, thou art in height;
> And that thy soule should give thy flesh her weight.
> Goe on, and doubt not, what posteritie,
> Now I have sung thee thus, shall judge of thee.
> Thy deedes, unto thy name, will prove new wombes,
> Whil'st others toyle for titles to their tombes.

In the first eight lines the defining is mainly by negatives ('a Muse, That serves nor fame, nor titles', 'Thou art not one . . .'). As the poem moves to the celebration of Nevil's qualities the verse texture thickens and engages the reader more closely.

> Thou rather striv'st the matter to possesse,
> And elements of honor, then the dresse;

To make thy lent life, good against the Fates:
And first to know thine owne state, then the States.
To be the same in roote, thou art in height;
And that thy soule should give thy flesh her weight.
Goe on, ...

The changing pattern of stresses, the cluster of emphases, the reinforcement of allied consonants and vowels, — all help to give the sense of steady movement, of actively engaging with life, ending with the finely dismissive,

> Whil'st others toyle for titles to their tombes.

Jonson's verse, I have tried to indicate is indeed 'plain', as Trimpi defines it, but not in any limiting sense. It has its music: something that suggests that, for all the hard rationality of his mind, it had its origins, at its best, not far from those regions where very different poets have first sensed their meanings in 'a worldless musical stir'. I should like to end by quoting 'To the Right Honourable, the Lord High Treasurer of England. An Epistle Mendicant. 1631' (*The Under-wood*, LXXI), even though Trimpi has already called attention to its moving qualities. The poem is not public in the sense of dealing directly with the behaviour and attitudes of public men, but it does reflect Jonson's convictions about the role of the poet in a world of men concerned with public affairs.

My Lord;
Poore wretched states, prest by extremities,
Are faine to seeke for succours, and supplies
Of Princes aides, or good mens Charities.

Disease, the Enemie, and his Ingineeres,
Wants, with the rest of his conceal'd compeeres,
Have cast a trench about mee, now five yeares.

And made those strong approaches, by False braies,
Reduicts, Half-moones, Horne-workes, and such close wayes,
The Muse not peepes out, one of hundred dayes;

But lyes block'd up, and straightned, narrow'd in,
Fix'd to the bed, and boords, unlike to win
Health, or scarce breath, as she had never bin.

Unless some saving-Honour of the Crowne,
Dare thinke it, to relieve, no lesse renowne,
A Bed-rid Wit, then a besieged Towne.

The poem, although explicitly a begging letter, is 'manly, and not smelling parasite', confessing the poet's wants and sufferings (it was written five years after his paralytic stroke[15]), but dissolving self-pity in a witty metaphor. Compact and firm, it reflects the kind of life that Jonson most admired, — 'All order, and Disposure still'.* But the order is not imposed or inert; as an expression of a genuinely 'resolved soul', it has an unmistakable vitality.

It is, I suppose, vitality—a life-enhancing energy—that is common to all good poetry, of whatever kind. In reading any dozen or so of Jonson's 'social' poems at a stretch we do indeed feel that we are in contact with the mind of a man who stands for social–moral attitudes, for shared, traditional norms, that it would be damaging to allow to be edged away to the fringes of our collective consciousness, just because they are not so exciting as many other things that claim our attention in literature. But it is an individual, powerful and distinctive mind, — with its own privacies. That is why poems that spring from and reflect a particular social milieu live on, independent of it.

* In defining the tone of this, it is interesting to compare the more excited movement of the couplet in *The Vanity of Human Wishes* that uses a similar metaphor (ll. 281–2, 'Unnumbered maladies his joints invade . . .'), which is of course splendid in a different way.

VII

All or Nothing
A theme in John Donne

NO ONE TODAY needs to be told that Donne is a poet of paradox and ambiguity. In the best of his poems the tensions generated by his heterogeneous ideas have at least the appearance of being resolved, if only by a skipping wit that dares the reader to challenge the apparent logic at the risk of appearing too solemn for such company. There is, however, one tension that seems to have had an especial importance for Donne, and that was too deeply rooted in his personality to allow the kind of successful handling that one finds in the best of the love poetry. I refer to the conflict between his sense of the enormous importance of his own immediate experience and the sense of his own inadequacy and unimportance, whether as John Donne or as a representative member of the human race: the immoderate and hydroptic thirst for 'all' (or at any rate for very widely inclusive experience) clashing with the feeling of being 'nothing'.

It is preoccupation that is not very bothersome for the reader of most of the *Songs and Sonets*, even though in them, as Professor M. M. Mahood pointed out, the verbal antithesis occurs frequently and significantly.[1] But that the preoccupation with a feeling of nothingness in a mind so eager to reach for 'all' was in fact very bothersome for Donne is plain from the recurrence in his letters and verse epistles of what is almost an obsessive formula. 'The Storme', addressed to Christopher Brooke (1597), begins:

> Thou which art I, ('tis nothing to be soe).

In the impressive companion piece, 'The Calme', there is an odd extension from the vividly rendered sense of the becalmed sailors' physical incapacity ('Wee have no will, no power, no sense'—only the sense of misery) to a generalized reflection on man's littleness:[2]

> What are wee then? How little more alas
> Is man now, then before he was? he was
> Nothing; for us, wee are for nothing fit;
> Chance, or ourselves still disproportion it.

Variations of the formula used to Brooke occur in later verse letters to Sir Henry Wotton (1604)—'For mee, (if there be such a thing as I)'—

and to the Countess of Bedford (1609)—'*nothings*, as I am, may/Pay all they have, and yet have all to pay'. And in a New-year's letter to the Countess (1600?):

> This twilight of two yeares, not past nor next,
>   Some embleme is of mee, or I of this,
> Who Meteor-like, of stuffe and forme perplext,
>   Whose *what*, and *where*, in disputation is,
>   If I should call mee *any thing*, should misse. . . .
>
> When all (as truth commands assent) confesse
>   All truth of you, yet they will doubt how I,
> One corne of one low anthills dust, and lesse,
>   Should name, know, or expresse a thing so high,
>   And not an inch, measure infinity.

Characteristically Donne, in a verse letter of hyperbolical compliment (mixed with discreet advice to the Countess not to spend too much time on Court frivolities), expresses one of the central problems of human life—how can the 'inch' (man) 'measure infinity'?—but the foundation is the same acutely felt sense of personal nullity that recurs in his intimate prose letters. Sending a 'ragge of verse' to Sir Henry Goodyer, he writes: 'Sir, if I were any thing, my love to you might multiply it, and dignifie it: But infinite nothings are but one such; yet since even Chymera's have some name and titles, I am also *Yours*'. And again, to the same close friend a little later: 'Therefore I would fain do something; but that I cannot tell what, is no wonder. For to choose is to do: but to be no part of any body, is to be nothing . . . for to this hour I am nothing, or so little, that I am scarce subject and argument good enough for one of mine own letters: yet I fear, that doth not ever proceed from a good root, that I am well content to be lesse, that is dead'.[3] Such sentiments are obviously related to Donne's wretched fortunes in the years between his marriage and his ordination. But it is difficult to avoid the feeling that they are rooted in personality problems that the critic can point to, if he cannot explain: for example to what D. W. Harding has called (with the implication that it is slightly abnormal) Donne's 'sense of the transience of satisfying experience'*— its inability, in fact, to be 'all'.

Donne has left us in no doubt of his drive towards death. No one expends so much logic and learning as are deployed in *Biathanatos*—not at all events with that kind of intellectual verve—unless there are com-

---

* D. W. Harding, 'Donne's Anticipation of Experience', in *Experience into Words* (1963). Harding related this to 'an attempted insurance against some such failure of experience (as in Hardy's 'The Self-Unseeding'). In one of its forms it shows as a prolonged effort of anticipation, as though to ensure full responsiveness to the event when it did come.'

pelling personal reasons. And the witty and compassionate Preface[4] is explicit: 'I have often such a sickly inclination [towards suicide] . . . whensoever any affliction assailes me, mee thinks I have the keyes of my prison in mine owne hand, and no remedy presents it selfe so soone to my heart, as mine owne sword.' What seems to have been a more or less permanent disposition is clearly expressed in the 'Anniversaries' written for Elizabeth Drury, where the very fact that he did not know the girl who is his ostensible subject allowed free rein for feelings to some extent necessarily curbed in more directly personal poems. Dame Helen Gardner speaks of Donne as 'a man of strong passions, in whom an appetite for life was crossed by a deep distaste for it'.[5] But 'deep distaste' hardly does justice to the strength of Donne's revulsion from the 'fragmentary rubbidge' of the world, with its sense of protesting disappointment, that one finds in these poems, especially in the first of them, 'An Anatomy of the World': 'There is no health', 'Wee are borne ruinous'. Things might have been better once, but—with a barely disguised glance back at the lost domain of childhood—

> mankinde decayes so soone,
> We'are scarce our Fathers shadowes cast at noone . . .
> And as our bodies, so our mindes are crampt:
> 'Tis shrinking, not close weaving that hath thus,
> In minde, and body both bedwarfed us.
> Wee seem ambitious, Gods whole worke t'undoe;
> Of nothing hee made us, and we strive too,
> To bring our selves to nothing backe; and wee
> Doe what wee can, to do't so soone as hee.

> This man, so great, that all that is, is his,
> Oh what a trifle, and poore thing he is!

> Shee, shee is dead; shee's dead: when thou knowest this,
> Thou knowst how poore a trifling thing man is.

It is of course true that the second poem dwells on the joys of heaven—

> Thou shalt not peepe through lattices of eyes,
> Nor heare through Labyrinths of eares . . .

—and throughout religious belief is recommended as the only way of escaping from the miseries of a world decayed in all its parts. But most of the emotional force springs from the negative feelings; and except for three Vaughan-like lines towards the end—

> Who with Gods presence was acquainted so,
> (Hearing, and speaking to him) as to know
> His face in any naturall Stone, or Tree

—the world considered in itself has no spiritual potential; very obviously here there is no question of holding Infinity in the palm of your hand and Eternity in an hour, or of giving imaginative realization to what Coleridge called 'that other world which now is':[6]

> Turn to Luther's Table Talk, and see if the larger part be not of that other world which now is, and without the being and working of which the world to come would be either as unintelligible as *Abracadabra*, or a mere reflection and elongation of the world of sense—Jack Robinson between two looking-glasses, with a series of Jack Robinsons *in saecula saeculorum*.

In a letter Donne may appeal to traditional, and healthier, doctrine: 'You know, we say in the Schools, that Grace destroys not Nature';[7] but in the 'Anniversaries' the dichotomy seems complete.

> Be more then man, or thou'rt lesse then an Ant.

> Then, as mankinde, so is the worlds whole frame
> Quite out of joynt, almost created lame.

Rejection is the only way of escaping 'this worlds generall sicknesse':

> thou hast but one way not t'admit
> The worlds infection, to be none of it.

The poem may be in some respects a Renaissance version of the *de contemptu mundi* theme; but the vigour of the verse, combined with the echoes of many other of Donne's writings, prevents us from seeing it as simply that: the personal vibrations are too strong.

It is of course idle—though probably, in the twentieth century, unavoidable—to speculate on the sources of Donne's pervasive 'disconsolate melancholy', even though this cannot be explained simply by reference to his very obvious personal misfortunes. Certainly in the 'Anniversaries' there is plenty to justify Harding's comment, that 'in the fantasy he created around Elizabeth Drury Donne expressed unwittingly the familiar personal theme that for many people, of whom he was one, an unwilling and protesting separation from the fantasy perfect mother of infancy leaves the world a permanently disappointing place'. Even though Donne's mother died only two months before he did, and lived her last years with him in the Deanery, she was in a sense 'separated' from the four-year-old boy when she re-married less than a year after the death of his father. (In Chapter IV of *Young Man Luther* Erik Erikson studies the inability to mediate between 'allness' and 'nothingness' in its pathological extreme—his example is Hitler—but he also suggests the prevalence of this kind of oscillation in men of constructive genius and in very many 'ordinary' men.) But, obsessive and exaggerated as Donne's feeling of nothingness may at times have been, it is one of the permanent possibilities of our sentient life—something 'to which by reason of our weaknesse, and this worlds encumbrances, our nature is too propense and inclined', as Donne said of the death-wish in *Biathanatos* (*ed. cit.*, p. 71). We can, in short, so little take a merely clinical and detached view of his 'case', that we hope, as we read or re-read, to find the poet not repeating, but exploring, his sense of nullity, the intellectual–emotional disturbances set up when the mere inch, man, confronts immensity. Donne of course in practice found his solution in a life of austere devotion and duty, accepting fully the admirable advice that he gives in *Essays in Divinity*: 'Let no smalness retard thee: if thou beest not Amber, Bezoar, nor liquid gold, to restore Princes; yet thou art a shrub to shelter a lambe, or to feed a bird; or thou art a plantane, to ease a childs smart; or a grasse to cure a sick dog.'[8] In the poetry, only 'A Litanie' comes to terms with the all or nothing antithesis in a sober recommendation of the middle way.

> From being anxious, or secure
> Dead clods of sadnesse, or light squibs of mirth,
>   From thinking, that great courts immure
> All, or no happinesse, or that this earth
>   Is only for our prison fram'd,
>   Or that thou art covetous
> To them whom thou lov'st, or that they are maim'd
> From reaching this worlds sweet, who seek thee thus,
> With all their might, Good Lord deliver us. . . .
>
>   That learning, thine Ambassador,
> From thine allegeance wee never tempt,
>   That beauty, paradises flower
> For physicke made, from poyson be exempt,
>   That wit, borne apt, high good to doe,
>   By dwelling lazily
> On Natures nothing, be not nothing too,
> That our affections kill us not, nor dye,
> Heare us, weake ecchoes, O thou eare, and cry.

It is, as Helen Gardner says, 'a singularly unbitter poem, although it was written at a bitter time'.[9] But although it deserves to be better known it has not the power of the Holy Sonnets or the Hymns, which deal with altogether different matters, and which, I think, do not reach across doctrinal barriers as do the no less Christian poems of George Herbert or T. S. Eliot's *Four Quartets*. Both Herbert and Eliot—like Blake in a different way—can make us feel with full imaginative power the relations between our littleness and a world of infinite possibilities, so that the 'all' is welcoming rather than frightening or oppressive. It is, however, useless to wish that a poet who has given us so much should be other than he is, especially since it is his confrontation of nothingness that results in one of his greatest poems. I refer of course to 'A Nocturnall upon S. Lucies Day'. A. Alvarez, in a fine analysis of this poem, says, 'Despite its theme, the piece has been driven continually forward by a curious restless energy. Yet that energy is entirely in the negatives.'[10] Which is true; but paradoxically the poem, by the very energy of the account of 'how it feels to reach absolute zero' and 'how it feels to *think* when you are there', becomes a kind of affirmation. After all, the poet has *made* something, alive in all its parts, which itself is a victory over chaos and the sense of nothingness that is its theme.

VIII

Shakespeare's Tragedies and the Question of Moral Judgment

WHEN I WAS invited to take part in this Symposium* it was suggested that I might be willing to accept the role of the 'Arnoldian' critic. This, I assumed, was not intended as a compliment, however undeserved, but was simply a suggestion that someone committed to a view of poetry as in some sense 'a criticism of life,' someone whose writings on Shakespeare are thought to have a moral slant, should try to define the nature of his approach to Shakespearian tragedy; should try, in particular, to throw some light on the part played by moral judgment in his response to those master-works that are not easily landed in the moralist's net. It is a task that I am glad to accept. And although at the end I may leave you with no more than some self-evident truths, there may be some profit in the journey.

It certainly has its difficulties. 'Moral,' says the Dictionary,

> Of or pertaining to character or disposition considered as good or bad, virtuous or vicious; of or pertaining to the distinction between right and wrong, or good and evil, in relation to the actions, volitions, or character of responsible beings.

A play is a moving image of life: it is concerned with men in action. If we are thinking about it at all, and not merely giving ourselves up to an interest in story—which is anyhow virtually impossible—we simply cannot help making moral distinctions between right and wrong. On the other hand, to describe a critic *tout court* as 'a moralist' is to suggest some kind of limitation or disability: he has not an adequately free or open mind; he sets off with preconceived, and perhaps narrow, moral standards and forces his material to conform, or finds fault if it does not; or his moral preoccupations lead him to substitute for the vivid particulars of the work before him some comparatively inert generalizations. Alternatively, of course, the objectors may be expressing a feeling that in the long run moral judgment has no place in the work of art or in criticism: in this view the business of the critic, like that of the artist, is

* 'Approaches to Shakespeare,' a symposium sponsored by the Glasgow Endowment Committee at Washington and Lee University, Winter 1968. The other speakers were C. L. Barber, Kenneth Burke, and Stanley Edgar Hyman.

simply to understand and to make intelligible. There is clearly a problem here for the critic who, while feeling the force of these objections, believes that criticism, like art though in a humbler way, is a contribution to the life of reason, and that 'he who thinks reasonably must'—in some sense—'think morally.' And the problem is not only a critical one: it reflects the very much wider question of how a man can be committed to values, and all that that implies by way of judgment, and yet believe (as I do) that moralizing is the devil.[1]

If we want testimony to the moral function of literature—and that from creative writers themselves—we shall find no lack of it. George Eliot, for example, for all her admirable 'passion for the special case,' and her 'repugnance to the men of maxims,' her insistence on the need for *'treatment,* which alone determines the moral quality of art,' on the need *not* to lapse 'from the picture to the diagram,' willingly accepted, as novelist, 'the office of teacher or influencer of the public mind.' Conrad spoke of 'the moral discovery that lies at the heart of every tale.' And D. H. Lawrence:

> The essential function of art is moral. Not aesthetic, not decorative, not pastime and recreation. But moral. The essential function of art is moral.

Lawrence of course went on to make the point that the morality he was concerned with was 'passionate', not 'didactic', and in the 'Study of Thomas Hardy,' he offered another criterion for distinguishing the morality of really great works of art which I shall come back to later. But the point is that all three of these great novelists are agreed that the function of their art is in some sense moral. I cannot imagine that any of them would demur when a recent critic of Henry James, Miss Dorothea Krook, invoking standards that she clearly expects to be taken for granted, writes of 'the double purpose of every great dramatist: that of a radical criticism of society . . . on the one hand, and, on the other, of a "criticism of life" in Matthew Arnold's sense—a radical exposure, sometimes in its comic aspect, more often in its tragic aspect, of some of the fundamental and permanent predicaments of human life.'[2]

All this of course is very general. Important as testimony, it means little more than that our concern with literature cannot be divorced from our normal human concerns in which the distinction beween right and wrong, or good and evil, is so inevitably present and active; that, in the words of L. H. Myers,

> When a novelist displays an attitude of aesthetic detachment from the ordinary ethical and philosophical preoccupations of humanity something in us protests.

But to say that tells us nothing at all about the way in which our moral sense enters into—or, for that matter, emerges from—a reading of any literary work, more especially when the work is a Shakespearian tragedy, which so completely refuses to be nailed down to a moral scheme. Dryden could sum up his *All for Love* in a couplet,

> And fame to late posterity shall tell,
> No lovers lived so great, or died so well;

you cannot treat *Antony and Cleopatra* so, not even if you stand that judgment on its head. When an eighteenth-century writer tells us, of *Hamlet*,

> all the moral we can deduce is, that murder cannot lie hid, and that conscience ever makes a coward of guilt,

or another, more subtly,

> The instruction to be gathered from this delineation is, that persons formed like Hamlet, should retire, keep aloof, from situations of difficulty and contention: or endeavour, if they are forced to contend, to brace their minds, and acquire such vigour and determination of spirit as shall arm them against malignity,[3]

something in us protests. What, then, is the nature of the moral consciousness to which a Shakespeare tragedy may properly be said to appeal, and what is the nature of the interaction between the two? The only way of throwing some light on these matters is to question ourselves as to what happens when we are engaged with a particular tragedy as fully and responsibly as we can. And we should take care that we do not sidestep that naïve, delighted and partly 'uncritical' engagement that is at the root of all good criticism, and that, in our search for profundity, we sometimes ignore.

When we read or watch a Shakespeare play, we are, I take it, much engaged with the story, with the question, What happens, what can possibly happen, next? This interest, I think, never entirely deserts us, and when we see a good performance of *Hamlet*, even if it is for the tenth time, we still wait for the end with a kind of agonized expectation, half hoping—though we know the hope is futile—that it need not end in catastrophe. And with the interest in story and situation goes some kind of emotional engagement with the persons who perform the action, movements of sympathy and antipathy that shift and change as the play goes on. We need not find Hamlet, as one critic has done, 'the most adorable of heroes,' but we could hardly be said to know the play if his fate left us entirely unmoved. Liking and disliking, approval and disapproval, are at work long before we begin to grasp the total pattern that the characters—their words and actions—compose. I suspect that even Professor Heilman was exasperated by and sorry for King Lear long before it began to dawn on him that what was even more deeply affecting him was a complex and magical web of meanings having to do with seeing and blindness, madness and reason, and the ambiguities of Nature.

It is at this naïve and indispensable level of response that our moral judgment is first engaged. Unless we were shocked by the murders in *Macbeth* and *Othello* we should hardly be human, let alone good readers. And some kind of moral assessment goes on even when we contemplate quite minor characters: Kent, for all his stubbornness and hot temper, is trustworthy, Osric is a moral cipher, and so on. And the fact that some cases are dubious—such as Brutus's decision to join the conspiracy—doesn't alter the matter: it may be a long time before we can come to any sort of clarity about Brutus's action, but the play makes us ponder its rightness or wrongness. And this spontaneous moral pondering operates not only when we stand back, as it were, and see characters and situations in their totality, but when we dwell on the minute details out of which our more massive reactions will be formed. When Iago says of Othello and Desdemona,

> His soul is so enfetter'd to her love,
> That she may make, unmake, do what she list,
> Even as her appetite shall play the god
> With his weak function,

we reflect not only that it is characteristic of Iago to see love simply as appetite, but that there is a curious and limiting distortion in that 'enfetter'd.' If we go on to reflect that Othello himself had indicated a view of marriage as in some sense a confinement—

> But that I love the gentle Desdemona,
> I would not my unhoused free condition
> Put into circumscription and confine
> For the sea's worth—

we are surely not indulging in gratuitous moral arithmetic, but following the dramatist's own lead to the significance of his action. The plays in short take for granted our moral interest and engagement as much as they take for granted our ability to understand the words and construe the language, even though linguistic and moral literacy alike may be forced to undergo a discipline of change and development.

There is of course, as I have indicated, another side to this basic and necessary *naïveté*, even more important than the unavoidable—though often tentative—habit of moral assessment that I have been discussing. It is simply openness and receptivity, a willingness to give oneself up, at least provisionally, to what the play offers, without any over-anxious or premature need to make sense of it all, which usually means to fit it into some preconceived intellectual or moral pattern. It is this dual process, simultaneously passive and active, simply receiving and yet actively relating what is received to our own permanent but developing moral life, on which we found our 'criticism' of Shakespeare's tragedies —that is, the way in which we describe to ourselves and others the furthest reach of meaning that we have been able to take from them. If, then, our accepted moral notions cannot be allowed to stand in the way of our openness and receptivity, and that in turn cannot inhibit the working of our moral consciousness, the question remains of how these interact in the full development of a tragedy, fully attended to.

What happens when we read or watch *Hamlet*? We see a young man in a state of intense melancholy because of the death of a loved father and the hasty remarriage of his mother to his father's brother. The young man has it revealed to him by a ghost that the supplanter is in fact the murderer of his father, and he is commanded to take vengeance. That task occupies the remainder of the play, and is only completed at the expense of seven other lives including Hamlet's own. The exciting action, with stratagem and counter-stratagem, is indeed enough to hold the most unsophisticated theatre-goer, as is abundantly proved. But of course Shakespeare gives us more than that. Our minds are engaged with the nature of the corruption that surrounds Hamlet and with the particular brooding darting consciousness that confronts that corruption, and of course, since the play heavily insists on it, with the ambiguity of the Ghost—'spirit of health, or goblin damned?'. It is Hamlet's reaction to the Ghost, his testing of it, and—'I'll take the Ghost's word for a thousand pounds'—his final submission to it, that is the main interest into which the interest in what-happens-next? is absorbed. The nature of that central consciousness, and its development in the course of the action, is something that, above all, we find ourselves trying to understand. It is of course something that comes home to us in a peculiarly intimate way: so much is compressed into that consciousness that we can hardly help seeing Hamlet, with D. G. James, as 'an image of modernity' or, with C. S. Lewis, as a kind of archetypal figure of a man who has lost his way. But in our attempt to understand, to bring home, questioning plays an essential part; and it is—we cannot avoid the word—moral questioning. What I do *not* mean should be clear. I do not mean that we judge Hamlet in relation to 'the ethics of revenge,' either our own, or those that we impute to the Elizabethans, for that would be to take him right outside the context in which he has his proper existence, the one that Shakespeare has created for him.* In coming to terms with a great work of art there are

* I am grateful to Miss Eleanor Prosser's scholarly and acute *Hamlet and Revenge*, not only for its challenge to rethink the play in detail. But her demonstration that the original audience was not likely to assume without

no short cuts. We do not hold our moral consciousness in abeyance (as though we were in the kind of cloud-cuckoo-land Lamb saw in Restoration comedy), for that would be impossible. But we do need to abandon any rigid moral stance, and to allow free intercourse between our moral notions and the great surge of fresh experience which is the play. What we attend to, in short, are those revealing tones and implications in their minutely appropriate words, which are the dramatic representatives of different attitudes in that complex play of attitudes-in-action which is the tragedy: the suspicious unction of Claudius's first speech, or the crass moral obtuseness with which Polonius, like his son before him, tramples on young love—'Affection! Pooh!'. Where Hamlet is concerned we respond not only to what he says but to its implications— the tone, the timbre, the lifestyle, all those subtle indications of consciousness as *displayed* in the developing drama. I am under the necessity here of cutting a long story short and appearing more dogmatic than I could wish. What I would say, then, is that as we attend to Hamlet in his inward communings and his multifarious relations with others, we become aware not only of a man trapped and imprisoned but of an imprisoning state of mind. The extent to which 'Denmark' is 'a prison' is clear from any attentive reading[4] and I do not intend to speak of it here, except to remind you that Hamlet's predicament is real and painful: in that society of spying, subterfuge and treachery there is certainly enough to make any honest man regard it as an unweeded garden: 'things rank and gross in nature possess it merely.' Among all the characters it is only Hamlet who has the potentialities of a strong, free mind: you see it in his prose rhythms, his range of interest and reference, the spontaneous eagerness with which he greets anyone who is, or seems to be, outside the circle of corruption. But Hamlet is not the moral norm: he too is subject to judgment—and by this I mean judgment by criteria that the play itself provides, that Hamlet provides, in terms of vitality, freemoving life and a capacity for relationships. From this point of view, what we are compelled to notice, from the moment that Hamlet gives himself up to an exclusive preoccupation with the Ghost's command, wiping from his memory,

> all trivial fond records,
> All saws of books, all forms, all pressures past,
> That youth and observation copied there . . . ,

---

question that Hamlet had a duty to avenge his father (as an older generation of scholars tended to assume) and was indeed likely to be highly suspicious of a ghost who commanded murder, can by itself do no more than free us from misleading assumptions. What Shakespeare himself 'meant' when writing the play can only be approached by the normal methods of literary criticism—i.e. by attending to what he says.

is an increasing entanglement in a self-consuming preoccupation with the very evil that he is required to set himself against: it is as though the world in which he feels himself required to play the avenger had a kind of fifth column in Hamlet's own consciousness; and the fifth column, if it never takes entire control, pretty thoroughly disrupts the autonomous system that is—or, we feel, ought to be—Hamlet. I have argued this at some length in some published lectures, and a recent thorough re-reading of the play has given me no reason to change my mind. Hamlet's capacity for life is diminished to the extent that an exclusive concentration on corruption awakens a corresponding corruption in himself. I am not referring simply to the crudities of action—such as the sending of Rosencrantz and Guildenstern to their deaths, 'not shriving time allowed'—though we cannot ignore these, but to the words of dialogue and soliloquy in which Shakespeare reveals states of mind and feeling that are only crudely defined by our moral and psychological labels: sexual obsession, an exaggerated sense of unworthiness, a nostalgic longing for an impossible simplification, death if need be, as an escape from life's complexities, self-dramatization, self-righteousness, and a cruelty that ranges from the obscenities directed at Ophelia to the reasons given for not killing the King at prayer. All these qualities co-exist with those finer qualities that go to make 'the other Hamlet', who is never entirely lost sight of. But not even the beautiful and touching lines that are given to Hamlet as his death draws near can obscure the fact that what we are concerned with is a study—one of the most profound studies in our literature—of a trapped and death-directed consciousness. And to say that is to commit ourselves to a moral judgment.

I am perfectly aware that what I have just said, with all the crudeness of brevity, does not command universal assent. It does represent an approximation to my own thoughts and feelings about *Hamlet*; but just now I have no desire to convince anyone of the rightness of my own views. For what I want to say is this. Supposing I am right, and that the tentative following through of qualities and attitudes embodied in words that the play calls on us to perform, issues in some such over-all or inclusive judgment as I have sketched, there is still an important sense in which we cannot moralize the play, or feel that we have done our duty as critics, let alone as human beings, when we have provisionally defined the flaw, indeed the evil, in the central consciousness. Moral judgment is like our knowledge of the dictionary meanings of words and their history; we cannot do without it, but no more than our construing of the sense is it adequate to our experience of a great tragedy such as *Hamlet*.

Hamlet, we may say—and by Hamlet I mean not a real-life figure we have extracted from the play, but the dramatic embodiment of a particular complex attitude to life who affects us, *within the conventions of Shakespeare's art*, as if he were a fellow human—Hamlet has followed a disastrously wrong path. But when we have *felt* the play, entered into it imaginatively, it seems worse than inadequate simply to say that: and this for three reasons. The first is contained in Yeats's saying that in great tragic drama 'it is always ourselves that we see upon the stage'— and this in a more profound sense than is contained in Coleridge's remark that he had 'a smack of Hamlet' in him. We are too deeply involved; for in following Hamlet's fortunes we are trying out our own attitudes to a world that is hardly as we would wish it to be, and that may indeed contain people who have done us some wrong. And when we are involved in this way our judgment, while sensitized beyond the normal, becomes something different from judgment in the usual sense, when we acquit, excuse or condemn in the light of an abstract code or previously defined standards. The second reason is suggested by Northrop Frye when he says that 'tragic heroes are wrapped in the mystery of their communion with that something beyond which we can see only through them, and which is the source of their strength and their fate alike.' 'As for the something beyond [he goes on], its names are variable, but the form in which it manifests itself is fairly constant. Whether the context is Greek, Christian, or un-defined, tragedy seems to lead up to an epiphany of law, of that which is and must be.'[5] In *Hamlet* I think we have an especially acute sense of the tragic hero as a person; but that sense is constantly taken up into the sense of law that Frye speaks of, the sense of *how things must be*, which tragedy gives us the courage to face. And this, we remark, is mediated through the 'flawed' hero himself—a tension that is recognized in all theories of tragedy from Aristotle onwards. And finally, of course, even when we condemn Hamlet, when, that is, our aroused sympathy recoils from what he offers or enacts, it is Hamlet himself who provides some of the norms against which we measure his swervings. And if one of the norms, and that the greatest of all—the 'rarer action' of Prospero's great speech in *The Tempest*—is absent from the play, except by implication, it remains true that almost all the positives against which we can define the evil of Denmark as a perversion of life, are mediated through him. To quote Professor Frye once more: 'The discovery or *anagnorisis* which comes at the end of the tragic plot is not simply the knowledge by the hero of what has happened to him . . . but the recognition of the determined shape of the life he has created for himself, with an implicit comparison with the uncreated potential he has forsaken.'[6] In *Hamlet* that uncreated potential, like the workings of Dîke or the law, is something we only know through the Prince himself. It is partly a matter of what others—Ophelia, Horatio—say about him; partly of what he himself says when we feel that he is most free.

But it also has to do with something less easily defined—a way of speech, flexible, ranging, responsive, capable of infinite modulation, that contrasts not only with the way of speech given, say, to Polonius or to Claudius, but with the speech of Hamlet himself when he is given over to his obsessions with corrupted sex or with revenge. In other words it is Hamlet himself, or Shakespeare speaking through Hamlet, who clarifies whatever standards of judgment we may feel bound to apply. But the play doesn't merely ask us for judgment; it asks us to stretch our imaginations. And at the end what we feel is not the desire to judge, but simply pity and fear.

At this point we may perhaps pause on what Coleridge liked to call a landing-place and look back over the course of the argument. At the beginning of this paper, when I was anxious to insist that literature has a moral function, I supported myself with some quotations. It will have been noticed that these were taken from novelists, or referred to the novel. The suggestion will by now, I hope, have entered your minds that what, with due qualification, is right and adequate for the novel is not necessarily right or adequate for great poetic drama.* Miss Dorothea Krook, in her study of Henry James in which she rightly considers his novels as being in a fairly direct sense a 'criticism of life', makes a further observation. She is considering the question of why James's heroes and heroines are often so very rich, and she writes:

> James's millionaires and heiresses have in his novels exactly the same dramatic function as the kings, queens and princes in Shakespeare's plays. They are 'representative' of all humanity in the modern world in exactly the same sense as Shakespeare's kings, queens and princes are representative: in the sense that they are the acknowledged symbols of supreme power and prestige in their society. . . . They embody, in short, the dominant (though not necessarily the exclusive) ideal of human possibility in that society; consequently, what 'happens' to them—their vicissitudes, their 'rise and fall', their suffering and joy—is exemplary and instructive for the purpose of drama in exactly the way that Shakespeare conceived the fate of a Hamlet, a Macbeth, a Lear to be exemplary and instructive.[7]

We may readily agree that James's heroes and heroines are, for all their money, representative. But, leaving on one side the question of whether Shakespeare's heroes do in fact embody 'the dominant . . .

---

* Though this may also be said of novels that in some way approach poetic drama, e.g. *Moby-Dick* or, perhaps, *Wuthering Heights*.

ideal of human possibility' in their society, we may well ask ourselves whether the comparison between the great novelist and the great tragic poet does not contain a quite misleading implication about the work of the latter. For the truth is, as I hope we have seen, that the fate of Hamlet isn't merely 'exemplary and instructive'. It may, perhaps, be that; but it is also very much more; and it is in the very much more that we find the defining qualities of great tragedy. Clearly you can't make too sharp a distinction between the varying modes of the novel and the varying modes of tragedy; but the fact remains that the attention we give to Hamlet is different in kind from the attention we give to Isabel Archer, or to Mr. Casaubon.

Perhaps we are now near the heart of the matter. At the level of human response, where we feel for the tragic hero *as though* he were a fellow human being—and even in the most patterned and stylized of tragedies, like the Greek, this is a necessary and unavoidable part of our total apprehension—at this level we admire, or sympathize with, the hero, for all his blindness, his faults and sins. Even with Macbeth, who is the most damnable of Shakespeare's heroes, even with Coriolanus, who is the least likeable, we assimilate some of 'their' energy, or the energy that is conveyed through them. Macbeth has made for us, so to speak, the terrible journey of fear, a journey backwards away from the 'good things of day' towards the meaningless dehumanized fragments of the Witches' cauldron; made it because the very thought that such things could be, inside him, fills him with a desperate panic which seems to demand actualization of the potential evil within. And in the very course of that journey he reveals for us qualities of courage and insight that, in the world of the play, we should not otherwise have known. And this counterbalancing energy does something to our unavoidable moral judgment. It is necessary that the 'butcher' should be removed; but we do not contemplate his end with any satisfaction, however grim.[8]

The fact remains, however, that in Shakespeare's tragedies what I have called the human response is only a part of our total engagement. Even in *Othello*, which everyone recognizes as the most domestic, in some ways one of the least metaphysical, of the tragedies, the human action engages with and reveals a psychological, indeed a metaphysical, pattern, that is part of the play (as Robert Heilman has shown in *Magic in the Web*), however much this may affect us in the theatre simply as suggestion and overtone. And it is at this more universal level that the normal mode of our moral judgment undergoes its most radical transformation. I have hinted at something of this in relation to *Hamlet*. Perhaps we may clarify the matter still further if we turn our attention, briefly, to the concluding movement of *King Lear*.

Nothing is more wonderful in Shakespeare's mature art than the assured and flexible technique that allows him to move without strain or apparent incongruity into quite different dramatic modes, whilst yet preserving the unity of the whole: to move, for example, from scenes where the focus is on the directly personal and individual (so that our immediate response is as though to this particular man in this particular situation) to the more or less overtly symbolic. And between these extremes are virtually infinite gradations, so that within our simply human response to *this* predicament wide-reaching overtones are evoked with different degrees of intensity, and even the most directly 'symbolic' situations and events (Prospero's storm, Hermione's statue) are firmly rooted in feelings and insights that belong to the common stuff of our humanity.

It would not be true to say that *King Lear* begins at the simply human and naturalistic level: from the start formalizing devices are at work that both concentrate and extend our attention. But it is true to say that we are aware of a powerful individual presence, Lear himself, whose behaviour as a man demands our judgment. King Lear, we say, made a wrong choice—a choice springing from the total personality that is revealed to us—and the rest of the play shows him learning the lesson of its consequences. This of course is an almost grotesque over-simplification: well before the central scenes on the heath we know that we are concerned not simply with the fate of one old man but with the nature and place of man in the world; our minds and imaginations are engaged, though always with a precise particular focus, with the relation of every man to the chaotic forces of 'nature', with the nature of reason and its relations to feeling and impulse, with in short the possibility of affirming any kind of humanity (what does that mean?) in the face of the forces that threaten it.

It is beyond any man's powers to describe briefly the massive meanings that are built up in the course of the play. My purpose is simply to remind you of those meanings that press on the play's final movement, on which I wish now to concentrate with an eye to the particular problem that is engaging us. The scene of Lear's reconciliation with Cordelia is directly and poignantly human in its appeal, the more effectively so not only because it follows Lear's greatest outbursts of despair but because in the preceding Edgar and Gloucester sequence the play had moved well in the direction of a kind of Morality sparseness.

> *Lear*   Do not laugh at me;
> For, as I am a man, I think this lady
> To be my child Cordelia.
> *Cor.*   And so I am, I am.

Lear Be your tears wet? Yes, faith. I pray, weep not;
    If you have poison for me, I will drink it.
    I know you do not love me; for your sisters
    Have, as I do remember, done me wrong:
    You have some cause, they have not.
Cor.   No cause, no cause.

Yet even here, in this most simply moving of scenes, there is some interplay of the natural and the formal, of personal feeling in a direct relationship and symbolic overtones; and before Lear wakes, Cordelia, in a dozen lines, recalls all that he has been through. In other words, Shakespeare wants us to hold in our imagination all that has happened in the storm, all those powerful overtones of universal meaning, together with what is now going on. It is as though all the questions that the play has forced on us—What is justice? what is madness? what is true need? all subsumed under the great question, 'Who is it that can tell me what I am?'—were here receiving an answer. The moral balance has now come down against those who embodied the belief that man is a merely natural force in a world of natural forces, and on the side of those who hold to the belief that man is utterly different from this, that what makes him man is his capacity to feel something other than his own immediate needs and desires.

The play however does not end here, and we are forced, as we watch, to continue our questionings. Cordelia's forces are defeated, and she and the King are sent to prison, where Edmund arranges for them to be killed. He in turn is killed in a judicial combat by Edgar, and although he sends word for his order to be countermanded—'some good I mean to do Despite of mine own nature'—it is too late. Cordelia is murdered, and Lear dies desperately trying to reassure himself that she still lives. What do we make of that sequence?

Perhaps we can obtain some hint of an answer if we call to mind the opening of the final scene (V.iii), where there is the same kind of alternation that occurs elsewhere between formal qualities, a rather severe stylization, and qualities that seem designed to express a human, personal response to the situation. Cordelia again uses the rhymed speech she had used in the play's opening, and uses it to the same effect:

        We are not the first
    Who, with best meaning, have incurr'd the worst.
    For thee, oppressed King, I am cast down;
    Myself could else out-frown false Fortune's frown.

But these impersonal and choric lines are at once followed by Lear's rapturous expression of his happiness at being reunited with his daughter, an expression that has something of the touching obliviousness of all else of a man who has recovered what is most dear to him after the most extreme hazards. Ignoring here the multiple ironies of these twenty-five lines, I suggest that in this blending of the formal and the intensely personal and individual you have an anticipation of the play's end, which is so hard to describe. For there you have the almost unbearable expression of personal agony framed by a ritual solemnity.

Lear	Lend me a looking-glass;
	If that her breath will mist or stain the stone,
	Why, then she lives.
Kent	Is this the promis'd end?
Edgar	Or image of that horror?
Albany	Fall and cease. . . .

The feeling that these interjections support is that we are not only watching a rending personal grief: it is a solemn ritual of mourning, as though a world were coming to an end: 'O ruin'd piece of Nature! This great world Shall so wear out to nought.' All the pettiness of ambition and intrigue seems infinitely far removed; and even when Edmund's death is reported, 'That's but a trifle here.' And this perhaps is why the play ends with those curiously hesitant and unemphatic lines of Edgar's,

> The weight of this sad time we must obey;
> Speak what we feel, not what we ought to say.
> The oldest hath borne most: we that are young
> Shall never see so much, nor live so long.

It is almost a confession of the inadequacy of words, as though words no longer matter.

At this culminating point, then, moral judgment steps down. Who are we to say that Lear was an egotist or a fool? That question contains its own answer. But what of those more universal insights, part psychological, concerning the nature of man, part moral, concerning what man ought to be, that, I have claimed, are released when we fully engage with the play? Certainly we do not disown these; but in relation to the imaginative world of the play we hold them in a different way from the propositions of the moralist. The point is well put by D. H. Lawrence in his 'Study of Thomas Hardy':

> Every work of art adheres to some system of morality. But if it be really a work of art, it must contain the essential criticism of the morality to which it adheres. And hence the antinomy, hence the conflict necessary to every tragic conception. The degree to which the system of morality, or the metaphysic of any work of art is submitted to criticism within the work of art makes the lasting value and satisfaction of that work.

That is, in reading *King Lear*, we are false to the experience that Shakespeare offers if we in any way ignore or tone down the image of almost unbearable suffering with which the play ends: 'All's cheerless, dark, and deadly.' The sense of *that*, clearly, is something that runs strongly through the whole play, and helps to account for the profound irony. The play as a whole, however, is neither pessimistic nor finally committed to the irony of the absurd; it is an affirmation of human values. But even our affirmations are forced to observe a certain reticence.[9]

I said at the beginning that the most you could hope for from my examination of this problem was a reaffirmation of some simple truths. Our criticism of Shakespeare's tragedies, of plays depicting men in tragic action, is unavoidably moral. When we have lived through the experience of *Hamlet* or of *Lear* we are not in some mysterious realm 'beyond good and evil'—that is to say beyond humanity—because without our capacity for sure and delicate discrimination of good and evil in terms of life or its denial we should not in any sense possess that energizing vision which is the tragic artist's gift to mankind. But vision, not judgment, vision in which judgment has been transformed into something different from its workaday self, is the word that we are compelled to use. Neither does this vision belong to some special realm of 'aesthetic' experience. For just as we encounter tragedy equipped with the ordinary interests of our lives, including what we call our ethical interests, so we go back from the work to 'life' not with 'what we have learned' (that would be the moralistic way of putting it) but certainly with our minds—our awareness, sympathies, insights—extended, enriched and capable of a sturdier working. Our experience, in short, re-enters the world of action and relationship, the world of moral choice and judgment; but the attitudes with which we confront that world have now a deeper hinterland. Which is simply to say that more of life is open to the transforming energies of the imagination.

IX

The Thought of Shakespeare

EVEN to a superficial view, it is clear that in Shakespeare's plays a mind of unusual power is at work: the structure and patterning of even the earliest plays is evidence enough that they were not done without thinking; and when we recall many of the best-known passages—Hamlet's 'To be or not to be', for example, or Polixenes' speech in *The Winter's Tale* on the relation of art and nature—we cannot deny that thought in the usual sense of the word has gone into them. But none of this justifies us in using my title phrase as though we were talking about something self-evident and requiring no explanations. 'The thought of Shakespeare' suggests a consecutive development of discursive reasoning—as we speak of the thought of Francis Bacon or Descartes or, at a less abstract level, the thought of George Bernard Shaw: something that can be followed from point to point, argued with, or even—without too much distortion—summarized. Obviously this is something we do not find in Shakespeare. Shakespeare read widely—far more widely than used to be supposed; he may even have read Hooker; but his handling of the laws of nature in *King Lear* is very different from anything we find in *The Laws of Ecclesiastical Polity*. And even when the plays—or characters within the plays—seem to be offering 'thought', we take it, not at its face value, and not as we should take the thought of a moralist or philosopher, but as one ingredient in something wider, and other.

Consider for a moment Ulysses' famous speech on degree in *Troilus and Cressida*.

> The heavens themselves, the planets, and this centre
> Observe degree, priority, and place,
> Insisture, course, proportion, season, form,
> Office, and custom, in all line of order . . .
> Take but degree away, untune that string,
> And, hark! what discord follows. . . .

Here surely is a piece of Shakespearian 'thought'. Not only does it reflect a good deal of Elizabethan teaching about the necessity of order and due subordination, it is an eloquently persuasive passage of ratiocination; and it ends with a strong imaginative vision of the chaos that comes 'when degree is suffocate'.

> Then every thing includes itself in power,
> Power into will, will into appetite;
> And appetite, an universal wolf,
> So doubly seconded with will and power,
> Must make perforce an universal prey,
> And last eat up himself. . . .

If we are looking for evidence of Shakespeare's thought on a matter of great and permanent concern it would be difficult to find anything more striking. And yet there are various considerations that forbid us to take the speech as straightforward rational exposition, a direct expression of its author's mind, as we might take a comparable passage in Hooker. To start with, it is always hazardous to jump to conclusions about what Shakespeare was thinking just because we find parallels to various passages in the writings of his contemporaries. Shakespeare's plays have been regarded as a treasury of Elizabethan commonplace on such matters as the heinousness of rebellion and the need for order in the state. But this—since we are dealing with a man of remarkable intelligence—is to see the matter too simply.[1] Ulysses' speech occurs in a particular dramatic context. It is almost immediately followed by the rather underhand plot against Achilles, in which Ulysses takes the lead, and Shakespeare takes particular pains to ensure that we shall not see the Greek generals quite as the dignified elder statesmen that they envisage themselves as being. As Aeneas says, enquiring for Agamemnon so that he may deliver his message,

> How may
> A stranger to those most imperial looks
> Know them from eyes of other mortals?

And even if we attend simply to the speech itself there is something in the tone—the prepared, oratorical, public manner—that prompts some questions about its validity. True, it offers a positive conception of public rule, but we do find outselves wondering whether Greek reason, thus expressed, is an entirely satisfactory alternative to Trojan impulsiveness, which is also given careful exposition. Perhaps I can make my point by remarking that another tradition of thought—other, I mean, than that contained in the Elizabethan commonplaces of degree—was also available to Shakespeare. I quote from *The Consolation of Philosophy* of Boethius, using Chaucer's translation:

> . . . all this accordaunce of thynges is bounde with love, that governeth erthe and see, and hath also commandement to the

hevene. . . . This love halt togidres peples joyned with an holy
boond, and knytteth sacrement of mariages of chaste loves; and
love enditeth lawes to true felawes.

(Book II, verse 8)

When, with some familiarity with Shakespeare's other plays, we listen
to Ulysses' speech, it is at least open to us to reflect that 'order' is not
a simple concept, that creative order cannot be divorced from love,
and that love needs for its expression something other than a rhetoric
that clearly has no roots in a personal life.

Similar considerations apply to every passage in Shakespeare where
an argument is pursued or a line of thought put forward. The kind and
degree of endorsement that we give the 'thought' is determined not
only by subtleties of tone, manner and implication—by expression in a
poetic form that is precisely so and not otherwise—but by the particular
context into which it enters. I think of such things as Richard II on the
divine right of kings, Brutus on the necessity of tyrannicide, and
Macbeth on the futility of life. What this means is that you cannot
equate Shakespeare's thought with the explicit thought of any of his
characters. Much less can you get at his thought by assuming that the
plays simply reflect contemporary ideas. And when you cast more widely
for what might be called the thought of a play, you find that you are
taking into account far more than 'thought'—far more, that is, than
discursive thought: you bring into focus the attitudes embodied in the
different speakers in their complex relationships, the implicit comment
of action on profession, emotional overtones, perhaps things even
more elusive.

Do we have to say, then, that there is no such thing as 'the thought
of Shakespeare'? Did he simply let his mind be a thoroughfare for all
thoughts? Do his plays simply reflect the richness and variety of life,
without—in Matthew Arnold's sense—offering a 'criticism' of it? An
affirmative answer to these questions also feels wrong. 'The poetical
Character,' said Keats in a famous passage, 'has no self—it is everything
and nothing—it has no character—it enjoys light and shade; it lives in
gusto, be it foul or fair, high or low, rich or poor, mean or elevated—it
has as much delight in conceiving an Iago as an Imogen. What shocks
the virtuous philosopher, delights the chameleon Poet.' There is, I
think, much truth in this. But to think of Shakespeare simply as a
'chameleon Poet', changing colour, as it were, according to the circumstances that he himself creates, to do this is to ignore the feeling of
coherence that we have when we contemplate not only a single play but
all the plays considered as a single work: it is to ignore the imaginative
drive that runs through Shakespeare's plays from first to last. Perhaps
what we have to do is to attempt to re-define 'thought'.

First of all, then, if by 'thought' we mean 'the formation and arrangement of ideas in the mind', then it is plain that there are other modes of thought besides the familiar discursive mode. In discursive thought the mind abstracts from the rich variety of experience, and the thinking consists of an orderly progression of ideas thus abstracted. It is this progression that, in spoken or written argument, is offered for inspection, so that each step of the mind may be tested before a conclusion is reached. But thought is not limited to what can be offered— abstractly, explicitly and discursively: it can also be stimulated. The way a great artist stimulates ideas is by the presentation of particulars. And these particulars are not simply presented in a temporal or linear succession like steps in an argument: they fall into a pattern which—ideally speaking—the mind perceives in a single complex act of attention.

One way in which Shakespeare promotes ideas is by the patterning of his plot. Professor Hereward T. Price, in an excellent study of *Construction in Shakespeare*,[2] says:

> The point that I want to make is that Shakespeare had an eminently constructive mind. . . . Shakespeare's work is a strict intellectual construction developed from point to point until he brings us to the necessary and inevitable conclusion. *He interrelates part to part, as well as every part to the whole. His main idea is manifested in an action, with which it is intimately fused, so that the crises in the action which move us most deeply reveal at the same time the inner core of Shakespeare's thought.* [My italics.]

One of Professor Price's examples is the way in which, in the First Part of *King Henry VI*, formal ceremony is three times interrupted, at the beginning of the first, third, and fourth acts, by dissension and disorder. What this means is, as Mr. Cairncross puts it in the Introduction to his edition of the play: 'Ceremony and degree have lost their hold. Not only is an extended ceremony not wanted dramatically in a play like this; there is just no place for it in the nature of things.'[3] Further—and stronger—examples are the pattern of retribution in *Richard III*, and the careful alternation of main plot and subplot in the central scenes of *King Lear*, so that Yeats could say:

> We think of *King Lear* less as the history of one man and his sorrows than as the history of a whole evil time. Lear's shadow is in Gloucester . . . , and the mind goes on imagining other shadows, shadow beyond shadow, till it has pictured the world.

But thought in Shakespeare is generated not only by a pattern of incidents, but by what may be called—rather pedantically—a pattern of attitudes embodied in different characters: different attitudes towards

Honour in *Henry IV*, Part I, towards liberty and restraint in *Measure for Measure*, towards Nature in *King Lear*. And when we attempt to elicit the thought of these plays we rarely find that it can be summed up in the explicit utterance of any of the characters: it lies behind the clash of opposites and needs the whole play for its expression; so that in *The Tempest*, for example, the question of 'nature' and 'nurture' isn't simply settled on the side of nurture: Caliban, we are made to feel, has his rights.

When we speak of Shakespeare's thought, then, we mean something that emerges from a dramatic pattern, that inheres in that pattern and is inseparable from it. What I now want to add is that Shakespeare's thought—his poetic thought—is far more than thought as commonly conceived. The point is a difficult one, but for my present purpose it can be put quite simply. *As You Like It* rings changes on the contrasting meanings of 'natural' (*either* 'adequately human' *or* 'close down to the life of instinct') and 'civilized' (*either* 'well nurtured' *or* 'artificial'), especially in relation to the passion of love. In a play by Shaw the ideas would be put forward in the form of argument and counter-argument. Shakespeare is subtler. His characters do not only advance ideas, they embody attitudes to life that lie deeper than 'ideas', and our judgment is directed not only to *what* they say but to *how* they say it: it is the *how* that reveals the feelings, tone, and—as it were—life-style that comes to expression in their explicit formulations about experience. Thus Jacques' melancholy world-view is not simply an intellectual ingredient. Our response to his famous speech on the seven ages of man, for example—'All the world's a stage . . .'—is not determined exclusively by the substance, as though Shakespeare himself were offering us a little homily on life: it is determined by our awareness of the weary cynicism, the languor and preening self-regard that is finally 'placed' so neatly and effectively by Rosalind.[4] In play after play—in relation to Richard II, Brutus, Hamlet, Troilus, Othello—Shakespeare plumbs the recesses of the mind beyond 'thought', so that a character's conscious and deliberate formulation of any matter of urgent interest and concern—

—For every man that Bolingbroke hath press'd
To lift shrewd steel against our golden crown,
God for his Richard hath in heavenly pay
A glorious angel. . . .

—It must be by his death, and for my part,
I know no personal cause to spurn at him,
But for the general. . . .

—It is the cause, it is the cause, my soul. . . .

—Life is a tale told by an idiot. . . .

—all such formulations are seen as having their full meaning only in the complex tissue of thoughts, feelings, desires, motives, valuations, and actions from which they emerge.

It is this hinterland of articulate thought—thought, often, in the very process of formation—that Shakespeare's developed verse can present so superbly. And this applies not only to the imputed thought of the major characters, so that every utterance of Othello or Macbeth carries something of a subliminal meaning, something from the fringes—or from beyond the fringes—of consciousness.[5] It applies also to all that is conveyed by the pervasive poetic medium within which the characters have their being, so that they can echo and re-echo each other without any sense of incongruity, as though they were—what indeed they are—symbols and projections of one mind actively constructing, or growing into, a single unified vision of life. Lady Macbeth's 'Come thick night' and Macbeth's 'Light thickens', Duncan's 'the air Nimbly and sweetly recommends itself Unto our gentle senses' and Malcolm's 'Your leavy screens throw down. And show like those you are', are not simply the utterances of individual characters: they are related aspects of a single vision of good as freedom and clarity, and evil as that which hinders and impedes. It is this 'pattern behind the pattern' that above all expresses itself in modes that may be impervious to the rational understanding—in imagery, rhythm, overtone, and suggestion —though they speak directly to the imagination.

When we speak, therefore, of the 'thought' of a Shakespeare play— the controlling 'idea' that determines not only the over-all design but the minutest details—we refer to a movement of mind, of imagination, that emerges *from* the structure of the plot, *from* the interplay of the characters and of the varied attitudes to experience that they represent; and we refer to a depth and energy of apprehension that, uniting all the characters in a single vision of life, enlists not only our cognitive and conceptual faculties but as much of our own wholeness as we can bring to bear. Shakespeare's thought is not something that can be paraphrased or summarized: it is something we imaginatively apprehend and assimilate to our own most personal life in a lifetime of discovery.

When this is recognized, and only when it is recognized, we are free to speak of Shakespeare's thought and to point to some of its main lines of growth. In the remainder of this paper I shall try, very briefly, to say something about the ways in which Shakespeare's mind and imagination grappled with the subject of power.

It was not an accident that Shakespeare's earliest plays, the three parts of *Henry VI* and *Richard III*, were concerned with power—power in the simple and obvious sense of who, in the state at large, gives orders to whom. It is important to realize this simple fact and to realize what the focus of attention really is. These plays take as their immediate subject events in England's still recent past—the faction and dynastic rivalry that began immediately after the death of Henry v, that broke out in the Wars of the Roses, and that culminated in the bloody triumph of the Yorkist Richard III, who in turn was overthrown by Henry Tudor at Bosworth Field. But they are not straight chronicle plays. Chronicle material is selected from, compressed, altered and added to, to form dramatic structures that are not designed solely to endorse the Tudor view of history. Even the first Part of *Henry VI*, as Professor Price observes, is not, as commonly supposed, 'artless, chaotic or merely discursive'; on the contrary, 'Shakespeare is imposing upon a body of historical data a controlling idea, an idea that constructs the play.' The idea is simple: it is that private faction undermines public order and the common cause—a process symbolized not only in the repeated scenes of interrupted ceremony to which I have already referred, but in the death of Talbot, who is betrayed by the rivalry of Somerset and York. 'This jarring discord of nobility . . . doth presage some ill event. . . . There comes the ruin, there begins confusion' (iv.i). In the two remaining Parts the pattern is equally schematic but the moral is less simple. It is as though the question, What is it that undoes the state?— answer: faction—were replaced by a further question, What is the nature of faction? The answer is given in the repetition and parallelism of the plot, in the apparently endless succession of revenges for wrong done. York kills Old Clifford; Young Clifford kills York's son, Rutland—'Thy father slew my father; therefore, die'—and joins the other Lancastrians in exulting over the defeated York, whose head is placed on the city gates; Young Clifford is killed in his turn, and his head replaces York's, for 'Measure for Measure must be answered.' And the whole senseless process is summed up in the two famous stage directions (*3 Henry VI*, II.v), 'Enter a son that has killed his father, dragging in the dead body', and 'Enter a father that has killed his son, bringing in the body'. *Richard III* is the most powerful and vivid member of this sequence of plays, but it grows directly from its predecessors. The victorious Yorkists are themselves divided and their dynastic triumph serves only to establish the dominating figure of Richard of Gloucester, in whom all the self-seeking of the earlier plays finds it fullest embodiment. Richard, however, does not stand alone; he is at the centre of what A. P. Rossiter calls "a basic pattern of retributive justice".[6] Mutual revenge is now seen as mutual punishment. Nemesis presides over the play, not as a convenient fiction, but because this is the way things happen: 'Wrong hath but wrong, and blame the due of blame.'

All this is obvious enough. What is, I think, equally obvious, though it gets less attention, is the total imaginative effect of these plays, which sometimes depends on hints and glimpses that cannot be subsumed in the rather rigidly controlled patterns of which I have spoken. In other words, to become aware of a play's main structural lines is only the beginning of understanding; even in dealing with these early plays whose pattern, as Professor Price says, can appear 'as schematic as the black and white squares on a chess board,' you have not really done very much when you have established the more obvious correspondences of plot structure. Even the Henry vi plays are something much more than pageant accompanied by illustrative dialogue. Structure includes, but is more than, a structure of events: it is a structure of value judgments, and value judgments are conveyed by words. For example, the contrast between the simple bloody-mindedness of most of the nobles—York's

> I will stir up in England some black storm
> Shall blow ten thousand souls to heaven, or hell—

and the religiously toned positives of the old Protector, Gloucester, or Henry himself,

> Thrice is he arm'd that hath his quarrel just,
> And he but naked, though lock'd up in steel,
> Whose conscience with injustice is corrupted;

even though the play puts the King's ineffective virtue in an ironic light—such a contrast is at least as integral to the pattern as the simpler effects of action. Nor indeed can we expect even the early Shakespeare to hand over his meanings with the explicitness of a morality play. As soon as we have recognized that living structure comes into being only when we ourselves are actively engaged, we see that the necessary process of putting two and two together—of holding in one focus different attitudes towards the main action—involves what is implied as well as what is explicit. Shakespeare from the start expects from his audience some alertness towards tone and implication. Take a small example from the third Part. At Act ii, scene iii, the Yorkists have suffered defeat at Towton. In addition to the familiar cry for revenge ('Warwick, revenge! brother, revenge my death!') there is Warwick's blasphemous vow 'to God above' to fight

> Till either death hath closed these eyes of mine
> Or fortune given me measure of revenge.

Edward of York then joins him on his knees, and applies to God— 'Thou setter up and plucker down of kings'—terms that, as C. H. Herford pointed out, were popularly assigned to Warwick himself, and that are in fact used by Margaret when addressing Warwick in a later scene—'Proud setter up and puller down of kings.' Shakespeare couldn't say more plainly that for these men God can only be envisaged —when He is envisaged at all—as a kind of super-Warwick. Of course, you hear what he is saying only when you make the connexion for yourself. But to make connexions is a main part of the understanding of Shakespearian drama.

There is a further point to make here. The Henry VI plays are structured so as to embody a controlling idea, and you can learn from them something of how to approach later and more complicated plays. But just as you have to be alert to what is implied, rather than explicitly stated or presented, so—even from the start—you have to notice not only the more or less obvious pattern, but also what breaks into or goes beyond it, or in some way doesn't fit in. Cast back for a moment to the simplest play of the series, the first Part of *Henry VI*. The play's latest editor quotes Alfred Harbage to the effect that this 'is a play about the courage, prowess and assumed righteousness of the English as represented by such loyal and able leaders as Salisbury, Bedford, Warwick, and, above all, Lord Talbot; and about the opportunism, treachery, and fox-like success of the French as represented by the fraud and moral depravity of La Pucelle' (New Arden edition, Introduction, p. xl). No doubt this fairly represents the general background of assumptions against which the theme of internal faction is developed. But it is not the whole story. Talbot is indeed presented for our admiration as the embodiment of English patriotism; but there are also suggestions that Talbot's single-minded patriotism, although it serves to measure the depravity and self-seeking of the factious nobles, is not an absolute standard: it is not, by itself, sufficient to measure the causes of chaos in a world given to violence. Nor is it simply assumed that values are embodied in the English cause if only the English would give up quarrelling among themselves. In Act III, scene iii, when Joan persuades the Duke of Burgundy to desert the English and return to his French allegiance, her speech has a genuine authority.

> Look on thy country, look on fertile France,
> And see the cities and the towns defac'd
> By wasting ruin of the cruel foe;
> As looks the mother on her lowly babe
> When death doth close his tender dying eyes,
> See, see the pining malady of France. . . .

I am not pretending that this is great poetry; but it is not the speech of a character intended only for contempt. Joan is indeed later presented as contemptible; but I hope it is not only hindsight if I say that just at this point something breaks through the prevailing tenor of English patriotism and points forward to the great speech of the Duke of Burgundy, in *Henry V*, when he pleads for peace.[7] And we recall how much else there is in the later play—though less than ten years later—to qualify the simple patriotic interpretation that is often put on it. You can see too how in *Richard II* conflicting values are held in tension with each other, forming a pattern of meanings of great complexity,[8] In *1 Henry VI* we can hardly speak of complexity; there is rather, when we keep the last scenes presenting La Pucelle in mind, simple contradiction. But the point I am making is a simple one: you can't extract the structure from a Shakespeare play like the backbone from a kipper. Shakespearian structure is a living thing; it emerges only as we relate this to that; it cannot be summed up in an easy formula. That is why we need to be alert not only to the main lines of development of a play but of what cuts across them, and makes us reassess the pattern of meaning we thought we had found.

And now there is one last thing I should like to say about these early plays before leaving them. It is in fact rather obvious, but not the less important for that, especially if we keep the later plays in mind. The meaning of the three parts of *Henry VI* may begin to become clear as we attend to dramatic structure—a pattern of events and of attitudes towards those events (at the same time not ignoring what cuts across and complicates the more obvious orderly arrangement). But even here —at all events in the second and third Parts—the total imaginative effect depends also on hints and glimpses that cannot be subsumed in any formal pattern. We are here of course in the realm of individual and intuitive, but not lawless, judgment. It seems to me, then, that what we are most aware of is the unending clash of tight, self-contained egos, without any reaching out towards 'the other', or towards anything that transcends the self. And the feeling we get as we read or watch is that life is delivered over to automatism because of a radical misdirection of energy. Public life is private life writ large (that truth came to Shakespeare early), and Richard of Gloucester is explicit:

> And am I then a man to be beloved?
> O monstrous fault, to harbour such a thought!
> Then, since this earth affords no joy to me,
> But to command, to check, to o'erbear such
> As are of better person than myself,
> I'll make my heaven to dream upon the crown.

The pursuit of power is a substitute gratification, and it is in Richard that Shakespeare reveals something of what happens in the person when power is envisaged as the sole desirable end. The soliloquy I have just quoted from *3 Henry VI*, III, ii continues:

And I,—like one lost in a thorny wood,
That rends the thorns and is rent with the thorns,
Seeking a way and straying from the way;
Not knowing how to find the open air,
But toiling desperately to find it out,—
Torment myself to catch the English crown.

In that central image Shakespeare puts into words the sense of night-mare and frustration that pervades these plays—a process in which there is literally *no end*, only a sterile and meaningless repetition: 'a perpetual and restless desire of power after power, that ceaseth only in Death.' Early in the last act of this same play Warwick—'Proud setter up and puller down of kings'—meets defeat and death at the hands of the Yorkists at Barnet. His last words are a formal, rhetorical lament on the vanity of power:

Thus yields the cedar to the axe's edge,
Whose arms gave shelter to the princely eagle,
Under whose shade the ramping lion slept. . . .

But before the end the speech shifts into another mode:

For who lived king, but I could dig his grave?
And who durst smile when Warwick bent his brow?
Lo, now my glory smear'd in dust and blood!
My parks, my walks, my manors that I had,
Even now forsake me, and of all my lands
Is nothing left me but my body's length.

Instead of rhetorical figures there is now the simplest and most natural expression of human feeling — 'my parks, my walks, my manors that I had . . .' The result is both a deepening of perspective (something that comes to be a major characteristic of the later historical plays[9]), and an intensification of the ironic light in which we see the play's conclusion. Warwick's words are still echoing in our minds when we hear the victorious Edward announce his security with that bland short-sighted-ness that we shall meet again (with different tones) in other of Shakespeare's 'successful' men of action.

And now what rests but that we spend the time
With stately triumphs, mirthful comic shows,
Such as befits the pleasure of the court?
Sound drums and trumpets! farewell sour annoy!
For here, I hope, begins our lasting joy.

Since Richard of Gloucester has just announced his intention of 'blasting' that 'harvest', the irony here is inescapable. But even without Gloucester's melodramatic asides, Edward's crude assumptions about the fruits of kingship are sufficiently placed, within the context of the play, as vanity. And the obviousness of the irony shouldn't prevent us from seeing the significance of it. Other princes in the Shakespearian drama—Henry Bolingbroke at the end of *Richard II* and again at the end of *I Henry IV*, Henry V at the end of his play—will be compelled to stand in the same steady light, of which they themselves are unaware. And this may serve as a reminder that Shakespearian irony is not simply a dramatic device. What it manifests is an intelligence that is at the same time a commitment to life and life's realities; and against *these* all kinds of sham, self-deception, substitute values—however loudly endorsed by society—must show themselves for what they are.

It seems plain, then, that in these early plays we have the beginning of much of Shakespeare's thought on the subject of power, even though it is not explicitly formulated *as* thought. The process in which, in play after play, he traces the intricacies of political power is far too large a subject for a single paper, much more for a concluding section. We will merely note that in the sequence of Shakespeare's plays there are four characteristics that bear directly on our question of what Shakespeare's 'thought' is on the question of power. First, there is the tendency (most marked in *Henry IV*) to put the political action in a wider setting that in various ways reflects back on it: there is an increase in depth and perspective. Second, for an explanation of conflict and failure at the political level we are more and more directed towards conflict and failure at the personal level: here the line runs from Richard II, to Brutus, to Coriolanus. Third, there is a growing sense of the inadequacy of action that is merely political, merely concerned with power, as in *Henry V*. Finally—and this is in some ways inseparable from the other three—the deepening insight into the inadequacies of power goes hand in hand with what may be called the celebratory aspects of Shakespeare's art, in which all is finally subsumed: the celebration, I mean, of life-values against which the distortions and subterfuges of partial life may be measured. This, too, was a long process, and it started early. Harold Goddard, remarking that in the reign of Henry VI Shakespeare came face to face with chaos, 'a subject that continued to enthral him to the end of his days,' says: 'It would be folly to try to subsume Shakespeare's works under one head, but, if we were forced to do so, one of the least unsatisfactory ways would be to say that they are an attempt to answer the question: 'What is the cure for chaos?'[10] That answer is to be found, not in the overtly political dramas but in the tragedies and final plays. Here, Shakespeare's handling of power, when it occurs, is always part of something far wider; it is always in implicit or explicit relation to positive values; and it can be defined only in terms of a total dramatic and poetic structure. His 'thought' about power, in short, is—inescapably—a function of the imagination: 'a man in his wholeness, wholly attending.'

At the end of a paper that has been necessarily discursive I must not attempt to dwell in any detail on one of the great tragedies, but we may briefly call to mind *Macbeth*. *Macbeth*, in one of its aspects, is a study in tyranny: dominative power, seeking to establish and support itself by violence, is traced as never before or since as a progress towards meaninglessness and chaos. It is not merely that Macbeth creates confusion around him; from the moment he yields to 'that suggestion Whose horrid image doth unfix my hair,' he *is* confusion. And what the poetry tells us in its imagery of unnatural strain and hysterical effort is, unmistakably, that violence towards another is violence towards the self—towards that innermost self that exists only in relationship—in the world where one gives and takes 'honour, love, obedience'. It tells us more too: not only that, as Martin Foss says, 'he who wants to possess will himself be possessed,'[11] but that apparent firmness and single-minded concentration on a purely egocentric purpose covers an underlying disintegration. But the telling is entirely in terms of the awakened imagination, that holds in one complex act of attention explicit thought, dramatic action, and symbolism, and all that is presented or suggested by rhythm and imagery.

> This castle hath a pleasant seat; the air
> Nimbly and sweetly recommends itself
> Unto our gentle senses.

> This guest of summer,
> The temple-haunting martlet, does approve,
> By his lov'd mansionry, that the heaven's breath
> Smells wooingly here; no jutty, frieze,
> Buttress, nor coign of vantage, but this bird
> Hath made his pendent bed, and procreant cradle:
> Where they most breed and haunt, I have observ'd
> The air is delicate.

Is this just a bit of 'poetry' or something put in to 'illustrate character'? I think not. The passage creates an imaginative 'atmosphere' that is important because it is so different from the atmosphere that we have come to associate with Dunsinane. But more: the birds are evoked with delighted attention to their free movements; and they are evoked in terms that make their sanctioned seasonal activities into something with a bearing on human life itself. What we have here, in short, is an image of life delighting in life; and it powerfully reinforces our sense of the ideal presence of a life-bearing order in the human commonwealth— something that Macbeth describes, when he has lost it, as 'Honour, love, obedience, troops of friends.' This, the play makes us feel, is the reality where man finds himself: when he steps outside that order—as Macbeth in his pursuit of power does by the murder of Duncan and the increasingly pointless murders that follow—he loses himself in a world that in one sense is real enough, but that in another sense is mere unreality—'where nothing is, but what is not.'

There is of course far more than that to say about Shakespeare's exploration of the nature of power. But the example may suffice to illustrate the point that it is the main object of my paper to establish. Shakespeare's 'thought' is not something that can be extracted from the body of his work or discursively paraphrased. We can point to certain preoccupations and describe in a general way some of the main directions of his mind. But in any fundamental sense, his 'thought'—in all its depth, fullness, complexity, and energy—can be apprehended only as an imaginative activity evoked and directed by all the resources of his art. We can never 'know about' Shakespeare's thought: we can only know it as living power.

X

Timon of Athens

ONE OF THE most interesting problems in Shakespeare criticism
—as indeed in the criticism of all great literature—is the problem
of divergent interpretations. I do not refer to shifts of emphasis and
approach inevitable as times change, or to the mysterious power of
works of art to reveal *more* meaning in the course of centuries, but to
radically incompatible accounts of 'the meaning' of a work among
readers who respect each other's standards and general powers of judgment. A glance at the history of opinion about Shakespeare's *Timon of
Athens*[1] suggests that the critic who chooses to write on this most
puzzling of Shakespeare's plays must take especial care to expose the
grounds of his judgment. An attempt to do this is my tribute to the
author of *The Wheel of Fire* and *The Imperial Theme*, works which, more
than any others available at the time, helped my generation in the
arduous and endlessly rewarding task of reading Shakespeare for
themselves.

There seems no doubt that *Timon of Athens* is an unfinished play: not
in the sense that it lacks a formal conclusion, but in the sense that it has
not been finally worked over for presentation on the stage.[2] It is,
however, very much more than a mere draft; it is a play moving towards completion; and although the great variety of critical opinion
warns us that it is not easy to get at the meaning, there is no reason why
we should not trust our impression that Shakespeare is saying something important, and use our wits to determine what that something
may be. Our best course, as usual, is to trust our immediate sense of
dramatic power, to begin by concentrating on those parts where our
minds and imaginations are most fully engaged, and to ask ourselves
how these are related to each other and to the remainder of the play—
to those parts of lesser intensity that serve to reinforce, to modify or to
cast a fresh light on what is more prominent. I am not advocating
simple concentration on dramatic highlights: all I am saying is that
understanding has to start somewhere, and we run less risk of going
astray if we start with whatever it may be that most engages us.

Timon is no exception to the rule that Shakespeare's plays are always
superbly well planned. When we look back on *Timon*, after directly

experiencing it, we recall three episodes or phases of great dramatic effectiveness. The first is the presentation of Timon in his prosperity, surrounded by suitors, friends and parasites. This begins about a third of the way through the first scene and continues throughout the second (that is to say, to the end of the first Act). The second is the scene of the mock banquet (III.vi), where Timon serves covered dishes of warm water to the friends whose utter falseness has been exposed, denounces them for the fawning parasites they are ('Uncover, dogs, and lap'), beats them, and drives them out. The third is the exhibition of Timon's misanthropy: this consists of the tirade of IV.i, and the tirades and curses of IV.iii, when Timon is confronted, in turn, with Alcibiades, Apemantus, the bandits, and other intruders on his solitude. There is in addition a kind of prologue, when Poet, Painter, Jeweller and Merchant congregate at Timon's house, and the Poet describes the common changes and chances of Fortune's Hill; and a kind of epilogue, where the cowed Senators of Athens submit to Alcibiades, Timon's death is reported, and Alcibiades speaks a formal valediction.

All these major scenes, and all but one of the intervening scenes, concentrate on Timon with an unremitting attention. The question that any producer, like any reader, must ask himself is, how is Timon presented? how are we to take him? Now it is obviously possible to take him as a truly noble man, ruined by his own generosity—'Undone by goodness', as the Steward says—someone, quite simply too good for the society that surrounds him. Roy Walker, in an interesting review of the Old Vic 1956 production, says, 'it was presumably the poet's intention to show how selfish society drives out true generosity.'[3] And another critic writes as follows:

> In the first part of *Timon of Athens* Timon appears as a man full of warmth, geniality and overflowing humanity. He is the incarnation of charity and hospitality, and believes in the supreme virtue of friendship, which his generosity is intended to foster. Gold plays an immensely important part throughout the play, but for Timon, before his fall, it is completely the servant of 'honour' (another key word) and of brotherly love. In the great feast of I.ii, he comes very near to enumerating an ideal of benevolent communism in which money merely provides the opportunity for men to express charity towards one another: 'We are born to do benefits; and what better or properer can we call our own than the riches of our friends? O what a precious comfort 'tis, to have so many, like brothers, commanding one another's fortunes' (I.ii. 105–9).[4]

Of remarks such as these I can only say that they seem to me completely to miss the point of the opening scenes. Timon is surrounded by the corrupt and the self-seeking: this is made very plain, and he must have been rather stupid or else possessed by a very strong emotional bias to have had no glimmer of it. Of course it is good to use one's money to redeem a friend from a debtor's prison or to enable a poor serving-gentleman to marry the girl of his choice. But it is not good to engage in a perpetual potlatch.

> No meed but he repays
> Seven-fold above itself: no gift to him
> But breeds the giver a return exceeding
> All use of quittance.   (I.i.288–91)

Gifts, to be meaningful and not part of a ritual of exchange or display, must be person to person. Timon, who does not pause to look at the Painter's picture or to glance at the Poet's book, hardly *attends* to anyone: in the words of one of the Lords, he simply 'pours it out' (I.i. 287). When, therefore, he voices the incontrovertible sentiments we have had quoted as an expression of his magnanimity—'We are born to do benefits. . . . O what a precious comfort 'tis, to have so many, like brothers, commanding one another's fortunes'—it is not moral truth that we recognize but self-indulgence in easy emotion. As for the significance of the great feast, Apemantus has already told us what to think of it:

> That there should be small love amongst these sweet knaves,
> And all this courtesy!   (I.i. 258–9)

And it is not long before the honest Steward sheds light retrospectively on the nature of Timon's hospitality:

> When all our offices have been oppress'd
> With riotous feeders, when our vaults have wept
> With drunken spilth of wine, when every room
> Hath blaz'd with lights and bray'd with minstrelsy. . . .
> (II.ii. 167–70)

Compared with those who have idealized the early Timon for his generosity, the eighteenth-century critic, William Richardson, surely came nearer to the truth when he wrote:

> Shakespeare, in his Timon of Athens, illustrates the consequences of that inconsiderate profusion which has the appearance of liberality, and is supposed even by the inconsiderate person himself to proceed from a generous principle; but which, in reality, has its chief origin in the love of distinction.*

* William Richardson, *Essays on Some of Shakespeare's Dramatic Characters*, Fifth edition (1797), p. 313. So too Dr. Johnson: 'The catastrophe affords a very powerful warning against that ostentatious liberality, which scatters

Tragedy of course takes us beyond bare moral judgment. But moral judgment necessarily enters into our experience of tragedy: and it is worth remarking how sharply, in this play, Shakespeare seems to insist on the moral issue, even to the extent of using techniques reminiscent of the morality plays. In the first part of the opening scene (in what I have called the Prologue) Timon's situation is presented with a formal simplification that suggests a moral *exemplum* rather than any kind of naturalistic portrayal. As the parasites gather—Poet, Painter, Jeweller, Merchant, and then certain Senators—the audience is invited (by one of them) to observe:

> See,
> Magic of bounty! all these spirits thy power
> Hath conjur'd to attend! (I.i. 5–7)

In the Poet's fable of Fortune's Hill we are given due warning of what to expect

> When Fortune in her shift and change of mood
> Spurns down her late beloved . . . (I.i. 84–5)

It is against this background that Timon appears and displays his undiscriminating, and ruinous, bounty; and it is here that the producer can help us a good deal, if he will let himself be guided by the hints that Shakespeare provides. The stage directions—both the explicit ones that seem to come direct from the author's working draft and those that are implicit in the text—are pretty clear indications of the intended theatrical effect. Timon's first entry is to the sound of trumpets. The 'great banquet' of the second scene is heralded by 'hautboys playing loud music'. And after the masque of Ladies as Amazons 'the Lords rise from table, with much adoring of Timon'. Throughout, there is much elaborate courtesy—'Serving of becks and jutting out of bums', as Apemantus puts it—and as the glittering pomp (which we now know can't be paid for) comes to an end, Timon calls for 'Lights, more lights' (I.ii. 234). All this obvious showiness serves the same purpose as similar elements in ballad or morality play: it tells us in straightforward visual terms that what we have before us is an example of vanity and pride of life decked out in tinsel. The last words of the scene are given to Apemantus:

> What needs these feasts, pomps, and vain-glories? . . .
>   O that men's ears should be
>   To counsel deaf, but not to flattery.
>   (I.ii. 248 ff.)

---

bounty, but confers no benefits, and buys flattery, but not friendship'. Johnson however thought that 'in the plan there is not much art'.

What we seem to be dealing with, then, is a play that, in some important ways, comes close to the Morality tradition. There is no attempt at characterization; many of the figures are simply representative types. When Timon, in need, appeals in turn to each of his false friends, all heavily indebted to him, what we watch is a *demonstration* of how right Apemantus had been when he said, at the feast,

> I should fear those that dance before me now
> Would one day stamp upon me. 'T'as been done.
> Men shut their doors against a setting sun.
>
> (I.ii. 148–50)

When Timon retires to the woods, naked and abandoned, he is Misanthropos, and his railings refer not to some sharply realized individual plight but to the human situation in general.

Now it is of course true that the tradition of didactic simplification was still active in Shakespeare's lifetime. A rather dull little Morality called *Liberality and Prodigality* was revived and acted before the Queen in 1601. As in our play Money is shown as in the gift of Fortune; Prodigality gets rid of Money with something of Timon's unthinking ease—

> Who lacks money, ho! who lacks money?
> But ask and have: money, money, money!

—and when Virtue hands over Money to 'my steward Liberality'— Prodigality having proved unworthy—her servant Equity preaches the golden mean ('Where reason rules, there is the golden mean') in the manner of Apemantus moralizing to Timon about 'the middle of humanity'. But we have only to put *Timon of Athens* beside *Liberality and Prodigality*, or beside a more sophisticated play in the same tradition such as Ben Jonson's *The Staple of News*, to see how inappropriate, here, any kind of Morality label would be. For myself I think we get closer to Shakespeare's play by recognizing the didactic elements than by a too ready responsiveness to Timon as the disillusioned idealist. But to see the play as straight didactic moralizing directed *at* Timon as Prodigality —as though he were merely an illustration of a moral thesis—that too feels inadequate. The verse is often too powerful to allow us that kind and degree of detachment as we judge.

We are still, then, left with the question on our hands: How is Timon conceived and presented? how are we to take him? Our answers so far have been mainly negative ones. If we want something more positive we must take a closer look at the play, paying special attention—as we always need to do—to those parts where we most find ourselves in difficulties of interpretation. There are various difficulties in *Timon*: and I mean more substantial ones than the identification of Timon's false friends, the name of the loyal Steward, or Shakespeare's confusion about the value of a talent.[5] One substantial difficulty concerns the dramatic function of III.v, where Alcibiades, failing to persuade the Senators to spare the life of his friend who has killed a man in hot blood, plans revenge against Athens. But this, together with the counterbalancing scene at the end, where Alcibiades is readmitted to the city, I want to put on one side for the moment in order to concentrate on Timon's invective, his display of satire and misanthropy in the fourth act.

The invective, of course, is largely about the power of money: and it has a superb force.

> O blessed breeding sun, draw from the earth
> Rotten humidity; below thy sister's orb
> Infect the air! Twinn'd brothers of one womb,
> Whose procreation, residence and birth
> Scarce is dividant—touch them with several fortunes,
> The greater scorns the lesser. Not nature,
> To whom all sores lay siege, can bear great fortune,
> But by contempt of nature.
> Raise me this beggar, and deny't that lord,
> The senator shall bear contempt hereditary,
> The beggar native honour.
> It is the pasture lards the brother's sides,
> The want that makes him lean. Who dares, who dares,
> In purity of manhood stand upright,
> And say this man's a flatterer? If one be,
> So are they all, for every grise of fortune
> Is smooth'd by that below: the learned pate
> Ducks to the golden fool . . .
>
> (IV.iii. 1–18)

Then, as Timon digs for roots and discovers gold:

> What is here?
> Gold? Yellow, glittering, precious gold?
> No, gods, I am no idle votarist.
> Roots, you clear heavens! Thus much of this will make
> Black, white; foul, fair; wrong, right;
> Base, noble; old, young; coward, valiant.
> Ha, you gods! Why this? this, you gods? Why, this
> Will lug your priests and servants from your sides,
> Pluck stout men's pillows from below their heads.
> This yellow slave
> Will knit and break religions, bless th'accurs'd,

Make the hoar leprosy ador'd, place thieves,
And give them title, knee and approbation
With senators on the bench. This is it
That makes the wappen'd widow wed again:
She whom the spital-house and ulcerous sores
Would cast the gorge at, this embalms and spices
To th' April day again . . .

(IV.iii. 24–41)

All this has an obvious relevance to the England of the late sixteenth and early seventeenth centuries. Professor Laurence Stone has documented very fully indeed the scramble for rewards at Court, the lavish expenditure on all forms of conspicuous display, the heavy dependence on credit and lucky breaks, the intense greedy competitiveness of those for whom Fortune's Hill was a vivid symbol for a very present reality.[6] There is no difficulty here. *Timon of Athens*, in so far as it is a direct satire on the power of money, can be seen as Shakespeare's response to certain prominent features in the economic and social life of his own day. And the satire, as we have just seen, has the kind of bite that makes it relevant to *any* acquisitive society, our own as much as Shakespeare's. (It was almost inevitable that Karl Marx should quote Timon's denunciation of 'gold . . . this yellow slave' in an early chapter of *Capital*.)

But—and here comes the difficulty—when Timon first gives expression to his outraged feelings and curses Athens, in forty lines of invective the only reference to money is short, incidental and indirect (IV.i. 8–12). He does, on the other hand, have a lot to say about sexual corruption; just as in encouraging Alcibiades to destroy Athens his catalogue of the city's vices, after a brief mention of usury, plunges into a lengthy diatribe against an anarchic sexuality. Nothing in the play has prepared us for this (apart from the dance of the Amazons in I.ii, Timon seems to have lived in an exclusively masculine society). And although Timon does of course denounce money, and although he subsequently gives some of his new-found gold to Alcibiades to pay troops levied against Athens, and some to the harlots to encourage them to spread diseases, it is not money-satire, or satire on ingratitude, that forms the substance of the long dialogue in the woods with Apemantus. In short, given the obvious data of the play, and given the obvious grounds for Timon's rejection of a society shown as corrupt and usurous, there is neverthelesss omething excessive in the *terms* of his rejection, just as there is something strange (and, if you see the play solely in terms of a *saeva indignatio* directed against society, even tedious) in the slanging match with Apemantus in the woods. What, then, is Shakespeare up to?

I suggest that as in all the greater plays Shakespeare is using the outward action to project and define something deeply inward. I do not mean simply that in *Lear* or *Macbeth* or *Othello* Shakespeare observes character with a rare psychological penetration, though he does of course do this. I mean that in a variety of ways he uses the forms of dramatic action, external conflict and event, to reveal inner conflicts and distortions, basic potentialities for good and evil, at a level where individual characteristics take second place to human nature itself. In short he demonstrates precisely what T. S. Eliot meant when he wrote:

> A verse play is not a play done into verse, but a different kind of play: in a way more realistic than 'naturalistic drama', because, instead of clothing nature in poetry, it should remove the surface of things, expose the underneath, or the inside, of the natural surface appearance.[7]

In *Timon*, as in *Lear* and *Othello*, Shakespeare is revealing what is 'underneath . . . the natural surface appearance'—sometimes in a naïve Morality way (as when the mock feast of steam and stones instead of nourishment shows us what the earlier feast really was—not a feast at all), sometimes with the force and subtlety of the great tragedies.

In *Timon* the surface appearance is lightly sketched in the suggestions of a corrupt society, where the business of individuals is very much to feather their own nests: more firmly, though in a rather schematized way, in the presentation of Timon's friends and parasites. But the surface appearance on which, in the first Act, attention is most sharply concentrated is Man in Prosperity, the ego sustained in a fixed posture by an endless series of reflections which show it just as it thinks itself to be:

> All those which were his fellows but of late,
> Some better than his value, on the moment
> Follow his strides, his lobbies fill with tendance,
> Rain sacrificial whisperings in his ear,
> Make sacred even his stirrup, and through him
> Drink the free air.
>
> (I.i. 78–83)

That this picture—of what the Steward, allowing himself a touch of satire, calls 'Great Timon, noble, worthy, royal Timon'—has to be drawn again and again betrays a compulsive need. What supports Timon in his self-idolatry, what buys him reassurance ('You see, my lord, how amply y'are belov'd'), is of course his wealth. But the wealth is secondary in dramatic importance to what it serves: means to the same end could have been extorted professions of filial affection, as in *Lear*, or any of the familiar tricks that we use to cut a fine figure in our own eyes. Towards the end of Act II the Steward points the action:

Heavens, have I said, the bounty of this lord!
How many prodigal bits have slaves and peasants
This night englutted! Who is not Timon's?
What heart, head, sword, force, means, but is Lord Timon's,
Great Timon, noble, worthy, royal Timon?
Ah, when the means are gone that buy this praise,
The breath is gone whereof this praise is made,
Feast-won, fast-lost . . .

(II.ii. 173–80)

At virtually one stroke the props to Timon's self-esteem are removed, and he is reduced to 'unaccommodated man'. He is stripped, so to speak, of his protective covering, and, as in *Lear*, his physical appearance reflects an inner state. 'Nothing I'll bear from thee But nakedness, thou detestable town!' (IV.i. 32–3).

There, I think, you have the central interest of the play. In a world such as the men of great tragic vision have always known it to be, a world where you clearly cannot remove all the threats—the inner and the outer threats—to your security, how, quite simply, do you keep going? Life only allows a limited number of choices. Either you live by some kind of integrating principle through which even potentially destructive energies can be harnessed, stability and movement combined; or, plumping for security—for 'a solid without fluctuation', like Blake's Urizen—you seek artificial supports for a fixed posture. Unfortunately the concomitant of a fixed posture is unremitting anxiety to maintain itself; and it is in the nature of artificial supports, sooner or later, to break down. This is what happens to Timon. When his supports are removed, 'when the means are gone that buy this praise', he is left, like Lear, with 'nothing'—nothing, that is, but a vision of a completely evil world that partly, of course, reflects a social reality, but is also an expression of his own self-hatred and self-contempt:

> . . . and his poor self,
> A dedicated beggar to the air,
> With his disease of all-shunn'd poverty,
> Walks like contempt, alone.

(IV.ii. 12–15)

It is this, surely, that explains the nature of Timon's first great speech of invective, where there is very little about money and nothing about ingratitude, but much about sexual incontinence and general anarchy.

> Let me look back upon thee. O thou wall
> That girdles in those wolves, dive in the earth
> And fence not Athens! Matrons, turn incontinent!
> Obedience fail in children! Slaves and fools,

Pluck the grave wrinkled senate from the bench,
And minister in their steads! To general filths
Convert, o'th' instant, green virginity!
Do 't in your parents' eyes! Bankrupts, hold fast;
Rather than render back, out with your knives,
And cut your trusters' throats! Bound servants, steal!
Large-handed robbers your grave masters are,
And pill by law. Maid, to thy master's bed;
Thy mistress is o' th' brothel! Son of sixteen,
Pluck the lin'd crutch from thy old limping sire;
With it beat out his brains! Piety and fear,
Religion to the gods, peace, justice, truth,
Domestic awe, night-rest and neighbourhood,
Instruction, manners, mysteries and trades,
Degrees, observances, customs and laws,
Decline to your confounding contraries;
And yet confusion live! Plagues incident to men,
Your potent and infectious fevers heap
On Athens ripe for stroke! Thou cold sciatica,
Cripple our senators, that their limbs may halt
As lamely as their manners! Lust and liberty
Creep in the minds and marrows of our youth,
That 'gainst the stream of virtue they may strive
And drown themselves in riot!   (IV.i. 1–28)

It is a little like what Conrad's Marlow glimpsed on his voyage up the
river to the heart of darkness, though perhaps more specifically realized.
Timon's horror is of anarchic impulses that he knows within himself
when the picture of noble Timon is destroyed. It is true of course that
Timon presently denounces the inequalities bred by fortune, the corruption caused by money; and throughout the scenes in the woods,
when he is visited by Alcibiades and the harlots, the bandits, and various
former hangers-on who have heard of his newly discovered wealth, the
satire on money-lust continues. All this is clearly very near the dramatic
centre of the play. But to treat it as *the* controlling centre, *the* dominant
theme, is to see things entirely from Timon's point of view, from the
point of view of a man who feels unjustly treated by others,—as
of course he is. But the play only makes sense as a whole when we
see him as self-betrayed, his revulsion against the city as equally a
revulsion against himself.* Midway in the indictment of money that
I quoted from the opening of IV.iii Shakespeare drops the necessary
clue:

* John Wain speaks of the 'neurotic and self-feeding' nature of Timon's
tirades—*The Living World of Shakespeare*, p. 195.

> ... all's obliquy;
> There's nothing level in our cursed natures
> But direct villainy. Therefore be abhorr'd
> All feasts, societies, and throngs of men!
> His semblable, *yea himself, Timon disdains.*
> Destruction fang mankind!   (IV.iii. 18–23)

If Shakespeare's intention was in fact, as I suppose, to portray self-revulsion, the shattering of an unreal picture and the flight from hitherto concealed aspects of the self that are found insupportable, this would also explain the drawn-out exchanges with Apemantus in the woods. In the opening of the play Apemantus, as professional cynic, is not an attractive figure. But he is no Thersites. It is from him, almost as much as from the Steward, that we get a true picture of Timon's 'bounty' and its effects:

> That there should be small love amongst these sweet knaves,
> And all this courtesy!
>   (I.i. 258–9)
> What a sweep of vanity comes this way.
> They dance? They are madwomen.
> Like madness is the glory of this life,
> As this pomp shows to a little oil and root.
> We make ourselves fools, to disport ourselves ...
>   (I.ii. 137–41)
>   Thou giv'st so long, Timon, I fear me thou wilt give away thyself
> in paper shortly. What needs these feasts, pomps, and vain-glories?
>   (I.ii. 246–8)

But if Apemantus is not Thersites, neither is he Lear's Fool, the disinterested teller of unwelcome truths: the emotional bias, like the ostentatious poverty, is too marked. It is this that explains his dual and ambiguous role in the later scene. On the one hand he is the objective commentator, a mentor that Timon ignores at his peril; and since this is so clearly intended it is a mistake to play him simply as the abject and railing cynic. His pronouncements have authority:

> This is in thee a nature but infected,
> A poor unmanly melancholy sprung
> From change of fortune [F. future]
>   (IV.iii. 202–4)
> If thou didst put this sour cold habit on
> To castigate thy pride 'twere well; but thou
> Dost it enforcedly. Thou'dst courtier be again
> Wert thou not beggar.
>   (IV.iii. 239–42)

The middle of humanity thou never knewest, but the extremity
of both ends.
(IV. iii. 300–1)

And th'hadst hated meddlers sooner, thou shouldst have loved
thyself better now.
(IV. iiii. 309–10)

On the other hand, and simultaneously, he is a kind of mirror image
of Timon. His first words on his reappearance are,

> I was directed hither. Men report
> Thou dost affect my manners, and dost use them, (IV.iii 198–9)

and not only is Timon's general manner identical in tone with that of
Apemantus in the opening scenes, each echoes what, at another time,
the other has said.[8] Geoffrey Bush remarks: 'Apemantus is what Timon
becomes. . . . Even in the first three acts, though Apemantus and Timon
are opposites, they are oddly drawn toward each other, as if they found
a peculiar importance in each other's company. They go together . . .
they are, as it were, two aspects of a single self, the extremes between
which the personality of a human being can alternate'.[9] And it is not
only cynicism about the world that they share. At the beginning of the
play Apemantus was described as one 'that few things loves better than
to abhor himself' (I.i. 59–60). Timon's echo of that we have already
heard: 'His semblable, yea himself, Timon disdains' (IV.iii. 22). The
final exchange of insults between the two, before Apemantus is driven
off with stones—

> —Would thou wert clean enough to spit upon!
> —A plague on thee, thou art too bad to curse. . . . (IV.iii. 364 ff.)

reads like a monologue of self-hate.

Some of this, perhaps, is matter for dispute. What is abundantly clear
is that Timon's misanthropy is in no essential way an approach to
reality; it is primitive rage at the destruction of an ego-ideal, horror and
hatred at what is revealed when support for that ideal picture is with-
drawn. Denied the absolute and one-sided endorsement that he had
claimed, the self-esteem that his wealth had enabled him to buy, he
refuses to see his claims for what they were. Instead he projects on to
the world at large his own desire to get what he wanted by means that
were essentially dishonest. He has been, in effect, a thief. Confronted
with the bandits, he declaims:

> I'll example you with thievery:
> The sun's a thief, and with his great attraction
> Robs the vast sea; the moon's an arrant thief,
> And her pale fire she snatches from the sun;
> The sea's a thief, whose liquid surge resolves

140

The moon into salt tears; the earth's a thief,
That feeds and breeds by a composture stol'n
From gen'ral excrement; each thing's a thief . . .
                                        (IV.iii. 438–45)

Shakespeare, who expected his audience to recognize a bad argument
when they heard one, knew that each of the elements mentioned here
in fact repays, or gives to another, what it takes. Timon, in becoming
nastier, has become sillier. But by now there is scarcely any pretence on
Timon's part that he is denouncing real corruption in a real world: he
is satisfying an emotional animus that can exhaust itself only in death.

> Come not to me again; but say to Athens,
> Timon hath made his everlasting mansion
> Upon the beached verge of the salt flood,
> Who once a day with his embossed froth
> The turbulent surge shall cover . . .
> Lips, let sour words go by and language end:
> What is amiss, plague and infection mend!
> Graves only be men's works and death their gain;
> Sun, hide thy beams, Timon hath done his reign.
>   (V.i. 217–26)

I am of course aware that this unfavourable view of Timon has
against it not only the opinions of many critics but, more important,
certain pronouncements within the play itself—pronouncements that,
unlike the eulogies of the parasites, are disinterested, and must therefore be given due weight. There is the unwavering loyalty of the
Steward, for whom Timon is

> Poor honest lord, brought low by his own heart,
> Undone by goodness . . .
>   (IV.ii. 37–8)

and there is the eulogy by Alcibiades that virtually concludes the play:

> Through thou abhorr'dst in us our human griefs,
> Scorn'dst our brains' flow and those our droplets which
> From niggard nature fall, yet rich conceit
> Taught thee to make vast Neptune weep for aye
> On thy low grave, on faults forgiven. Dead
> Is noble Timon . . .
>   (V.iv. 75–80)

But I do not think that either substantially modifies the account that
I have given. The Steward, playing Kent to Timon's Lear, reminds us
in his devotion that love and loyalty see further than the eye of the mere
spectator; there is no need to doubt the potentiality of goodness that is

in Timon. But in the play it remains unrealized. The most that his old servant's undemanding devotion can wring from Timon is the recognition that his undiscriminating condemnation of mankind must allow of one exception:

> You perpetual-sober gods! I do proclaim
> One honest man. Mistake me not, but one,
> No more, I pray . . .
>
> (IV.iii. 503–5)

The current of his feeling remains entirely unchanged:

> Go, live rich and happy,
> But thus conditioned: thou shalt build from men;
> Hate all, curse all, show charity to none,
> But let the famish'd flesh slide from the bone
> Ere thou relieve the beggar . . .*
>
> (IV.iii. 532–6)

As for Alcibiades, the fact that his role is only roughly shaped forces us back on intelligent guessing. But the general intention seems clear. The point of the central scene in which he pleads unsuccessfully with the Senators for the life of the soldier who has killed a man in a brawl is partly to emphasize the greed and corruption of society (that much of Timon's indictment is true):

> . . . I have kept back their foes,
> While they have told their money, and let out
> Their coin upon large interest; I myself
> Rich only in large hurts. All those, for this?
> Is this the balsam that the usuring Senate
> Pours into captains' wounds?
>
> (III.v. 106–11)

* I find myself in complete agreement with Mr. H. J. Oliver when he writes in the Introduction to the New Arden edition (pp. l–li): 'The presence of the Steward among the characters, then, so far from being the puzzle or contradiction that Chambers found it, is essential to the meaning of the play and expressly forbids us from identifying *our* judgment (or Shakespeare's) with Timon's . . . Timon's misanthropy, like everything else in Shakespeare's plays, is part of a dramatized situation and is in no sense a lyrical statement of the poet's own belief; and Timon's invective for which the play has received most of such praise as has generally been given it, is all the more remarkable when one pauses to reflect that it states an attitude from which, through the presence of the Steward, Shakespeare has dissociated himself completely.' All I would add is that, as we have seen, it is not only the presence of the Steward that 'places' Timon's misanthropy.

But there is more to it than this. Both Alcibiades and the Senators are right in the general truths they enunciate:

> *Alcibiades*   For pity is the virtue of the law,
> And none but tyrants use it cruelly.

> *First Senator* He's truly valiant that can wisely suffer
> The worst that man can breathe,
> And make his wrongs his outsides,
> To wear them like his raiment, carelessly . . .
> (III.v. 8–9, 31–4)

What we are forced to question, by Alcibiades' special-pleading and the Senators' complacency, is the reliability of the speakers. Alcibiades' claim that his friend acted 'in defence' (l. 56), with 'sober and unnoted passion' (l. 21), is undercut by his own admission that the man 'in hot blood Hath stepp'd into the law' (ll. 11–12), and this not in self-defence but, 'Seeing his reputation touch'd to death' (l. 19). And although the Senators profess to stand for law and the virtues of restraint there is something very disagreeable in their legalistic morality.

> *First Senator* My lord, you have my voice to't; the fault's
> Bloody; 'tis necessary he should die;
> Nothing emboldens sin so much as mercy.
> *Second Senator* Most true; the law shall bruise 'em.
> (III.v. 1–4)

Neither side is trustworthy. In this respect, then, the scene is a variation on the main theme. Much of what a man says may be true, as much of what Timon says is true; but what really matters is the integrity and self-knowledge, or the lack of these qualities, in the person speaking. If the Senators are clearly untrustworthy, Alcibiades does not represent an acceptable norm.

It is the recognition of this that prevents us from taking the last scene of all with the moral earnestness that both Alcibiades and the Athenians would like to impart. These eighty-five lines raise far more questions than they answer. Some of our perplexities may be due to the play's unfinished state. But if we take the scene in conjunction with III.v— the previous confrontation of Alcibiades with apparently representative Athenians—it suggests a world of hazy verbiage. (What right has Alcibiades to reproach Athens with being 'lascivious'? When last seen he was trailing about with a couple of mistresses. As for the Senators, anything goes, so long as they can save their skins and plaster the situation with appropriate platitude.) And this does not only contrast with Timon's blazing hatred, it offers a parallel. Men set themselves up for judges, when the underlying attitudes, from which their judgments spring, are distorted by evasions, self-exculpations, and lack of self-knowledge. All that is said in this final scene is, for Alcibiades and the Senators, an easy way out—the world's way when confronted with any kind of absolute, of negation or affirmation. In this context, 'Dead is noble Timon' suggests a bitter irony. Timon's self-composed epitaph was not noble; and his wholesale condemnation of the world, though not an easy way, was easier than the pain of self-recognition.

Presumably we shall never know when *Timon of Athens* was written, nor why it was not finally completed. The best of the verse puts it firmly in the period of Shakespeare's great tragedies. There are very many parallels—verbal and substantial parallels—with *King Lear*. Coleridge jotted down that it was 'an after vibration' of that play.[10] But why should a man try to repeat an unrepeatable masterpiece? My own guess, for what it is worth, is that *Timon* was drafted when *Lear* was already taking shape in Shakespeare's mind. Both plays are about a man 'who hath ever but slenderly known himself', who tries to buy love and respect, who has genuine reason to feel wronged, and whose sense of betrayal releases an indictment of the world that can't be shrugged off as 'madness' or 'misanthropy', but a man also whose sense of betrayal by others masks a deep inward flaw; in both the stripping away of all protective covering reveals with fierce clarity a world of evil. But there the major resemblances cease. *Timon of Athens* contains a loyal and decent Steward; it does not contain a Cordelia. Timon goes almost as far in hatred and revulsion as Lear; there is nothing in his mind that corresponds to Lear's gropings towards self-knowledge. And it is the active presence in *King Lear* of positive and affirmative elements that, paradoxically, makes its presentation of pain and evil so much more deeply disturbing. You can disengage from *Timon of Athens,* for all its power: you have to live with *King Lear*. And when the greater theme took possession of Shakespeare's mind, the more partial one could be abandoned: Timon had 'done his reign'.

XI

The Tempest

(i)

O F ALL THE greatest works of art it seems true to say that they
contain an element of paradox, that what imposes itself on our
imaginations as a unified and self-consistent whole contains contradictory elements tugging our sympathies—and therefore our judgments—
in different ways: part of the continuing life of the great masterpieces
springs from the fact that they will not allow the mind of the reader to
settle down comfortably with the sense that he has finally reached *the*
meaning which can now be put in a pocket of the mind with other
acquired certainties producible at need. More than is the case with any
other of Shakespeare's plays, with the exception of *King Lear*, paradox
is of the essence of *The Tempest*, a fact that is reflected in the history of
Shakespeare criticism. I am not referring to the truism that every work
of art, without exception, 'means' something different for every age
and every reader, but to the completely contradictory accounts that
have been given of this play. It is not so long since critics, identifying
Prospero with Shakespeare, saw the play either as embodying the
serene wisdom of age or as a deliberate turning aside from the harsh
realities of life to the more easily manageable world of romantic fantasy.
More recently the views to which I have alluded have been sharply
challenged, most notably by Jan Kott—in *Shakespeare our Contemporary*
—for whom *The Tempest* is 'a great Renaissance tragedy of lost illusions',
its ending 'more disturbing than that of any other Shakespearean
drama'. Others have written to much the same effect. And even for
those who are not unduly swayed by critical opinion there is difficulty
in saying simply and clearly where one feels the play's greatness to
reside. Because of its obvious impressiveness and mystery, and because
it is probably Shakespeare's last play without a collaborator, there is a
temptation to read in large significances too easily, as I think we may
tend to do with *Cymbeline*. On the other hand, to say that *The Tempest*,
like *Cymbeline*, points to more than it contrives to grasp and hold in a
unified dramatic structure—that also feels wrong. Perhaps we should
start by pondering what everyone would agree to be there, in the play:
I mean prominent aspects of the play's dramatic mode, its technique.
Not everyone will agree as to the significance to be attached to these,

but to consider them may clear the ground for criticism. I. A. Richards has remarked of the interpretation of poetry that 'whatever accounts are offered to the reader must leave him—in a very deep sense—free to choose, though they may supply wherewithal for exercise of choice'. This, he added, 'is not . . . any general licence to readers to differ as they please. . . . For this deep freedom in reading is made possible only by the widest surface conformities'; for 'it is through surfaces . . . that we have to attempt to go deeper'.[1]

There are four aspects of 'surface' technique that deserve attention. The play observes the unities of time and place; it is related to the contemporary masque; it makes great use of music and song; it employs a very great variety of modes of speech.

Alone among Shakespeare's plays the action of *The Tempest* keeps well within the limits of a natural day: indeed Prospero is rather insistent on getting the whole business completed in three or four hours. Clearly this means compression, and it is compression of a particular kind. There are plays that keep the unities that obviously have great depth and spaciousness, for example *Oedipus*, or *Phèdre*. Here the effect is different—as though important experiences were rendered by a rather spare, and at times almost conventional, notation, that only gets its effect when the reader or spectator is prepared to collaborate fully, to give apparently slight clues full weight. We notice in particular two things. (i) There is a form of symbolism developed out of the earlier plays (notably *King Lear*), as when Stephano and Trinculo fall for the 'trumpery' hung up on the line (or linden tree); and the potentially healing and cleansing power of the tempest is indicated by the information about the shipwrecked party—'On their sustaining garments not a blemish, But fresher than before'; and 'Though the seas threaten, they are merciful' (which it may not be fanciful to associate with Jung's dictum, 'Danger itself fosters the rescuing power'). Or again, love's labours are simply represented by Ferdinand carrying logs. (ii) Psychological states are briefly, even if pungently, represented. We know that Antonio was ambitious ('So dry he was for sway') and that Sebastian is a would-be murderer; but neither state of mind is developed as it might have been in the tragedies. Alonso undergoes a storm in which he learns to listen to his own guilt; but this is reduced to,

> O, it is monstrous, monstrous!
> Methought the billows spoke, and told me of it;
> The winds did sing it to me; and the thunder,
> That deep and dreadful organ-pipe, pronounc'd
> The name of Prosper: it did bass my trespass. . . .

So too with the young lovers: compared with Florizel and Perdita they have very little to say to or about each other, but what they do say is often telling and beautiful; and the harmony in diversity of the sexes is given in a simple tableau—'Here Prospero discovers Ferdinand and Miranda playing chess'. It remains to be seen whether we are justified in giving to these brief 'notations' the kind of weight that I have implied we should give.

The Tempest is also distinguished from Shakespeare's other late plays in its relation to the contemporary masque. Apart from the formally presented masque of Ceres at the betrothal in Act IV, there are various masque-like tableaux, as when 'several strange shapes' bring in a banquet for the shipwrecked party, and then, as they approach it: 'Thunder and lightning. Enter Ariel like a Harpy; claps his wings upon the table; and, with a quaint device, the banquet vanishes'. This has been often noticed;[2] and indeed Shakespeare had often used what is seen on the stage to emphasize what is said, as in the formal and ceremonious grouping of his characters, their pairing off or drawing apart; but The Tempest puts a special emphasis on modes of formal, masque-like, presentation, and we need to be fully aware of the language of visual suggestion that is developed in the play.

'Suggestion': the critic does well to be careful when he uses the word, but he can hardly avoid it when speaking of a play in which music and song have so important a part. Ariel sings to Ferdinand, to the sleeping Gonzalo, to Prospero as he robes him and anticipates his own freedom; Stephano sings 'a scurvy song'; Caliban sings. At key points in the action Ariel plays music to the actors. The banquet is presented to the King's party with 'solemn and strange music' and vanishes to the sound of thunder. The masque of Ceres is accompanied by 'soft music' and vanishes 'to a strange, hollow and confused noise'. In short 'the isle is full of noises . . .'. Now not only is music—harmony—the polar opposite of tempest, as Professor Wilson Knight has rightly and so often reminded us,[3] it is the art furthest removed from the discursive mode. In all Shakespeare's plays music and song had been functional to the action, and so they are here; but they make their contribution to the changing moods of the play by unexpected and almost undefinable means, as W. H. Auden has pointed out in his essay, 'Music in Shakespeare'.[4] Perhaps we may have to allow to the play as a whole a power of controlled suggestion greater than any formulable meaning we can attach to it.

Finally, in this brief glance at 'technique'—the surface characteristics which everyone would agree to be there, whatever the interpretation attached to them—we should notice the great range of style and manner: from the delicate allusiveness of Ariel's songs to the decidedly not delicate speech of the 'low' characters; from the slightly stylized verse of the masque to the passionate intensity of some of Prospero's speeches. Nor is it only the low characters who command a pithy idiom directly related to everyday speech. It is Antonio who gives us,

> For all the rest,
> They'll take suggestion as a cat laps milk;
> They'll tell the clock to any business that
> We say befits the hour;

and it is Ariel himself who describes the effect of his music on the drunken butler and his followers—'they prick'd their ears . . . lifted up their noses As they smelt music'. In the poetry of the play there is at least as much of the earthy as there is of the ethereal.

With this, of course, we find our attention focusing on far more than 'technique'. To the range of style there corresponds an equal range of interest and awareness. It is well known that the play makes direct reference to contemporary matters. It is, among many other things, a contribution to the debate on 'nature' and 'nurture'; and F. R. Leavis, making the point that *The Tempest* is 'much closer [than *The Winter's Tale*] to the "reality" we commonly expect of the novelist', is clearly right in saying that 'Caliban . . . leads the modern commentator, quite appropriately, to discuss Shakespeare's interest in the world of new discovery and in the impact of civilization on the native'.[5] Important as this is, it is even more important to see how much of 'the real world' comes into the play by way of reference, imagery and allusion. The opening storm proves to be merciful, but, as Gonzalo says,

> Our hint of woe
> Is common; every day, some sailor's wife,
> The masters of some merchant, and the merchant,
> Have just our theme of woe. . . .

Ariel's songs are balanced by the coarse life of Stephano's song. Gonzalo's Utopia, remembered from Montaigne, inevitably calls to mind its opposite—the more familiar world of 'sweat, endeavour, treason, felony, Sword, pike, knife, gun . . .'. The masque of Ceres conjures up images of the English countryside at its most peaceful:

> You sunburn'd sicklemen, of August weary,
> Come hither from the furrow, and be merry:
> Make holiday; your rye-straw hats put on, . . .

but we are also reminded of the wilder, undomesticated, aspects of nature—not only the storm-tossed waves, the 'roarers' that 'care nothing for the name of King', but 'long heath, broom, furze . . .', 'the green sour ringlets . . . whereof the ewe not bites', the lightning-cloven oak. The island, for all its magical qualities is very much a part of the everyday world: even one of the most delicate of Ariels songs has for

burden, 'Bow wow' and 'Cock a diddle dow . . . the strain of strutting
chanticleer', as though it were dawn in an English village. And at the
centre of these specific references is a vision of 'the great globe itself',
which, with all its towers, palaces and temples, as Prospero reminds us,
is as transient as 'this insubstantial pageant faded'. In other words, the
island mirrors, or contains, the world; what we have to do with is not
exclusion and simplification but compression and density, vibrant with
its own unique imaginative life. The point has been well put by Dr.
Anne Barton:

> Spare, intense, concentrated to the point of being riddling, *The
> Tempest* provokes imaginative activity on the part of its audience
> or readers. Its very compression, the fact that it seems to hide as
> much as it reveals, compels a peculiarly creative response. A need
> to invent links between words, to expand events and characters in
> order to understand them, to formulate phrases that can somehow
> fix the significance of purely visual or musical elements is part of
> the ordinary experience of reading or watching this play.[6]

(ii)

With so much, perhaps, all readers would agree. Any attempt to say
more, to define the centre of interest to which these different aspects of
Shakespeare's technique direct our attention, is unavoidably personal
and partial. As so often when a play has made a strong impact on the
mind and we know we are still far from understanding, it is useful to
face directly the more obvious difficulties. Consider, for example, the
abrupt ending of the masque that Prospero had arranged for Ferdinand
and Miranda.

> *Enter certain Reapers, properly habited: they join with the Nymphs in a
> graceful dance; towards the end whereof Prospero starts suddenly, and
> speaks; after which, to a strange, hollow, and confused noise, they heavily
> vanish.*

> Pros. [*Aside*] I had forgot that foul conspiracy
> Of the beast Caliban and his confederates
> Against my life: the minute of their plot
> Is almost come [*To the Spirits*] Well done! Avoid; no more!
> Fer. This is strange: your father's in some passion
> That works him strongly.
> Mir.　　　　Never till this day
> Saw I him touch'd with anger, so distemper'd.

It is indeed strange, and Professor Kermode finds the motivation
inadequate, wondering 'that Prospero should so excite himself over an
easily controlled insurrection'.[7] But it is only strange if we forget that

Caliban, like Ariel, stands in some kind of special relationship with Prospero. ('We cannot miss [i.e. do without] him', and, near the end of the play, 'This thing of darkness I Acknowledge mine'.) Caliban, although his mother was a witch, is also a 'native' of new-found lands who raises the whole question of man before civilization and of the relation of 'natives' to European settlers. It is also Caliban, who knows the island better than anyone else, who speaks some of the most beautiful poetry in the play:

> Be not afeard; the isle is full of noises,
> Sounds and sweet airs, that give delight, and hurt not.
> Sometimes a thousand twangling instruments
> Will hum about mine ears; and sometimes voices,
> That, if I then had wak'd after long sleep,
> Will make me sleep again: and then, in dreaming,
> The clouds methought would open, and show riches
> Ready to drop upon me; that, when I wak'd,
> I cried to dream again.

But he is also a brute 'on whose nature nurture can never stick'; and the play gives us no warrant for supposing that each man has not a Caliban inside himself—even Prospero. In the passage I have referred to we have had an elaborate, slightly artificial masque of Ceres—a vision of nature fertile and controlled. But life isn't as simple as that: Caliban, pure instinct, is still plotting; and it is the sudden memory of this that puts Prospero into a 'passion That works him strongly'. No one is put into that kind of temper by external danger (especially when the danger, such as it is, is largely represented by a couple of drunks), only by self-insurrection. Perhaps we have here an explanation of Prospero's tensed-up attitude towards Caliban at the beginning of the play and his spiteful and childish punishings of him—'I'll rack thee with old cramps, Fill all thy bones with aches. . . .' What I am suggesting is that the play is mainly the drama of Prospero, a man who, even by Elizabethan standards, is not old, but one who is looking towards the end of his days, trying to sort out and to come to terms with his experiences. Prospero is not simply above the action, controlling it, he is intimately involved. The play is about what Prospero sees, and, above all, what he is and has it in him to become. 'Prospero,' says Harold Goddard, 'when expelled from his dukedom, is a narrow and partial man. Thanks to his child, the island, and Ariel, he gives promise of coming back to it something like a whole one. But an integrated man is only another name for an imaginative man.'[8]

I have said that no single, clearly defined interpretation can be extracted from—much less put upon—this play. But when it is seen in some such way as this the action at least falls into an intelligible shape, which still allows the working of other promptings. Consider briefly a few major phases in the action. The play opens with a storm, conjured up by magic, but real enough not to make its nautical technicalities out of place. In some sixty lines Shakespeare—as in all his masterful openings—is doing several things simultaneously. The human characteristics of various people who will play a part in the subsequent action are revealed—from the detachment of Gonzalo to the panicky blustering of Antonio and Sebastian. The storm is also a reminder of fundamental equalities—'What care these roarers for the name of King?'. But like all Shakespearian storms it carries overtones: indeed it is explicitly related (I, ii, 207 ff.) to inner storms. The second scene is sometimes regarded as a contrast to the first, and so—in some ways—it is; but it is also a continuation. The storm has prepared us for something in the mind of Prospero, a mental turmoil that is sharply contrasted with the music of Miranda's compassion—'O, I have suffered with those that I saw suffer.' The tortured syntax of many of his speeches, with their abrupt dislocations, his interjections to Miranda (more, surely, than a clumsy attempt by the dramatist to hold the attention of the audience throughout a long exposition)—these mark the tumultuous strength of his anger against his brother: 'I pray thee, mark me, that a brother should Be so perfidious', ''Thy false uncle—Dost thou attend me?'. And underneath the anger (which to be sure is natural enough) is an admission of at least partial responsibility.

> I pray thee, mark me.
> I, thus neglecting worldly ends, all dedicated
> To closeness and the bettering of my mind
> With that which, but by being so retir'd,
> O'er-prized all popular rate, in my false brother
> Awak'd an evil nature. . . .

The New Arden note on this passage, rightly admitting that 'no paraphrase can reproduce its involved urgency', offers as the main sense: 'The fact of my retirement, in which I neglected worldly affairs and dedicated myself to secret studies of a kind beyond the understanding and esteem of the people, brought out a bad side of my brother's nature. . . .' Apart from the fact that a ruler's business is to rule—not at all events to be 'all dedicated' to study—the paraphrase misses the point. In the phrase, 'in my false brother Awak'd an evil nature', the verb has a subject, and it is not 'the fact of my retirement' but the pronoun 'I'. Auden is surely right when in *The Sea and the Mirror* he makes Prospero say, 'All by myself I tempted Antonio into treason.' From at least as early as *Richard II* Shakespeare had used incoherence *dramatically*; and Prospero's involutions contain at least some admission of hidden guilt.

The main movement of the play, it has been suggested, is Prospero's movement towards restoration, renewal of the self. He is certainly human enough—not simply the wise controller of other people's fate—to make us interested in his fluctuations of mood. True, as white magician he is in some ways analogous to the artist, and within the conventions of the play his magic can control much of the action. But even within the play magic cannot do what is most essential. It is not magic that determines Gonzalo's decency or the falling in love of Ferdinand and Miranda. Magic can help to demonstrate how evil mistakes the goal or desires what proves to be trash, just as art can set out telling *exempla*. But magic cannot help Prospero in his most extreme need. When, in the passage already referred to, he breaks off the masque because he has recalled the 'foul conspiracy of the beast Caliban and his confederates', his 'old brain' is genuinely 'troubled', and he needs to walk 'a turn or two . . . To still my beating mind'. The conspiracy, as it turns out, is easily dealt with: the conspirators are very stupid, and Prospero certainly puts too much effort and too much venom into punishing them. To 'a noise of hunters heard', Caliban and his associates are hunted by dogs, one of whom is called 'Fury' and another 'Tyrant'. Prospero clearly relishes the hunting:

> Go charge my goblins that they grind their joints
> With dry convulsions; shorten up their sinews
> With aged cramps; and more pinch-spotted make them
> Than pard or cat o' mountain.

It is not the first time that he has appeared like a bad-tempered martinet, so that you want to ask, What is he afraid of? It is immediately after his grim enjoyment at handing out punishment that he announces,

> At this hour
> Lies at my mercy all mine enemies.

Any actor playing the part of Prospero would have to ask himself, What is the *tone* of this? It certainly isn't a calm announcement of a further stage in the magician's demonstration: to my mind it is very close to the lines immediately preceding. The question of what Prospero intends to do with his enemies (which means also, What is he going to do with himself?) is a genuine one, and at this stage we have no right to assume that the answer will be comfortably acceptable.

If we agree that in this play comparatively slight clues do in fact bear a great weight of implication, then the opening of Act V, which immediately follows the hounding of Prospero's minor enemies, is a genuine crisis, and we miss what Shakespeare is doing if we see it as leading smoothly into a pre-ordained 'happy ending'. Everything now depends on how Prospero handles the situation. When the Act opens he is tugged two ways. Miranda—'a third of mine own life'—loves his enemy's son, and he furthers and approves, though putting mock obstacles in the way. But he has been in a thundering bad temper (which he has tried to overcome); he wants to get his own back—to hunt his enemies with the dog, Fury. The question is whether he can stop dwelling on his own wrongs, real as these are, stop nagging about Caliban, and trust his best self. That, surely, is the significance of the opening exchange with Ariel—his intuitive self. Ariel describes the plight of the King of Naples and his party.

> Your charm so strongly works 'em,
> That if you now beheld them, your affections
> Would become tender.
> *Pros.*　　Dost thou think so, spirit?
> *Ari.* Mine would, sir, were I human.
> *Pros.*　　　　And mine shall.
> Hast thou, which art but air, a touch, a feeling
> Of their afflictions, and shall not myself,
> One of their kind, that relish all as sharply,
> Passion as they, be kindlier mov'd than thou art?
> Though with their high wrongs I am struck to th' quick,
> Yet with my nobler reason 'gainst my fury
> Do I take part: the rarer action is
> In virtue than in vengeance: they being penitent,
> The sole drift of my purpose doth extend
> Not a frown further. Go release them, Ariel:
> My charms I'll break, their senses I'll restore,
> And they shall be themselves.*

It is *after* this—and in the acting there should be a marked pause before 'And mine shall'—that Prospero can 'abjure' 'this rough magic', and we hear the 'heavenly music' that he has called for. As Goddard points out, not only does Prospero obey Ariel, instead of commanding him—'Music replaces magic'.[9]

What follows is of great importance. Once more, music and formal movement add an undefinable suggestion to the spoken word. But the words are clear enough. The royal party, shepherded by Ariel, enter to

---

* It is interesting—though not, I think, essential for our understanding of the play—to note that some of Prospero's lines are a direct translation from the opening paragraph of Montaigne's essay 'Of Cruelty'. I owe this reference to Miss Eleanor Prosser; see her *Hamlet and Revenge*, (Stanford University Press) pp. 83–4, and 'Shakespeare, Montaigne and the "Rarer Action"', *Shakespeare Studies* I (1966) pp. 261–6.

'a solemn music', Alonso 'with a frantic gesture', and 'all enter the circle which Prospero has made'. As they come to themselves the feeling is of a more-than-individual return to consciousness.

> The charm dissolves apace;
> And as the morning steals upon the night,
> Melting the darkness, so their rising senses
> Begin to chase the ignorant fumes that mantle
> Their clearer reason.

(It is the same image as in George Herbert: 'As the sun scatters with his light All the rebellions of the night'.)

> Their understanding
> Begins to swell; and the approaching tide
> Will shortly fill the reasonable shore,
> That now lies foul and muddy.

Prospero is not simply *arranging* this: as 'one of their kind, that relish all as sharply, Passion as they', he is himself involved. As the King's party come to themselves, so he resumes his full human nature, not as magician but as man:

> I will discase me, and myself present
> As I was sometime Milan.

The often quoted 'the rarer action is In virtue than in vengeance' is of course the key. Prospero has come to terms with his experience, and —so far as their individual natures permit—with his enemies. There is a special emphasis on the rejoicings of the good Gonzalo.

> O, rejoice
> Beyond a common joy! and set it down
> With gold on lasting pillars: in one voyage
> Did Claribel her husband find at Tunis,
> And Ferdinand, her brother, found a wife
> Where he himself was lost, Prospero his dukedom
> In a poor isle, and all of us ourselves
> When no man was his own.

Prospero 'found his dukedom' in a more than literal sense 'in a poor isle', and you certainly have to include him among those who 'found' themselves 'when no man was his own'. But Gonzalo is not Shakespeare's chorus to the play. Antonio makes no reply to the 'hearty welcome' that Prospero offers all (V.i. 110–111), and it is his silence that comes between Prospero's first address to him—'Flesh and blood, You, brother mine. . . . I do forgive thee'—and the second, where 'forgive' is used in the barest legal sense:

For you, most wicked sir, whom to call brother
Would even infect my mouth, I do forgive
Thy rankest fault,—all of them; and require
My dukedom of thee, which perforce, I know,
Thou must restore.

It is with some reason that Auden, quoting these lines, finds that the play ends 'more sourly' than *Pericles, Cymbeline,* or *The Winter's Tale.* I myself don't feel that 'sourly' is the word. The harmony that is achieved is valuable,—but there is no final all-embracing reconciliation. Prospero may draw his circle of relationship, but some people will choose to stay outside, and Prospero will somewhat tartly respond. The music remains something that Caliban dreams of, and that humans hear from time to time—and can sometimes actualize in their own lives. The play claims no more than that. The end is an acceptance of the common conditions and common duties of life: 'Every third thought shall be my grave'. Those characters who have proved themselves capable of it have undergone a transforming experience. Now they go back to the workaday world, to confront once more the imperfect, paradoxical and contradictory nature of life.

Paradox runs through the play. Again and again the double and contradictory nature of things is insisted on. To Miranda's question, 'What foul play had we, that we came from thence? Or blessed was't that we did?' Prospero answers, 'Both, both, my girl'. Miranda's 'O brave new world, That has such people in't' is counterpointed by Prospero's ''Tis new to thee', which is not merely cynical and disillusioned. And the great speech in which Prospero dwells on the transience of all things human, which it would be both perverse and simple-minded to see as 'pessimistic',* begins,

You do look, my son, in a mov'd sort,
As if you were dismay'd: be cheerful, sir . . .

It is in these tensions that man has to live. Gonzalo, we remember, had tried to cheer up his king by painting a picture of the ideal commonwealth:

All things in common Nature should produce
Without sweat or endeavour: treason, felony,
Sword, pike, knife, gun, or need of any engine,
Would I not have; but nature should bring forth,
Of its own kind, all foison, all abundance,
To feed my innocent people.

* 'Prospero's great speech is an utterance neither of pessimism nor of ennui but of awe'—Enid Welsford, *The Court Masque,* p. 346.

Life, however, is more stubborn and intractable than that, and part of the greatness of *The Tempest* is that it forces us to recognize it. It helps us to face with something that is neither wishfulness nor despair—with something that is both resigned and positively affirming—the intractabilities and the limitations of our lives.

XII

Shakespeare: Four Histories

(i)

THE BACKGROUND

Shakespeare wrote ten plays on subjects taken from English history, and although only four of them will be dealt with in this essay some general observations on 'the Histories' may be allowed to introduce the discussion of *Richard III, King John, Richard II* and *Henry V*.

To start with, although we shall all go on using the term 'Shakespeare's Histories', it would be as well if we could free ourselves from some misleading notions that go with it. 'The Histories' are better thought of not simply as History Plays—the dramatization of past events—but as political plays. The Histories or Political Plays, moreover, do not form an entirely distinct and homogeneous species of Shakespearian drama: as with 'Shakespearian Tragedy' the blanket-term covers very great variety, and we need to be aware of this as well as of important common elements; there is continuity, development, but there is no mere repetition, no common formula for each member of the series. Finally, even though a rough grouping of plays on 'historical' themes clearly has its uses, these plays are properly understood only when they are seen in relation to others that are not historical or, in any obvious sense, political.

The political plays have of course a more obvious reference to events and accepted ideas outside themselves than is the case, for example, with *Othello*, and this raises the question of the kind of equipment necessary for the student. Here again there are a few simple distinctions to be made. To understand, to enjoy and to profit from these plays what we most need is of course an interest in men and affairs, a lively feeling for literature, and a capacity for responding to each play as a work of art. Given that basic and indispensable equipment however (and without it book-loads of information are of little use), some kinds of knowledge extraneous to the plays can help to sharpen our vision. Shakespeare was not, as was once believed, almost entirely ignorant of formal history, keeping by him, as was suggested in the eighteenth century, a 'chuckle-pated Historian' to give him facts which he after-wards vamped up.[1] He read for himself in Hall and Holinshed, and his reading did more than give him events that could be represented on the stage; it prompted his thinking about actions and reactions in the public world. As readers of the Histories therefore, we need to know something of the Tudor view of history; even more, perhaps, we need to know something of the main assumptions behind men's thinking about politics in the sixteenth century, of the clash of ideas about such subjects as law, power, government, and the relations of men in society. It remains to add that when we have equipped ourselves with some information of this kind we shall be very careful not to assume that Shakespeare, in any play, is simply reflecting 'Tudor ideas', or that he is accepting them uncritically as premises for a dramatic action—not, at all events, unless we have good warrant from the play itself. In almost all his plays Shakespeare combined in a remarkable way a sense of tradition—the ability to assimilate and learn from the past—and the freshness and independence of one who sees and thinks for himself; even when he seems to put most emphasis on traditional and received ideas he has a way of subjecting those ideas to the keenest scrutiny: which of course is how tradition is kept alive, and part of the debt we owe to genius.

The major themes and assumptions of English historical writing in the sixteenth century have been admirably described by E. M. W. Tillyard in the second chapter of his *Shakespeare's History Plays*—a book indispensable to the student. In the historians' treatment of the comparatively recent past the great theme was of course the slow and painful working out of the consequences of the deposition of Richard II and the providential accession of Henry Tudor by which the civil strife of more than half a century was brought to an end: 'So that all men'—in Hall's often quoted words—'(more clearer than the sun) may apparently perceive, that as by discord great things decay and fall to ruin, so the same by concord be revived and erected.' Nowadays we may feel a little ironic about the Tudor view of history, so convenient for the Tudor monarchs, just as we find it hard to stomach the use of Homilies appointed to be read in churches for absolutist propaganda. Perhaps fully to enter into the Tudor dread of renewed internal dissension it would be necessary to have some first-hand experience of the miseries of civil war—of how 'one doth rend the other of those that one wall and one foss shuts in' (*Purgatorio*, vi, 83–84). But a very little historical imagination should be enough to check our irony. When in 1548 Hall asked, 'what noble man liveth at this day or what gentleman of any ancient stock . . . whose lineage hath not been infested and plagued with this unnatural division?' it was no mere rhetorical flourish. For sixteenth-century Englishmen it must have been virtually self-evident that 'the union of the two noble and illustre families of Lancaster and York' was an act of Providence.

But the events that loomed largest in the eyes of English historians of the sixteenth century—the miseries of the Wars of the Roses—were only the most striking examples of processes at work in all times and all places. History, for all its immediate appeal to the human interest in story, in character and action, was essentially the record of a moral process: it taught lessons that could be applied to the understanding of the present and the conduct of affairs. As Louis B. Wright says, in his great work on the reading habits of the Elizabethans: 'The faith in the didactic value of history was not confined . . . to any social group in Tudor and Stuart England, because the belief was almost universal that a knowledge of the past furnished a valuable guide to the present.'[2] And when history was transposed into semi-fictional forms it was still the moral issue that was predominant. It was, in the words of one of the most popular compilations of the mid-sixteenth century, 'a mirror'. Thomas Baldwin, in his dedication of the first edition of *A Mirror for Magistrates* (1559) to 'the nobility and all other in office', declaring that God dealt sternly with corrupt governors, wrote:

> How he hath dealt with some of our countrymen your ancestors, for sundry vices not yet left, this book . . . can show: which therefore I humbly offer unto your honours, beseeching you to accept it favourably. For here as in a looking glass, you shall see (if any vice be in you) how the like hath been punished in other heretofore, whereby admonished, I trust it will be a good occasion to move you to the sooner amendment.[3]

We need not concern ourselves just now with the rather sweeping assumption behind this (Baldwin himself admits that 'some have for their virtue been envied and murdered'); the important fact is that those who bought the *Mirror* in its successive editions—and its popularity continued until well into the seventeenth century—expected something more than information or entertainment; they expected moral examples drawn from the field of public life and great affairs.

Similar expectations and interests were also satisfied in the theatre. It is a matter of common knowledge that the last ten or fifteen years of the reign of Queen Elizabeth I saw the performance of a very large number of plays on subjects drawn from English history. Some of these can properly be covered by the familiar description of 'chronicle play'— 'a history transformed into a play' (Schelling); but a considerable number, including the most distinguished, are related more closely to the old political and social moralities—like, say, Skelton's *Magnyfycence* (1529–32), Sir David Lindsay's *Ane Satyre of the thrie estaitis* (c.1540–52), or the anonymous *Respublica* (1553)—than they are to the straight 'chronicles': to use the convenient term coined by A. P. Rossiter, they were Moral Histories—'chronicle patterned on an abstract design'. In the Preface to his edition of the anonymous *Woodstock* (c.1591–4) Rossiter wrote:

> 'Moral History' is a form to be critically recognized, not as a primitive survival, with flat Abstractions masking as characters; but as a useful name for history-plays where the shadow-show of a greater drama of state plays continually behind the human characters, sometimes (as in Shakespeare) upon something as large as the cyclorama of the stars . . . However historical an Elizabethan play is, it is very little 'period': the writer's mind, like the stage itself (with its Elizabethan dresses and weapons), largely operated in a timeless sphere. Within that sphere, history was often presented as the conflict of principles.[4]

'Moral History'—in the sense in which *Woodstock* is a Moral History— is a category into which none of Shakespeare's plays fits with any ease. (Rossiter himself made this plain in his later book, *Angel with Horns*.) All the same, to recognize the existence of this *kind* of play is to bring about an important shift of focus when we try to see Shakespeare's Histories for what they are: for they too use historical material as a means of exploring fundamental principles of man's life in a political society.

Little can be said by one who is not a specialist in these matters about the political principles most likely to have influenced the mind of the young Shakespeare. Perhaps the best known principle of state concerned the necessity for authority, order and degree. There was as yet no fully developed theory of the divine right of kings, but it was natural that supporters of the Tudor monarchy should put a good deal of weight on the virtue of obedience in the subject. Not only was firm order in the state the only alternative to anarchy (in the later part of the century contemporary France seemed to reinforce the lesson of the Wars of the Roses), society was seen as part of the cosmic order with its parallel and corresponding 'planes of being', so that disorder at one level was echoed in the others. In the First Book of Homilies (1547), *An Exhortation Concerning Good Order and Obedience to Rulers and Magistrates* speaks of order in the heavens, on the earth, in man's body and mind, and in the state, and proceeds:

> So that in all things is to be lauded and praised the goodly order of God: without the which no house, no city, no commonwealth can continue and endure; for, where there is no right order, there reigneth all abuse, carnal liberty, enormity, sin and Babylonical confusion. Take away kings, princes, rulers, magistrates, judges, and such estates of God's order, no man shall ride or go by the highway unrobbed; no man shall sleep in his own house or bed unkilled; no man shall keep his wife, children, and possessions in

quietness; all things shall be in common; and there must needs follow all mischief and utter destruction both of souls, bodies, goods and commonwealths.[5]

This is the note that, after the failure of the Rebellion of the North, is formidably developed in the *Homily against Disobedience and Wilful Rebellion* (1570). Since the miseries of mankind sprang from Adam's disobedience, 'it is evident that obedience is the principal virtue of all virtues, and indeed the very root of all virtues, and the cause of all felicity'. Rebellion, on the other hand, is 'worse than the worst government of the worst prince':

> How horrible a sin against God and man rebellion is, cannot possibly be expressed according to the greatness thereof. For he that nameth rebellion nameth not a singular or one only sin, as is theft, robbery, murder and such like; but he nameth the whole puddle and sink of all sins against God and man; against his prince, his country, his countrymen, his parents, his children, his kinsfolk, his friends, and against all men universally; all sins, I say, against God and all men heaped together nameth he that nameth rebellion.[6]

This aspect of Tudor theory has been admirably described in recent works of scholarship, and in a general way is now sufficiently well known to students of Elizabethan literature. But it is also important to remember that at no time did absolutist propaganda have an entirely free field. Besides positive law, there was Natural law (so powerfully expounded by Hooker); beside the idea of royal supremacy there was the idea of the moral responsibility of the ruler—the idea, even, of the ruler as the 'representative' of the commonwealth: 'kings and princes ... are but members ... without a commonwealth there can be no king.' This last quotation is from John Ponet's *A Shorte Treatise of Politicke Power* (1556) which, according to Ponet's modern editor, was one of the signs, in mid-century, of a partial return to medieval conceptions of the limits of a prince's power: 'Even with the rise of strong national monarchy, the old restrictions did not entirely disappear from the English consciousness.'[7] How far these different currents of thought —derived from contemporary need and practice and from medieval tradition, from the Bible, Aristotle and Aquinas, and from many other sources—conflicted with and modified each other is something not easily determined. For the literary student there are perhaps two points in especial to be emphasized. The first is the simple fact that 'Tudor thought' on social and political matters was not entirely homogeneous: there was at all events sufficient diversity—indeed contradiction—to incite thoughtful men to thinking. The second is that a loyal and intelligent subject of Elizabeth I was likely to be conscious of other political matters besides what was due to the Prince. At the beginning of his masterly and lucid survey, *Political Thought in England: Tyndale to Hooker*, Mr. Christopher Morris remarks of sixteenth-century Englishmen:

> Most of all they discussed the importance to Society of obedience to authority, although they remained aware of limits which, in a healthy society, no authority would think of over-stepping. The King, moreover, was only one of the authorities. There were others—the Law, the People, the Church, God, and (according to some thinkers) Conscience. None of these authorities had as yet been conflated or confused with any other; and the problem facing social theorists was that of rendering to each authority its due.

In the early 1590's the author of *Woodstock* knew what response he would get from his audience when he made the bad Judge, Tresilian, say, 'It shall be law, what I shall say is law . . . I rule the law'.*

Where, then, did Shakespeare take his start? To that question only a study of the plays can provide an adequate answer. It can safely be asserted however that he was well aware of the 'educated' view of English history since the deposition of Richard 11, and of the prevailing doctrine of the need for strong rule, order and degree, and of the heinousness of rebellion: aware of them, but not uncritical of them; for each view, right up to a point, oversimplified. The belief in historical nemesis, with its corollary of some kind of mundane happy ending once guilt had been expiated, left no room for a fact of history as fully attested as the coming home of sins to roost:

> Just or unjust alike seem miserable,
> For oft alike both come to evil end.

For neither Shakespeare nor Milton was that a final answer: all the same it represents a different order of thinking from the easy moralizing of *A Mirror for Magistrates*, and it was a thought not unlikely to have occurred to the author of *King Lear*. As for the necessity for order, so often expounded in this period, I know it is sometimes claimed that Shakespeare was a convinced exponent of what we should nowadays call the right-wing assumptions of his time; and there are indeed passages in his work that testify to a horror of anarchy. But order—especially order dependent on absolute rule and unargued acceptance of

---

* cf. Morris, op, cit., p. 83: 'Without doubt there was general agreement among Elizabethans that the king was not absolute in any but a highly technical sense, that he was not above the law, that law was not what he willed, that in so far as he ever made law, he made it in and through his parliament.' On Shakespeare's attitude to these matters Mr. Morris has some wise remarks in a later essay: 'Shakespeare's Politics', *The Historical Journal*, VIII, 3 (1965).

the powers that be—was not for Shakespeare a simple and unquestioned value: essential order, simultaneously political and more-than-political, was something that needed his full mature powers to define and assert. What he gained from the historical writing and the political assumptions of his time, though not from these alone, was a conviction that politics and morals cannot be separated without falsification and disaster. That conviction lasted him a lifetime. More narrowly formulated doctrines of the kind touched on above served him in organizing historical material in his earliest work; but as his mind played on them, the current simplifications were dissolved into something more subtle, more far-reaching, more firmly related to the pressures of experience. As A. P. Rossiter said: 'The Tudor myth system of Order, Degree, etc., was too rigid, too black-and-white, too doctrinaire and narrowly moral for Shakespeare's mind: it falsified his fuller experience of men.'[8] The plays now to be examined show Shakespeare developing a view of history, of politics and public life, more searching than anything to be found in his 'sources'.

(ii)

RICHARD III

To call Shakespeare's Histories 'political' plays is simply one way of indicating that they deal with such matters as the nature of power—and the conflict of powers—within a constituted society, and with the relation of political exigencies to the personal life of those caught up in them. In other words, they belong not with the limited class of Elizabethan chronicle plays, but with that extensive range of world literature that includes *Antigone, Athalie, The Possessed* and *Under Western Eyes*. To say this is not of course to offer a definition: it merely suggests the nature of the interest that we bring to bear. What that interest finds to engage and direct it in such plays as *Richard III* and *Julius Caesar* is a matter for particular criticism: there is no formula that will help us. But there is one preliminary generalization that may be made. Shakespeare's early plays show an increasingly subtle relation between observation and what—for want of a better word—we may call inwardness. It is observation that strips off pretence, shows us how the world goes, points a useful moral. But at its furthest reach it can do no more than offer a truth that we acknowledge about other people—the Bastard's 'Commodity, the bias of the world', or Dr. Stockman's summing up in *An Enemy of the People*:

> I only want to drum into the heads of these curs the fact that the liberals are the most insidious enemies of freedom—that party programmes strangle every young and vigorous truth—that considerations of expediency turn morality and justice upside down.

Inwardness on the other hand is not only the probing of character and motive, it involves the observer: some revelation of what is usually concealed prompts not only dramatic sympathy but a sense that something potential in the spectator is being touched on. It is the development of this quality that, above all, links the political plays with the great tragedies—with *Macbeth*, for example, which is simultaneously political play and universal tragedy. In the plays before us there is indeed no clear line of progression, but we shall, I think, appreciate more vividly what each play has to offer if we see it not simply as an isolated achievement but as pointing towards the masterpieces that lie outside the scope of this study.

Richard III (1592–3) is clearly linked to the three parts of *Henry VI* by what Dr. Tillyard calls 'the steady political theme: the theme of order and chaos, of proper political degree and civil war, of crime and punishment'; but it is very much more than a dramatic presentation of the Tudor view of history. It is not simply a play about the providential accession of the House of Tudor; it is, in the first place, an elaborately formal dramatization of power-seeking in a corrupt world, held together by what Rossiter calls a 'basic pattern of retributive justice'.*

The formal pattern of the play has often been described, and certainly it is a contrivance of great ingenuity. Basically (as Dover Wilson, following Moulton, points out), it is composed of a complicated system of nemeses: crime brings punishment, for, in the words of York in *3 Henry VI*, 'Measure for measure must be answered', or, in the words of Buckingham in this play, 'Wrong hath but wrong, and blame [*sc.* fault] the due of blame'. Clarence (who broke his promise to Warwick and was one of those who killed Edward, the Lancastrian Prince of Wales) goes to his death in the Tower just as Hastings is released. Hastings, hearing of the death of the Queen's kindred at Pomfret, exults in his own security:

> Think you, but that I know our state secure,
> I would be so triumphant as I am? (III.ii. 81–82)

just before he is hustled to his death by Richard and Buckingham. Buckingham, 'the deep revolving, witty Buckingham', who plays his part as Richard's 'other self' with something of his master's swagger, breaks with Richard partly because of the proposed murder of the Princes, partly because he can't get payment for his services: when he

---

* Whether directly, or mediately through the chronicles, Shakespeare was deeply indebted to More's Life of Richard, which was 'an attack on the non-moral statecraft of the early Sixteenth Century'—R. W. Chambers, *Thomas More* (1935), p. 117.

too falls and is led to execution, he recalls the false oath with which he sealed his reconciliation with the Queen's party:

> That high All-seer, which I dallied with,
> Hath turn'd my feigned prayer on my head,
> And giv'n in earnest what I begg'd in jest.   (V.i. 20–22)

As for the arch-contriver, there is the succession of eleven ghosts before Bosworth to remind him—and us—what he is now paying for. This kind of repetition in the action gives an effect of irony both to the mutual pledges and to the boastful self-assertion of the characters; whilst at the same time the device of formal accusation of one character by another keeps the crimes committed constantly in view—each is, as it were, his brother's bad conscience. The effect is to present almost all these people as interlocked in a 'destiny' made of 'avoided grace' (IV.iv. 219).

The formal patterning of the action is of course paralleled in the verbal structure: 'the patterned speech of the dialogue ... is fundamentally one with the ironic patterns of the plot' (Rossiter). I do not know whether rhetorical devices are more numerous here than in any other of Shakespeare's plays; they are certainly more obtrusive. No purpose would be served by listing the various figures of speech—alliteration, repetition, antithesis, stichomythia, and more recondite Elizabethan 'figures'—it is enough if we notice the stiff formal texture of so much of the verse:

> *Anne.* Lo, in these windows that let forth thy life
> 　　　　　　[the wounds of the dead Henry VI]
> I pour the helpless balm of my poor eyes.
> O cursed be the hand that made these holes!
> Cursed be the heart that had the heart to do it!
> More direful hap betide that hated wretch,
> That makes us wretched by the death of thee,
> Than I can wish to adders, spiders, toads,
> Or any creeping venom'd thing that lives!   (I.ii. 12–20)

> *Gloucester.* Fairer than tongue can name thee, let me have
> Some patient leisure to excuse myself.
> *Anne.* Fouler than heart can think thee, thou canst make
> No excuse current but to hang thyself.
> *Glou.* By such despair, I should accuse myself.
> *Anne.* And, by despairing, shouldst thou stand excused
> For doing worthy vengeance on thyself,
> That did unworthy slaughter upon others.   (I.ii. 81–88)

> *Q. Elizabeth.* If you will live, lament: if die, be brief.
> 　　　　　　　　　　　　　　　　　　　　　　　(II.ii. 43)

Duchess of York. Dead life, blind sight, poor mortal living
ghost,

Woe's scene, world's shame, grave's due by life usurp'd,
Brief abstract and record of tedious days,
Rest thy unrest on England's lawful earth,
Unlawfully made drunk with innocent blood! (IV.iv. 26–30)

These are characteristic examples; and the internal patterning of the verse is emphasized by the formal stance of the characters, as when Richard and Anne engage in a 'keen encounter of our wits', or when Queen Margaret makes a late appearance (clean contrary to historical fact and probability—'Here in these confines slily have I lurk'd') solely that she may join with Queen Elizabeth and the Duchess of York in a prolonged antiphonal lament that serves, once more, to recall the crimes and miseries of the past that have made the wretched present. Together, the elements of rhetorical speech and carefully balanced action combine to produce a complicated echoing effect of revenge and mutual wrong.

Yet what we have to do with is not a self-enclosed world of evil. The characters, it is true, move in a dense atmosphere of hatred, suspicion, treachery and fear, but the standards against which we, the spectators, are expected to judge 'the grossness at this age',* are firmly presented. This is not only a matter of explicit religious reference, as when the Second Murderer of Clarence surprisingly quotes Scripture—

How fain, like Pilate, would I wash my hands
Of this most grievous murder— (I.iv. 272–3)

Shakespeare had already at command more varied means of awakening the moral imagination. When compared with the second part of Clarence's dream, which is explicitly about hell, the first part may at first seem almost extraneous to the matter in hand: in fact it is an effective symbolist transformation of the more explicit moral commentary:

Methought I saw a thousand fearful wracks,
A thousand men that fishes gnaw'd upon,
Wedges of gold, great anchors, heaps of pearl,
Inestimable stones, unvalu'd jewels,

---

* Buckingham, objecting to the Cardinal's reluctance to fetch the young Duke of York from sanctuary:

<blockquote>
You are too senseless-obstinate, my lord,
Too ceremonious and traditional.
Weigh it but with the grossness of this age,
You break not sanctuary in seizing him. (IIIi.44–47)
</blockquote>

All scatter'd in the bottom of the sea,
Some lay in dead men's skulls; and, in the holes
Where eyes did once inhabit, there were crept,
As 'twere in scorn of eyes, reflecting gems. . . . (I.iv. 24–31)

This, we may say, is a Shakespearian condensation of the contrast
that runs all through Tourneur's *The Revenger's Tragedy*. At the other
extreme is the dialogue on conscience between the murderers of
Clarence:

> *First Murderer.* How dost thou feel thyself now?
> *Second Murderer.* Faith, some certain dregs of conscience are
> yet within me.
> *First Murderer.* Remember our reward, when the deed's done.
> *Second Murderer.* 'Zounds! he dies! I had forgot the reward.
> *First Murderer.* Where's thy conscience now?
> *Second Murderer.* O, in the Duke of Gloucester's purse.
> *First Murderer.* When he opens his purse to give us our reward,
> thy conscience flies out.
> *Second Murderer.* 'Tis no matter, let it go: there's few or none
> will entertain it.
> *First Murderer.* What if it come to thee again?
> *Second Murderer.* I'll not meddle with it: it makes a man a coward:
> a man cannot steal, but it accuseth him; a man cannot swear, but
> it checks him; a man cannot lie with his neighbour's wife, but it de-
> tects him. 'Tis a blushing shamefast spirit, that mutinies in a man's
> bosom; it fills a man full of obstacles; it made me once restore a
> purse of gold that by chance I found; it beggars any man that
> keeps it; it is turn'd out of towns and cities for a dangerous thing;
> and every man that means to live well endeavours to trust to him-
> self and live without it.   (I.iv. 120ff.)

Irrelevant from the point of view of 'plot', this—which has obvious
parallels in the later plays—is clearly a low-life variation on the main
theme. ('Conscience', says Richard when he has just suffered his worst
defeat at its hands, 'is but a word that cowards use.') Nor, if we remember the Seven Deadly Sins in *Piers Plowman*, shall we find anything in-
congruous in the humour. The serious comedy of this scene is one
more reminder that behind *Richard III* is the tradition of the morality
play.*

Now all this, although necessary, has done little to bring into focus
what it is that makes the play worth watching or reading, what makes it

---

* cf. Dover Wilson's Introduction to his edition of the play, pp. xvi–xvii.
There is of course more sardonic humour in the scene (III.vii) in which
Gloucester is 'persuaded' to accept the crown.

indeed characteristically Shakespearian: that is, the felt presence of a
creative energy centring in, but not confined to, the figure of Richard of
Gloucester. It is something that takes possession of our imagination as
soon as Richard declares himself in his opening soliloquy:

> . . . Grim-visag'd War hath smooth'd his wrinkled front;
> And now, instead of mounting barbed steeds,
> To fright the souls of fearful adversaries,
> He capers nimbly in a lady's chamber,
> To the lascivious pleasing of a lute.
> But I, that am not shap'd for sportive tricks,
> Nor made to court an amorous looking-glass;
> I, that am rudely stamp'd, and want love's majesty,
> To strut before a wanton ambling nymph;
> I, that am curtail'd of this fair proportion,
> Cheated of feature by dissembling Nature,
> Deform'd, unfinish'd, sent before my time
> Into this breathing world, scarce half made up,
> And that so lamely and unfashionable,
> That dogs bark at me as I halt by them;
> Why, I, in this weak piping time of peace,
> Have no delight to pass away the time,
> Unless to spy my shadow in the sun,
> And descant on mine own deformity.
> And therefore, since I cannot prove a lover,
> To entertain these fair well-spoken days,
> I am determined to prove a villain. . . .   (I.i.9ff.)

There is a colloquial vividness here that reminds us of Mosca's self-
revelation at the opening of the third act of *Volpone*, but the total
effect is quite un-Jonsonian. The idiomatic gusto—the pleasure in speaking words that have the well-directed aim of caustic popular speech—
points forward to the Bastard, and will be an element in the poetry of
all the greater plays. And this blends unobtrusively with effects of
rhetoric and artifice: consider, for example, how the alliteration insists
on a slight meaningful pause after 'spy' and 'descant' in the lines,

> Unless to spy my shadow in the sun,
> And descant on mine own deformity.

What is not Jonsonian is the felt presence of a world behind the lines
—a world of strutting gallants and affected ladies, with, by contrast,
the dogs barking at the malformed Richard; and behind this, pressing
on it, is the private world of the man who has always felt himself to be
outside the world's game and will, in consequence, simply play his
own.[9]

It is the energy with which Richard plays his part—forthright wooer, plain blunt man, reluctant king ('O! do not swear, my Lord of Buckingham'), satirical commentator on the world's affairs and Machiavellian schemer—it is this that makes him into a commanding figure. But we should certainly be wrong to regard him solely as an 'engaging monster' to whose successful contrivance we give a reluctant admiration. Not only is Richard, like the other political figures, placed firmly within a framework of explicit moral reference, the energy that informs his language also manifests itself in other ways. I do not intend to take up again the question of 'character' in Shakespeare.[10] It is clear that if Shakespeare was intent on something more than—something different from—the presentation of life-like characters, his figures are never merely embodied abstractions: in some sense we feel them as if they were persons, and we are made explicitly aware of those aspects of their assumed life history (Othello's generalship, Coriolanus' ties to his mother) that are relevant to the main design. In the case of Richard of Gloucester this means that Shakespeare compels us to take into account, and to give full weight to, his deformity—and his rancour at his deformity—that is insisted on in his first soliloquy. When, in Act II, scene iv, young York retails the gossip, picked up from his mother, that his uncle Gloucester was born with teeth, it seems a mere repetition of the legend to which Gloucester had himself subscribed in *3 Henry VI* (V.vii. 53–54 and 7off.). The effect, however, is very different; for whereas in the earlier play the abnormality seemed little more than part of the stock legend of the monster ('which plainly signified That I should snarl and bite and play the dog'), the present context enforces a change of tone and implication. Gloucester—his mother has just told us—'was the wretched'st thing when he was young', and this unobtrusive substitution of the real for the conventional momentarily shifts the balance of our sympathies and antipathies, just as when, later, young York gives his uncle a 'scorn' about his hunchback (III. i. 128–35). There is to be sure no attempt to blur judgment with a sentimental 'understanding'. But the fact remains that in the presentation of the zestfully sardonic villain there are some disturbing reverberations:

A grievous burthen was thy birth to me;
Tetchy and wayward was thy infancy;
Thy school-days frightful, desperate, wild and furious. . . .
(IV.iv. 168–70)

It does not seem fanciful to say that this—from a further exchange between mother and son—presents in miniature the Delinquent's Progress to a manhood that is 'proud, subtle, sly, and bloody' (IV.iv. 172).[11]

In *Richard III*, although the various conventions are not yet welded into a unity, the connexion between linguistic vitality and energy of moral insight is already apparent. It is not only that Richard's lively idiom 'cuts through the muffled hypocrisies of language'.* Even in the elaborately stylized scenes Shakespeare is aiming at something more subtle than a self-conscious display of rhetorical skill: these too can precipitate a moment of lucid truth about human nature; as when Anne gives a somnambulistic half-assent to Richard ('would I knew thy heart') when he has woven round her his net of sophistries, which she knows to be such (I.ii. 33–224), or when Queen Elizabeth, engaged in a formal rhetorical duel with Richard (IV. iv. 376–80), shows him, step by step, that there is nothing he can swear by and be believed—neither honour, nor self, nor religion:

> *Q. Eliz.* Swear then by something that thou hast not wrong'd.
> *K. Rich.* Then, by myself—
> *Q. Eliz.*   Thyself is self-misus'd.
> *K. Rich.* Now, by the world—
> *Q. Eliz.*   'Tis full of thy foul wrongs.
> *K. Rich.* My father's death—
> *Q. Eliz.*   Thy life hath it dishonour'd.
> *K. Rich.* Why then, by God—
> *Q. Eliz.*   God's wrong is most of all.

But perhaps the most striking example of artifice working in the service of psychological realism is the climactic scene of Richard's visitation before Bosworth by the ghosts of his victims (V.iii. 119ff.). Judged by the standards of the later Shakespeare the stiffly formal projection of suppressed guilt is crudely done. But this 'morality masque', this 'homily in fancy dress', does not stand alone; it leads directly to Richard's soliloquy on awakening:

> O coward conscience, how dost thou afflict me!
> The lights burn blue. It is now dead midnight.
> Cold fearful drops stand on my trembling flesh.
> What do I fear? myself? there's none else by:
> Richard loves Richard; that is, I am I.
> Is there a murderer here? No. Yes, I am.
> Then fly. What, from myself? Great reason: why?
> Lest I revenge. What, myself upon myself?
> Alack, I love myself. Wherefore? for any good
> That I myself have done unto myself?
> O, no! alas, I rather hate myself
> For hateful deeds committed by myself. . . .

* 'In scorn or indignation, such writers as Dickens, Heine and Baudelaire sought to cut through the muffled hypocrisies of language.' George Steiner, *Tolstoy or Dostoevsky* (1960), p. 25.

Touches of melodrama should not prevent us from seeing that Richard's dialogue with himself is, as Palmer says,[12] 'no empty catechism, but a dialogue pointed at the heart of the eternal problem of conscience and personality'. It not only points forward to the deeper searchings of the self-division caused by evil in *Macbeth*, it helps to explain why *Richard III* is so much more than an historical pageant, more even than a political morality play. It is one instance among others of Shakespeare's sure sense—his sane, sure probing—of what lies behind the heavy entanglements of public action.

(iii)

KING JOHN

Shakespeare's *King John* (c. 1594) has no relation to Bale's *King Johan* (c.1539; revised 1560–3), which may be mentioned here for two reasons. Bale's play is violent Protestant propaganda, his King virtually a martyr to the corrupt power of Rome:

> This noble King John, as a faithful Moses,
> Withstood proud Pharaoh, for his poor Israel,
> Minding to bring it out of the land of darkness. . . .

Some at least of Shakespeare's first audience must have been familiar with this tradition and have noticed what he did *not* say. Secondly, although John is supposed to stand for an historical person, the other characters are either allegorical ('England, a widow') or hover uneasily between allegory and history (Sedition is also Stephen Langton, and Private Wealth, Cardinal Pandulph): in other words the play takes its place in a category only recently recognized in which the old morality technique is used for contemporary religious or social purposes.

Shakespeare's direct source is the anonymous *The Troublesome Reign of King John*, published in two parts in 1591, in which the action makes some claim to being historical. *The Troublesome Reign*, although not so tedious as Bale's play, and although it provides a first sketch of the Bastard, is a sprawling affair. If Shakespeare's dramatic skill is evident in the form that he imposed on mere chronicle material it is because he shaped his original, and thereby transformed it, in the light of an idea— something of which *The Troublesome Reign* is innocent. It wasn't merely a matter of toning down the anti-Roman Catholic bias, or of excising the less promising scenes and reshaping the rest, or, even, of developing the Bastard into a vigorous 'character'. What Shakespeare set himself to do was to present international power politics in the realistic spirit in which he had presented the manoeuvring for power within one country in *Richard III*.

The attempt is not entirely successful. Partly this is because the chronicle material was recalcitrant. More important, if we exclude Constance and Arthur (and the rhetoric of Constance's laments has little to do with true feeling), there is no point at which any kind of inward life is seen: the play is entirely governed by 'observation'. Within these marked limitations what we are given is of course often superb; and Faulconbridge, the main commentator on the action, represents the clear emergence in Shakespeare's work of an element that he was to transcend but never entirely to abandon. In spite of his royal blood the Bastard is, in the society in which he finds himself, an outsider—the shrewd young man up from the country; and his vigorous colloquial speech matches the keenness of his perception of all forms of humbug, whether social or diplomatic. The tone is set in the sprightly imaginary dialogue in which he sees himself engaging in the inanities of polite conversation in 'worshipful society' (I.i. 189ff.). He is the solvent of all that is pretentious and unreal, whether it is the political rhetoric of the Citizens of Angiers ('He speaks plain cannon fire, and smoke and bounce'), or the love rhetoric of the Dauphin and some Elizabethan sonneteers, or diplomatic profession not matched by performance.

The world into which he is introduced is the world of 'policy', of Machiavellian statecraft. John is a usurper, whose 'strong possession' is much more than his 'right'. This however does not prevent him from publicly announcing himself as 'God's wrathful agent'. On the other side King Philip of France, joining the Duke of Austria in 'a just and charitable war', makes much of the religious sanctions of his support of Arthur, of his 'hospitable zeal' in the young Prince's cause, and so on. None of which prevents him from patching up a peace with England by means of a politic marriage between John's niece and the Dauphin, in which the bride is to bring four provinces as her dowry. That the peace is immediately broken at the instigation of the papal Legate does not affect the force of the Bastard's pivotal speech on 'commodity', or self-interest, which closes the first section of the play:

> Mad world! mad kings! mad composition!
> John, to stop Arthur's title in the whole,
> Hath willingly departed with a part:
> And France, whose armour conscience buckled on,
> Whom zeal and charity brought to the field
> As God's own soldier, rounded in the ear
> With that same purpose-changer, that sly devil,
> That broker, that still breaks the pate of faith,
> That daily break-vow, he that wins of all,
> Of kings, of beggars, old men, young men, maids,
> Who, having no external thing to lose
> But the word 'maid', cheats the poor maid of that,

That smooth-faced gentleman, tickling Commodity. . . .
And this same bias, this Commodity,
This bawd, this broker, this all-changing word
Clapp'd on the outward eye of fickle France,
Hath drawn him from his own determined aid,
From a resolved and honourable war,
To a most base and vile-concluded peace. . . .   (II.i. 561ff.)

This looks forward to the remainder of the action as well as back. There is indeed none of the anti-Catholic bias of the earlier John plays, but Pandulph is a worldly prelate, playing the world's game: having broken the league between the French and English kings he coolly expounds to the Dauphin how the news of his invasion of England is likely to cause John to put Arthur to death, thus strengthening the Dauphin's claim to the English throne. On John's politic submission he thinks to dismiss the French forces that he has used for his own purposes:

It was my breath that blew this tempest up,
Upon your stubborn usage of the Pope;
But since you are a gentle convertite,
My tongue shall hush again this storm of war. . . .

(V.i. 17–20)

The 'gentle convertite' meanwhile has become a murderer—in intention if not in effect—whose bad conscience is reflected in political ineptitude and an inglorious end. The Dauphin, on the other hand, has attempted to double-cross the English lords who, deserting from a bad king to a foreign invader, are caught in the contradictions of political action:

. . . such is the infection of the time,
That, for the health and physic of our right,
We cannot deal but with the very hand
Of stern injustice and confused wrong.   (V.ii. 20–23)

The weakness of the play is seen in the conclusion. The revolted English lords, learning of the Dauphin's treachery, return to their allegiance. Salisbury has a lofty speech about this:

We will untread the steps of damnéd flight,
And like a bated and retired flood,
Leaving our rankness and irregular course,
Stoop low within those bounds we have o'erlooked,
And calmly run on in obedience,
Even to our ocean, to our great King John. . . .

(V.iv. 52–57)

The last line, severely qualified though it is by the context of the play, does not seem to be intended ironically: it is simply preparing the way for the patriotic finale which can be contrived when John is dead and a new king proclaimed who does not share his guilt:

> This England never did, nor never shall,
> Lie at the proud foot of a conqueror,
> But when it first did help to wound itself . . .
>   . . . nought shall make us rue,
> If England to itself do rest but true.   (V. vii. 112ff.)

This passage is certainly an improvement on the corresponding lines in *The Troublesome Reign*, and there is no reason to doubt Shakespeare's patriotism. But it is difficult to see here, as some have done, an explicit statement of the main theme of the play. In none of Shakespeare's plays does the ending simply cancel out—though it may modify—anything that has been strongly built into the body of the action, and on most of what has been unfolded before us our comment can only be the Bastard's 'Smacks it not something of the policy?' It is 'policy' and its entanglements that is engaging Shakespeare's interest. And although this may be seen with an almost cynical amusement, as in the Commodity speech, there are hints of a deeper awareness of what is involved in the clash of rival interests, as in the sombre poetry of the Bastard's comment as Hubert carries away the body of the dead Arthur:

> I am amazed, methinks, and lose my way
> Among the thorns and dangers of this world.
> How easy dost thou take all England up!
> From forth this morsel of dead royalty,
> The life, the right and truth of all this realm
> Is fled to heaven: and England now is left
> To tug and scamble and to part by th'teeth
> The unowed interest of proud-swelling state. . . .
> Now happy he whose cloak and cincture can
> Hold out this tempest.   (IV.iii. 140ff.)

Observation of the public world, when as keen-edged as the Bastard's, ends in perplexity and misgiving, and by itself can go no further. In order to explore the nature of the 'tempest' caused when right and truth are fled, leaving only appetite and interest, naked or disguised, Shakespeare needed to relate more firmly his portrayed public action to the inner lives of men.[13]

RICHARD II

Richard II (1595) is a political play with a difference. Drawing on events known to everyone as leading to the English civil wars of the fifteenth century, it presents a political fable of permanent interest: for what it shows is how power—hardly conscious of its own intentions until the event fulfils them—must necessarily fill a vacuum caused by the withdrawal of power.[14] But behind the public framework attention is concentrated on *the kind of man* who plays the central role. Richard is more than an unkingly king, he is an egotist who, like egotists in humbler spheres, constructs an unreal world that finally collapses about him. And it is because the political interest cannot be separated from the psychological interest—is indeed dependent on it—that *Richard II* is a different kind of play from *King John*: in some important ways it looks back to *Richard III* and forward to *Julius Caesar* and *Macbeth*.

That Richard is a king, and not simply a man, and that the play is about the deposition of a king—these are cardinal dramatic facts; and most of Richard's actions have to do with the exercise of kingly power, or the failure to exercise it. What we should think of the King the play leaves in no doubt. Of the king-becoming graces named in *Macbeth* (IV.iii. 91ff.) Justice stands first, and Richard is not just. The matter of Gloucester's death, though referred to with some explicitness (I.ii), lies outside the action of the play, but the whole of the first two acts portrays an arbitrariness and self-will that respects neither persons nor established rights. Richard is an extortionate landlord of his realm; he is brutal and unjust towards Gaunt; and in depriving Bolingbroke of his inheritance he strikes at the foundations of his own power:

> Take Hereford's rights away, and take from time
> His charters and his customary rights;
> Let not tomorrow then ensue today;
> Be not thyself; for how art thou a king
> But by fair sequence and succession? (II.ii. 195–9)

Action is reinforced by explicit commentary. Richard's behaviour is a 'rash fierce blaze of riot' (II.i. 33); it is 'vanity' (II.i. 38); it is a 'surfeit' that will inevitably bring its 'sick hour' (II. ii. 84). At the turning point of the action the gardeners are introduced for no other purpose than to moralize the event:

> *First Servant.* Why should we, in the compass of a pale,
> Keep law and form and due proportion,
> Showing, as in a model, our firm estate,
> When our sea-walled garden, the whole land,
> Is full of weeds? . . .

Gardener. Hold thy peace—
He that hath suffered this disordered spring
Hath now himself met with the fall of leaf . . .
. . . and Bolingbroke
Hath seiz'd the wasteful king. O, what pity is it
That he had not so trimm'd and dress'd this land
As we this garden! . . .
Superfluous branches
We lop away, that bearing boughs may live;
Had he done so, himself had borne the crown,
Which waste of idle hours hath quite thrown down.*

(III.iv. 40ff.)

If however 'the political moral of *Richard II* is clear . . . it is not simple' (Brents Stirling). Richard's misdeeds do not justify his deposition—and this not because Shakespeare has passively accepted the doctrine of the sanctity of kingship and the sinfulness of rebellion. Gaunt, it is true, proclaims passive obedience before 'God's substitute, His deputy anointed in His sight', but this is balanced by the unavoidable questions prompted by Richard's own development of the theory of divine right (III.ii. 36ff.). What guides us here is simply Shakespeare's appraisal of necessary consequences. It may be argued that Carlisle's impassioned prophecy before the deposition is prophecy only in appearance—Shakespeare had read Holinshed and knew what happened in the fifteenth century. But Shakespeare is not merely offering wisdom after the event; he is intent on causes and consequences, on the laws of human behaviour, as in Richard's rebuke to Northumberland after the deposition:

thou shalt think,
Though he divide the realm and give thee half,
It is too little, helping him to all. . . .
The love of wicked men converts to fear,
That fear to hate. . . . (V.i. 60ff.)

This is the way things happen in the game of power, and although Bolingbroke returns initially to claim what is justly his, he is no more—even if, confronting Richard's 'vanity', he is no less—than a man of power. In short, the play presupposes no possibility of a simple solution to the political situation: as Rossiter says, 'Richard is wrong, but

* It is a mistake to play this scene as a simple mixture of humour and pathos: the Gardener, who is not a stage rustic, has a genuine 'authority'. For the history of the comparison of the state to a garden see Peter Ure's Introduction to the New Arden edition, pp. li-lvii.

Bolingbroke's coronation is not right; and Richard's murder converts it to blackest wrong'. York's words apply to *both* sides—'To find out right with wrong—it may not be' (II.iii. 145).

Within this clearly delineated framework of a political dilemma—this soberly realistic mapping of one of history's cunning passages—interest centres on the man who is Richard II. He is early shown as petulant and wilful; but what the play focuses with especial clarity is the fact that he is a self-deceiver, a man who imagines that a habitable world can be constructed from words alone. As with many figures in the later plays, essential attitudes are embodied in a manner of speech which simultaneously 'places' them. On Richard's return from Ireland some sixty lines are devoted to this purpose alone:

> I weep for joy
> To stand upon my kingdom once again.
> Dear earth, I do salute thee with my hand,
> Though rebels wound thee with their horses' hoofs.
> As a long-parted mother with her child
> Plays fondly with her tears and smiles in meeting,
> So weeping, smiling, greet I thee, my earth,
> And do thee favours with my royal hands;
> Feed not thy sovereign's foe, my gentle earth,
> Nor with thy sweets comfort his ravenous sense,
> But let thy spiders that suck up thy venom
> And heavy-gaited toads lie in their way,
> Doing annoyance to the treacherous feet,
> Which with usurping steps do trample thee;
> Yield stinging nettles to mine enemies. . . .   (III.iii. 4ff.)

—and so on. There follows Richard's elaborate comparison of the king to the sun, leading into an assertion of divine right:

> Not all the water in the rough rude sea
> Can wash the balm off from an anointed king:
> The breath of worldly men cannot depose
> The deputy elected by the Lord;
> For every man that Bolingbroke hath press'd
> To lift shrewd steel against our golden crown,
> God for his Richard hath in heavenly pay
> A glorious angel. . . .   (III.ii. 54ff.)

The sequence prompts various reflections. Most obviously Richard has not been a 'mother' to his land (we last saw him ordering the seizure of Bolingbroke's possessions, and we have been told of his other exactions): this bit of make-believe is almost as fantastic as the notion that Bolingbroke would be troubled by spiders. Richard of course does not expect to be taken seriously—'Mock not my senseless conjuration, lords', he says: the trouble is that it is impossible to draw a line between this fanciful self-dramatization and the more seriously intended assertion of royal power that follows. Not only does the repeated use of the first person singular ('my earth'!) undermine the royal 'we' when it appears (III.ii. 49–50), Richard's assumption that heavenly powers will aid a king is seen, in this context, as not very different from the admittedly fanciful invocation of the English soil; indeed the religious references— as with the 'three Judases' later (III.ii. 132)—only serve to underline the fearful discrepancy between Richard's self-deceiving rhetoric and reality. On a later speech in which self-dramatization is followed by foolish and irrelevant fantasy (III.iii. 143ff.) Dr. Johnson commented, 'Shakespeare is very apt to deviate from the pathetic to the ridiculous'; but it is Richard, not Shakespeare, who thus deviates.

Shakespeare however is using the figure of Richard for a more serious purpose than the exhibition of a particular kind of kingly incompetence. *Richard II* is not universal tragedy, as *Macbeth* is; nevertheless what lifts it above the previous political plays is the way in which reality breaks into the closed world of the self-deceiver. The deposition scene (IV.i. 162ff.) begins equivocally: there is dignity and pathos, but there is also the familiar self-regarding dramatization and habit of word-play. It is at the end of a passage of restrained rhetoric—beginning, characteristic-ally, 'Now, mark me how I will undo myself'—that the process of recognition begins. There is indeed no sudden illumination, and the process is difficult to define without extensive quotation, but there is something that can properly be called a break-through from the depths of the nature that Shakespeare has imagined. It can be felt in the changed tone. Whereas Richard's earlier manner had been almost feminine, it is now masculine and direct. At the end of Richard's speech of self-deposition, the question, 'What more remains?' (IV.i. 222) may be read as 'exhausted' (Traversi) or as an abrupt descent from rhetoric. What can be in no doubt is that from now on Richard sees himself without disguise:

> Must I do so? and must I ravel out
> My weaved-up follies? . . .
> Nay, if I turn mine eyes upon myself,
> I find myself a traitor with the rest. . . .
>   . . . I'll read enough
> When I do see the very book indeed
> Where all my sins are writ, and that's myself.   (IV.i. 228ff.)

It is this new tone that underprops the pathos ('Mine eyes are full of tears, I cannot see'), and makes the subsequent play with the mirror something different from mere self-indulgent theatricality: as Derek

Traversi says, 'artificiality, conscious self-exhibition, and true self-exploration are typically blended':

> Was this the face
> That every day under his household roof
> Did keep ten thousand men? Was this the face
> That like the sun did make beholders wink?
> *Was this the face that faced* [trimmed] *so many follies* . . .?
>
> (IV.i. 281ff.)

In more senses than one Richard is a man at bay, for he is exposed to himself as well as to his enemies.* It is a bleak awakening, as he admits with a sparse directness in the moving scene of his parting from his wife (V.i):

> Learn, good soul,
> To think our former state a happy dream;
> From which awak'd, the truth of what we are
> Shows us but this.

Richard still *sees* his own story (V.i.40ff.); but he also sees his own 'profane hours', and the verse in which he foretells to Northumberland the consequences of usurpation (V.i.55ff.) is unusually forthright.

The scene of the murder firmly establishes this new movement. Richard's thought is still fanciful (something not unlikely in solitary confinement) and his expression 'conceited'; but the more fanciful passages end with a return to the idiomatic and forthright:

> While I stand fooling here, his Jack o' the clock. . . .

> Spurr'd, gall'd, and tir'd by jauncing Bolingbroke;

and there is no turning away from the painful reality. Richard recognizes his own sins:

> And here have I the daintiness of ear
> To check time broke in a disorder'd string;
> But for the concord of my state and time
> Had not an ear to hear my true time broke:
> I wasted time, and now doth time waste me. . . .   (V.v. 45ff.)

* It is worth noticing how Shakespeare contrives to give the *feel* of Richard's isolation, not only by what is said but by what is not said: like Richard, we are aware of Bolingbroke's meaningful taciturnity ('Mark, silent king . . .') and of the eyes fixed on the central figure. The climax ('Then give me leave to go.'—'Whither?'—'Whither you will, so I were from your sights') is masterly.

And this in turn is accompanied by a recognition of the vanity of a life lived without some transforming principle that takes the self beyond the self:

> Nor I, nor any man that but man is,
> With nothing shall be pleas'd, till he be eas'd
> With being nothing. (V. v. 39ff.)

The expected death comes abruptly—'How now! what means death in this rude assault?' Editors find this line perplexing, but the meaning is surely clear: death has not come in any of its fancifully imagined forms (III.ii. 155ff.), it is simply brutal. In a sense the play ends with the heavily stressed monosyllabic line,

> thy fierce hand
> Hath with the king's blood stain'd the king's own land.
> (V.v. 109–10)

Those scenes of the last act from which Richard is absent, showing glimpses of the new world in which Bolingbroke rules, seem in some ways perfunctory and immature, and it is hard to take much interest in Aumerle's abortive conspiracy or the scene in which the Duchess of York pleads for her son's life. Sometimes the verse descends to doggerel, which may perhaps be, as Dover Wilson thinks, left over from an older play—though it is hard to see why Shakespeare should have let his attention lapse at just these points. It is indeed difficult to be sure of the reason for the unevenness of the last act, but certainly the poor verse of V.iii and V.vi makes the scene of the murder (V.v) stand out in strong contrast—and this not only in an easy theatrical effectiveness. Bolingbroke exercises kingly power with more firmness than Richard had done, and he shows clemency to Aumerle; but—and there is a parallel here with the opening scenes of the play—behind the public exercise of kingly rights lies illegality, and an act so bad that it can only be hinted at. It seems at least possible that the explanation of the silly rhymes and the almost farcical note of parts of the Aumerle scenes is that all this is intended to emphasize the superficial character of authority divorced from the moral foundations of rule. The reality is murder:

> Riddles lie here, or in a word—
> Here lies blood. . . .

As Traversi, in his excellent study of the play,[15] suggests, Bolingbroke's 'absorbing pursuit of power' is, in the nature of things, not likely to lay firmer foundations than Richard's abnegation of responsibility. The world of the unsuccessful egoist has collapsed; the nature of the world constructed by the realist politician, Henry IV, will be shown in the plays that bear his name.

V

HENRY V

Between *Richard II* and *Henry V* stands *Henry IV*, and neither of the two Parts of that play fits very happily into any generalizations we might be tempted to make about 'the Histories'. Indeed, as I have suggested elsewhere,[16] the second Part is at least as closely related to the tragedies as it is to the historical sequence. All the same, *Henry IV* is in one of its aspects a political Morality of the kind that Dover Wilson describes in *The Fortunes of Falstaff*: Justice triumphs over Iniquity, and Hal, escaping from Feigning Flatterers, emerges as the type of the Prince, the Ruler. Now, in *Henry V* (1599), Shakespeare—a popular playwright after all—finds himself committed to showing the Ruler in action. If the play doesn't entirely succeed it is partly because it is ostensibly devoted to a public theme in which we cannot quite believe; and the impression we get from the play is that Shakespeare didn't believe in it either.

Certainly there is much in the play that can be cited by those who believe that Shakespeare's king is simply the hero of popular legend:

> Never came reformation in a flood,
> With such a heady currance, scouring faults. . . . (I.i. 33–34)

Canterbury and Ely describe him at length as the Renaissance complete man—able to reason in divinity and state affairs, eloquent, and yet a man of action. We may not entirely trust these worldly prelates, but it is a Chorus that speaks of him as 'the mirror of all Christian kings'; Henry emphatically declares that his 'passions' are subject to his 'grace' (I.ii. 242); and he wishes to wage war with equity:

> . . . we give express charge that in our marches through the country there be nothing compelled from the villages, nothing taken but paid for, none of the French upbraided or abused in disdainful language; for when lenity and cruelty play for a kingdom, the gentler gamester is the soonest winner. (III.vi. 105ff.)

He is aware of 'the fault my father made in compassing the crown', and he hopes by penitence to cleanse his rule of that stain. He is the embodiment of military heroism, the successful leader in war; he is 'free from vainness and self-glorious pride' (V. Chorus); and he shows himself capable of mixing easily with the common people. Nevertheless the play is something very different from a simple glorification of the warrior king. When we give full weight to all its parts—not simply to those in which Henry is favourably presented—we see that Shakespeare's attitude is complex and critical.

The patriotic theme is developed in the declamatory and unsubtle verse of the Choruses.* But what they give is only the public view of the public theme—'an abstract of average public opinion' (Goddard): there are also realistic 'close-ups' which bring in some deflationary irony. The second Chorus for example ('Now all the youth of England are on fire ... and honour's thought Reigns solely in the breast of every man') is immediately followed by the first meeting of Bardolph, Nym and Pistol. Pistol 'shall sutler be Unto the camp, and profits will accrue'. As he says later (II.iii. 52–54):

> Yoke-fellows in arms,
> Let us to France; like horse-leeches, my boys,
> To suck, to suck, the very blood to suck.

We shouldn't of course make too much of the sociological significance of Pistol & Co.: they are obviously stage-comics, and Bates and Williams are the genuinely representative figures among the common soldiers. But Shakespeare knew that they were among the 'cull'd and choice-drawn cavaliers' eulogized in the third Chorus; he knew what the war meant to them; and he knew what was likely to happen to the disbanded riff-raff when the war was over (V.i. 83–85):

> Old I do wax, and from my weary limbs
> Honour is cudgelled. Well, bawd I'll turn,
> And something lean to cut-purse of quick hand. . . .

A similar qualifying irony plays round some (not all) of the more famous passages of military exhortation. In Henry's long speech calling on the citizens of Harfleur to capitulate, Shakespeare's voice speaks through—and in a sense opposed to—the voice of the King, thus firmly 'placing' the sentiments expressed:

> The gates of mercy shall be all shut up,
> And the flesh'd soldier, rough and hard of heart,
> In liberty of bloody hand shall range
> With conscience wide as hell, mowing like grass
> Your fresh-fair virgins and your flowering infants. . . .
> What rein can hold licentious wickedness
> When down the hill he holds his fierce career?
> We may as bootless spend our vain command
> Upon the enraged soldiers in their spoil
> As send precepts to the leviathan
> To come ashore. . . .   (III.iii. 10ff.)

---

* 'The lines given to the Chorus have many admirers; but the truth is, that in them a little may be praised, and much must be forgiven' —Dr. Johnson.

There is much more to the same effect. Now Henry is of course painting the bloodiest possible picture in order to win Harfleur without fighting: when the city gives in his order is, 'Use mercy to them all'. All the same, Shakespeare has been at pains to describe in detail some of the almost inevitable consequences of war. And this is not the only occasion on which he reminds the audience that there is more than one way of responding to a successful military campaign. We can for example put side by side the English and the French versions of the battle of Crecy:

> *Canterbury.* ... Edward, the Black Prince,
> Who on the French ground play'd a tragedy,
> Making defeat of the full power of France;
> Whiles his most mighty father on a hill
> Stood smiling to behold his lion's whelp
> Forage in blood of French nobility. (I.ii. 105 ff.)

> *French King.* ... Edward, Black Prince of Wales;
> Whiles that his mountain sire, on mountain standing,
> Up in the air, crown'd with the golden sun,
> Saw his heroical seed, and smil'd to see him,
> Mangle the work of nature, and deface
> The patterns that by God and by French fathers
> Had twenty years been made. (II.iv. 56 ff.)

We have here in little—in the clash between the admiring 'Forage in blood' and the regretful 'Mangle the work of nature'—an example of something that is not made fully explicit until the play is near its end: it is the contrast between a limited and inadequate ideal of manliness and one that is fully adequate and mature. Henry's first speech before Harfleur—'Once more unto the breach, dear friends' (III.i)—does not represent the war poetry of the play at its best. It is rhetorical in the bad sense, the imagery is forced and unnatural, and it compares very unfavourably with the King's address to his men before the battle of Agincourt (IV.iii). All the same, it is not only the speech from the play that every schoolboy knows, or used to know, it represents an important part of the attitude to life embodied in the figure of the hero-king. How inadequate this is is fully revealed when, in the last scene, Burgundy makes his great plea for peace (V.ii. 31 ff.):

> ... let it not disgrace me
> If I demand before this royal view,
> What rub or what impediment there is,
> Why that the naked, poor, and mangled Peace,
> Dear nurse of arts, plenties, and joyful births,
> Should not in this best garden of the world,

Our fertile France, put up her lovely visage?
Alas! she hath from France too long been chas'd,
And all her husbandry doth lie on heaps,
Corrupting in its own fertility.
Her vine, the merry cheerer of the heart,
Unpruned dies; her hedges even-pleach'd,
Like prisoners wildly overgrown with hair,
Put forth disorder'd twigs; her fallow leas
The darnel, hemlock and rank fumitory
Doth root upon, while that the coulter rusts
That should deracinate such savagery;
The even mead, that erst brought sweetly forth
The freckled cowslip, burnet, and green clover,
Wanting the scythe, all uncorrected, rank,
Conceives by idleness, and nothing teems
But hateful docks, rough thistles, kecksies, burrs,
Losing both beauty and utility.
And as our vineyards, fallows, meads, and hedges,
Defective in their natures, grow to wildness,
Even so our houses and ourselves and children
Have lost, or do not learn for want of time,
The sciences that should become our country,
But grow like savages, as soldiers will
That nothing do but meditate on blood,
To swearing and stern looks, defus'd attire,
And every thing that seems unnatural. . . .

This beautiful passage—which in its ease and complexity reminds us that Shakespeare is now reaching the height of his powers—is not only free from the emotional straining that marks the Harfleur speech; it offers a positive ideal of civilization that is no mere abstraction but that brings with it the felt presence of the lived activities in which the ideal may be embodied. 'Behind the image of life and nature run wild for lack of human care is the implied ideal of natural force tended and inte-grated into a truly human civilization';[17] human, but still rooted in nature: in Milton's words, 'Growth, sense, reason, all summ'd up in man'.

Seen in this light it is hard to regard the play as a simple glorification of heroic leadership, even if, with Dover Wilson, we find that Henry's character is deepened and humanized after Harfleur. Rather I should agree with Mr. Traversi that the effect of the play as a whole is 'to bring out certain contradictions, human and moral, which seem to be inherent in the notion of a successful king'.[18] Although Shakespeare presents with understanding the heightened fellowship of those sharing a common danger, and the responsiveness of the good general to the needs of the situation, there is only one scene where Henry gains a full measure of our sympathy—and that in spite of the fact, or because of the fact, that we don't entirely agree with him. I refer of course to the masterly scene near the opening of Act IV, where the King, disguised and under cover of darkness, talks with the common soldiers before the battle of Agincourt. There is no need to comment on the surface realism—admirably done—of the soldiers' comments:

> *Bates.* He [the King] may show what outward courage he will, but I believe, as cold a night as 'tis, he could wish himself in Thames up to the neck, and so I would he were, and I by him, at all adventures, so we were quit here. (IV.i. 112ff.)

The ensuing conversation—so unforced in tone, and yet so telling in all its details—poses the dilemma of political leadership when force is accepted as a necessary instrument of policy: and it is a real dilemma, not one admitting of any simple solution. To the King's claim that his cause is just and his quarrel honourable Williams replies with a curt, 'That's more than we know'; and he goes on to insist on the grave moral responsibility of the ruler:

> But if the cause be not good, the king himself hath a heavy reckoning to make, when all those legs and arms and heads, chopped off in a battle, shall join together at the latter day, and cry all 'We died at such a place'; some swearing; some crying for a surgeon; some upon their wives left poor behind them; some upon the debts they owe; some upon their children rawly left. . . . Now, if these men do not die well, it will be a black matter for the king that led them to it; who to disobey were against all proportion of subjection.
> (IV.i. 133ff.)

Henry replies with a variety of arguments, too long to quote here, leading to the conclusion, 'Every subject's duty is the king's; but every soldier's soul is his own': *how* each soldier dies is his own concern. It is an interesting speech, in conscious intention sincere, and each statement in it taken singly is true or, at least, more than merely plausible. But it doesn't all add up to what Henry thinks it does. The analogies on which Henry relies so heavily are not perfect analogies: the master who sends his servant on a journey, in which the servant is set upon and killed 'in many irreconciled iniquities', is not an exact equivalent for the king who leads his subjects to war. The King has brought his men to fight ('Then imitate the action of the tiger'), and, says Williams, 'I am afeard there are few die well that die in battle; for how can they charitably dispose of any thing when blood is their argument?' That contention could, I think, be answered, but Henry does not answer it. He simply shifts the responsibility. And the mood of the whole tragic argument finds its natural issue in the famous soliloquy:

> Upon the king! let us our lives, our souls,
> Our debts, our careful wives,
> Our children, and our sins lay on the king!
> We must bear all. O hard condition!
> Twin born with greatness. . . .   (IV.i. 126–30)

—ending with the nostalgic vision of a life free from the weight of responsibility which is all the king gets in return for his vain 'ceremony'. The even division of sympathy in this scene—with the cutting edge of the argument, all the same, directed against Henry—suggests something of the complexity of attitude that informs the play as a whole. It is not resolved.

In *Julius Caesar*, written in the same year as *Henry V*, Shakespeare examined even more closely the complexities of political action. But is *Julius Caesar* a History, a Political Play, or a Tragedy? In a sense the futility of the question provides an answer to it. When history is conceived in terms of a living present, it becomes a spur to the political intelligence; when the political intelligence is that of a Shakespeare—nourished, moreover, by a tradition in which political action is seen primarily as social, and ultimately as individual, action—then the action of that intelligence on its material will almost necessarily bring into view some of the profoundest questions of human nature. What gives Shakespeare's early political plays their distinctive quality is the fact that they are part of the same continuous, and continually deepening, exploration of the nature of man that includes the great tragedies. Why that should be so I have tried to indicate in the preceding pages, and by way of summary I should like to use the words of a critic whose understanding of Shakespeare was informed by a rare wisdom and humanity. Speaking of the material that Shakespeare made use of for the very first of his Histories, Harold Goddard wrote: 'Here, writ large, was the truth that chaos in the state is part and parcel of chaos in the minds and souls of individuals, that the political problem is, once and for all, a function of the psychological problem.' Later in the same study Professor Goddard says: 'Perhaps education will some day revert to a perception of what was so like an axiom to Shakespeare: that psychology goes deeper than politics and that a knowledge of man himself must precede any fruitful consideration of the institutions he has created.'[19]

Notes

(Place of publication is London unless otherwise stated)

I. Literature and the Teaching of Literature

1 Charles Olson on 'Projective Verse', *The New American Poetry*, ed. Donald M. Allen (1960), p. 387.

2 Northrop Frye has some good remarks about this in 'The Road of Excess', published in *Myth and Symbol*, ed. Bernice Slote (University of Nebraska Press, 1960).

3 Seymour Chatman, *The Later Style of Henry James* (Blackwell: Language and Style Series, 1972).

4 Vernon Lee, *The Handling of Words* (The Bodley Head Week-End Library, 1927), pp. 249–50.

5 *The Handling of Words*, p. 271.

6 *The Listener,* September 25, 1969.

7 See D. W. Harding, 'Considered Experience: the Invitation of the Novel', *English in Education*, 1, 2.

8 *Selected Letters of Anton Chekhov*, ed. Lillian Hellman (1955), p. 57; author's emphasis retained.

9 On the dangers of 'relevance' as a criterion, see Stuart Hampshire's 'Commitment and Imagination', in *The Morality of Scholarship*, ed. Max Black (1967), p. 51.

10 This is a crude summary of some notable passages in Edwin Muir's 'The Public and the Poet', the last of his Charles Eliot Norton Lectures 1955–56, published as *The Estate of Poetry* (Hogarth Press, and Cambridge, Mass.: Harvard University Press, 1962).

11 A. N. Whitehead, *The Aims of Education* (1929: Mentor Books, 1961), p. 24.

12 I. A. Richards, 'The Future of the Humanities in General Education', in *Speculative Instruments* (1955), p. 61.

13 Published in *Memories and Studies* (1911).

14 'Stanford's Ideal Destiny', in *Memories and Studies*.

15 *Hope against Hope*, p. 70, cf. p. 187.

16 *Modes of Thought* (1938: Capricorn Books, N.Y., 1958), p. 178.

17 *Religion in the Making* (1926: Meridian Books, N.Y., 1960), p. 146; *Modes of Thought*, p. 8.

18 *The Aims of Education* (1929), Chap. 3.

II. Henry James and Human Liberty

1 *The Letters of Henry James*, ed. Percy Lubbock, Vol. II, pp. 398, 402.

2 Leon Edel, *Henry James*, Vol. II, *The Conquest of London, 1870–1883*, p. 327.

3 *Letters*, I, p. 125. D. W. Jefferson writes briefly and well of James's ambivalent but increasingly critical attitude towards upper-class English life in *Henry James* (Oliver and Boyd; Writers and Critics Series), Chapter IV, 'English Themes'. The ambivalence comes out in a letter of 1878 to Alice James (quoted by Jefferson), where he says of the British country house that it 'has at moments, for a cosmopolitanised American, an insuperable flatness. On the other hand, to do it justice, there is no doubt of its being one of the ripest fruits of time'.

4 *Young Man Luther* (Norton Library, N.Y., 1962), p. 210. More recently D. W. Harding has returned to the subject in 'The Concept of Peace': *The Science of Society and the Unity of Mankind: a Memorial Volume for Morris Ginsberg*, ed. Ronald Fletcher.

5 *Little Review*, August 1918; *Literary Essays of Ezra Pound*, ed. T. S. Eliot, p. 296.

6 Edel, *Henry James*, Vol. II, pp. 176ff.

7 *Henry James: The Critical Heritage*, ed. Roger Gard, pp. 94, 99–100.

8 R. H. Hutton in *The Spectator: The Critical Heritage*, p. 88.

III. Two Notes on Coleridge

(i) *Coleridge as Critic*

1 Written as an Introduction to *Coleridge's Variety: Bicentenary Studies*, edited by John Beer (Macmillan, 1974). Besides the editor the contributors were George Whalley, Earl Leslie Griggs, Kathleen Coburn, M. H. Abrams, Thomas McFarland, Dorothy Emmet, D. M. MacKinnon, and Owen Barfield.

2 Dorothy Emmet, 'Coleridge on the Growth of the Mind', *Bulletin of the John Rylands Library* (Manchester), XXXIV (March 1952); reprinted in *Coleridge*, ed. Kathleen Coburn (Twentieth-Century Views. Englewood Cliffs, N. J., 1967).

3 William Walsh, *Coleridge: The Work and the Relevance* (1967), pp. 85, 89.

4 S. T. Coleridge, *Biographia Literaria*, ed. J. Shawcross (1907), I 15.

5 S. T. Coleridge, *Shakespearean Criticism*, ed. T. M. Raysor, 2 vols (1930), I 68–9; II 270; I 20, 54–6, 67.

6 *Ibid.*, I 74.

7 S. T. Coleridge, *The Friend*, ed. Barbara Rooke, 2 vols (1969) (*Collected Coleridge*).

8 I borrow the phrase from J. A. Appleyard, *Coleridge's Philosophy of Literature* (Cambridge, Mass., 1965), Preface, ix, where, in the singular, it is used as a synonym for 'idea'.

9 S. T. Coleridge, *Miscellaneous Criticism*, ed. T. M. Raysor (1936), 136.

10 For this and the following examples see *Biographia Literaria*, ch. xv.

11 *Biographia Literaria* I 19, II 117. Cf. *Essays on his own Times*, ed. Sara Coleridge (1850) II 543.

12 *Biographia Literaria* II 117.

13 René Wellek, *A History of Modern Criticism, 1750–1950* (1955) II *The Romantic Age*, 186.

14 *Biographia Literaria* II 117.

15 *Political Tracts of Wordsworth, Coleridge and Shelley*, R. J. White (ed.) (Cambridge 1953), Introduction, xvi.

16 I 115.

17 *Cambridge Essays, by members of the University* (1856), pp. 324–5.

18 *Shakespearean Criticism* II 94.

19 *Collected Letters of Samuel Taylor Coleridge*, ed. Earl Leslie Griggs, 6 vols (Oxford, 1956–71), II 680.

(ii) A Tract for the Times: Coleridge and The Friend

1 *The Friend* by Samuel Taylor Coleridge, edited by Barbara E. Rooke, Bollingen Series LXXV. 4, Princeton University Press, 2 volumes.

2 Thomas McFarland, *Coleridge and the Pantheist Tradition* (Oxford University Press, p. viii). This is an opportunity to recommend this very remarkable study of Coleridge's religious thought, its place in the main stream of European philosophy from Spinoza to the nineteenth century, and its relevance for the present.

IV. Early Blake

1 Margaret Ruth Lowery, *Windows of the Morning: a Critical Study of William Blake's Poetical Sketches, 1783* (Yale University Press), p. 88.

2 *Milton*, Book the Second, 32 (35 in earlier editions); virtually repeated from *Vala or the Four Zoas*, Night the Eighth, 11. 379–80,
There is a State nam'd Satan; learn distinct to know, O (Mortals *del.*) Rahab!
The difference between States & Individuals of those States.
All references are to *The Complete Writings of William Blake*, edited by Geoffrey Keynes (The Nonesuch Press, 1957).

3 Susanne Langer, *Mind: an Essay on Human Feeling* (Johns Hopkins Press, Baltimore, 1967), Vol. I, p. 81.

4 Professor D. G. Gillham, in his book, *Blake's Contrary States: The Songs of Innocence and of Experience as Dramatic Poems* (Cambridge University Press, 1966) deals well with the essentially dramatic method employed in so

many of the poems. It was my privilege to work with Mr. Gillham when he was writing this book, and whatever my occasional disagreements with his conclusions, my debt to him is very great. See also the same author's *William Blake* (C.U.P. 1973). Since drafting this essay I find that Harold Bloom writes well of 'Mad Song', of which he says that it is 'the direct ancestor of poems like "The Tyger", or the dramatic speeches of unintended self-revelation made by the mythic figures throughout Blake's major works'.—*Blake's Apocalypse*, pp. 19–20.

5 *Poetical Sketches*, with an Introduction on Blake's Lyrical Poetry by Eric Partridge, and an essay on the Metric of William Blake by Jack Lindsay (Scholartis Press, 1927), p. 3.

6 *Nollekens and his Times . . . and Memoirs of Several Contemporary Artists* (1828), Vol. II, p. 458.

7 Mona Wilson, *The Life of William Blake* (revised edition, 1948), pp. 29–30.

8 Annotations to Lavater, *Complete Writings*, p. 88.

9 *Jerusalem*, Plate 3, 'To the Public', *Complete Writings*, p. 621.

10 *Wings of the Morning*, p. 160.

V. George Herbert

1 *The Works of George Herbert*, edited with a Commentary by F. E. Hutchinson (Oxford University Press). Dr. Hutchinson's essay on Herbert in *Seventeenth-Century Studies Presented to Sir Herbert Grierson* should also be consulted.

2 In *Literature and Pulpit in Medieval England*.

3 *Seven Types of Ambiguity*, pp. 163–65. Mr. Empson also has some excellent criticism of other poems by Herbert.

4 *A Priest to the Temple or, The Country Parson*, Chapter xxi.

5 *Seventeenth-Century Studies Presented to Sir Herbert Grierson*, p. 154.

6 *The Discharge*.

7 A few seem to be early work. Some contain references to the priesthood, and poems that appear in the Bodleian, but not in the Williams Manuscript, may be assumed to be later than the others: see Dr. Hutchinson's Introduction, pp. l–lvi, and pp. lxvii–lxix. It is worth remarking that *The Pilgrimage, Vertue, Life* and *The Flower* are among the poems found only in the Bodleian MS.

VI. Ben Jonson: Public Attitudes and Social Poetry

1 J. B. Bamborough, *Ben Jonson* (Hutchinson University Library), pp. 159–60.

2 The obvious and inescapable reference here is to Lawrence Stone, *The Crisis of the Aristocracy, 1558–1641*, especially Chap. v, Section II ('The Face of Violence') and Chap. viii ('Office and the Court').

3 '. . . if I have praysed, unfortunately, any one, that doth not deserve; or

if all answers not, in all numbers, the pictures I have made of them: I hope
it will be forgiven me, that they be no ill pieces, though they be not like
the persons'.—*Epigrammes*, Dedication (Muses Library edition of Jonson's
Poems, ed. George Burke Johnston, p. 5. I have used this edition throughout).

4 See Lawrence Stone, *Crisis of the Aristocracy*, Chap. xii ('Education and
Culture'), especially Section V (i) ('Literature and Scholarship'), and
Patricia Thomson, 'The Literature of Patronage, 1580–1630', *Essays in
Criticism*, 11 (1952).

5 *Ben Jonson and the Language of Prose Comedy*, p. 279.

6 Ted Hughes, *Poetry in the Making* (Faber paperback), p. 17.

7 *Conversations with Drummond*, Herford and Simpson, *Ben Jonson*, Vol. I, p.
143.

8 See p. 21 above.

9 For a striking example see Jon Stallworthy's account of the making of
'The Second Coming', *Agenda*, Autumn–Winter, 1971–2, pp. 24–33.
Stallworthy refers to his *Between the Lines: Yeats's Poetry in the Making*.

10 T. S. Eliot, Preface to Leone Vivante, *English Poetry and its Contribution to
the Knowledge of a Creative Principle*, pp. ix-x.

11 Wesley Trimpi, *Ben Jonson's Poems: a Study of the Plain Style*, pp. 105ff.

12 For 'Poetry as Discovery' I may refer to my essay in *Reality and Creative
Vision in German Lyrical Poetry*, ed. A. Closs. For 'The Hinterland of
Thought' see D. W. Harding's essay with that title in his *Experience into
Words*.

13 Hugh Maclean, 'Ben Jonson's Poems: Notes on an Ordered Society', in
*Essays in English Literature from the Renaissance to the Victorian Age, Pre-
sented to A. S. P. Woodhouse*, ed. M. MacLure and F. W. Watt (Toronto
University Press, 1964). See also Geoffrey Walton, *Metaphysical to Augustan*,
Chap. ii, 'The Tone of Ben Jonson's Poetry'.

14 Recognition of the virtues of the native plain style has been made easier by
practitioners and critics such as Yvor Winters and J. B. Cunningham. See
also the Introduction to John Williams, *English Renaissance Poetry: a
Collection of Shorter Poems from Skelton to Jonson* (Anchor Books, 1962) with
its interesting shift of emphasis from older anthologies in the choice of
poems. More recently Penguin Books (in the 'Poet to Poet' series) have
brought out a selection of Jonson's poems, made by Thom Gunn, to
which the modern poet contributes a splendid critical Introduction.

15 For Jonson's personal circumstances at this time, see Herford and Simpson,
I, pp. 91ff.

VII. All or Nothing: A Theme in John Donne

1 M. M. Mahood, *Poetry and Humanism* (1950) pp. 95ff. Professor M. C.
Bradbrook reminded me of this after I had written my first draft. Miss
Mahood's two chapters on Donne have an obvious bearing on the argu-
ment pursued here.

2 In a note to this passage, W. Milgate (*The Satires, Epigrams and Verse Letters of John Donne* (1967), p. 210) points out that 'the same cluster of ideas is found in *Sermons*, iii, 97, where Donne discusses the question of personal identity'. Quotations from Donne's verse letters are from this edition.

3 John Donne, *Selected Prose*, chosen by Evelyn Simpson, edited by Helen Gardner and Timothy Healy (1967), pp. 126, 129–30.

4 It is good to find Donne choosing such deeply charitable quotations from the Fathers to support his argument against 'peremptory judgements' on others.

> A devout and godly man, hath guided us well, and rectified our un-charitablenesse in such cases, by this remembrance. . . . *Thou knowest this mans fall, but thou knowest not his wrastling; which perchance was such, that almost his very fall is justified and accepted of God* . . . An uncharitable mis-interpreter unthriftily demolishes his owne house, and repaires not another. He loseth without any gaine or profit to any. And, as *Tertullian* comparing and making equall, him which provokes another, and him who will be provoked by another, says, *There is no difference, but that the provoker offended first, And that is nothing, because in evill there is no respect of Order or Prioritie.* So wee may soone become as ill as any *offender, if we offend in a severe increpation of the fact.* For *Climachus* in his *Ladder of Paradise,* places these two steps very neere one another, when hee says, *Though in the world it were possible for thee, to escape all defiling by actuall sinne yet by judging and condemning those who are defiled, thou art defiled,* etc. *Biathanatos* (first published 1646), pp. 18–19; *Selected Prose*, p. 27.

5 *The Divine Poems of John Donne*, ed. Helen Gardner (1952), Introduction, p. xxxv.

6 Coleridge, 'Dialogue between Demosius and Mystes', *Church and State*, ed. H. N. Coleridge (1839), p. 190.

7 *Selected Prose*, p. 153.

8 *Ibid.*, p. 78.

9 *The Divine Poems of John Donne*, p. xxxvi. Dame Helen deals well with Donne's contribution to the ideal of 'reasonable piety' in seventeenth-century Anglicanism.

10 A. Alvarez, *The Savage God* (1971), pp. 133 ff.

VIII. Shakespeare's Tragedies and the Question of Moral Judgment

1 See John Wren-Lewis, 'Love's Coming of Age', in *Psycho-analysis Observed*, ed. Charles Rycroft (Constable, 1966).

2 Dorothea Krook, *The Ordeal of Consciousness in Henry James*, p. 10.

3 I have taken the first of these quotations from R. W. Babcock, *The Genesis of Shakespeare Idolatry*, p. 131. The second is from William Richardson, *Essays on Some of Shakespeare's Dramatic Characters* (1797 edition), p. 120.

4 It has been well brought out by H. D. F. Kitto in his chapter on the play in *Form and Meaning in Drama*.

5 *Anatomy of Criticism* (Atheneum, N.Y.), p. 208.

6 *Ibid.*, p. 212.

7 *The Ordeal of Consciousness in Henry James*, p. 13.

8 See Wilbur Sanders, *The Dramatist and the Received Idea: Studies in the Plays of Marlowe and Shakespeare* (C.U.P., 1968), Chapter 13—a valuable, if sometimes puzzling, account of the play's disturbing power that was much in my mind whilst writing parts of this paper.

9 I should like to refer here to three recent studies that, in very different ways, enforce the difficulty of 'judgment' in a tragedy as great as *King Lear*: Marvin Rosenberg, *The Masks of King Lear* (University of California Press, Berkeley and London, 1972), Stanley Cavell, 'The Avoidance of Love: a Reading of *King Lear*', in *Must We Mean What We Say?* (Scribners, N.Y., 1969), and S. L. Goldberg, *An Essay on 'King Lear'* (C.U.P., 1974).

IX. The Thought of Shakespeare

1 Compare H. D. F. Kitto, *Form and Meaning in Drama*, p. 248.

2 University of Michigan, *Contributions in Modern Philology*, p. 17.

3 *The First Part of King Henry VI* (New Arden Shakespeare), edited by Andrew S. Cairncross, Introduction, p. liii.

4 This is brought out in James Smith's brilliant essay on the play: *Scrutiny* IX, 1, June 1940, now included in the posthumous *Shakespearian and Other Essays* (C.U.P., 1974).

5 See J. I. M. Stewart, *Character and Motive in Shakespeare*.

6 A. P. Rossiter, 'The Unity of Richard III' in *Angel with Horns*.

7 Discussed later in this volume, p. 184.

8 E. W. Talbert writes interestingly on this in *The Problem of Order: Elizabethan Political Commonplaces and an Example of Shakespeare's Art* (Chapel Hill), Chapter VI.

9 See Erich Auerbach, *Mimesis: the Representation of Reality in Western Literature*, tr. Willard R. Trask (Princeton University Press), Chapter 13, 'The Weary Prince'.

10 Harold Goddard, *The Meaning of Shakespeare* (University of Chicago Paperbacks), Vol. I, pp. 28–29.

11 Martin Foss, *Symbol and Metaphor in Human Experience* (Bison Book edition: University of Nebraska Press), p. 33. See also pp. 112–13.

X. Timon of Athens

1 A full account is given in Francelia Butler's *The Strange Critical Fortunes of Shakespeare's 'Timon of Athens'* (Iowa State University Press, 1966).

2 The evidence of incompleteness is fully presented by H. J. Oliver in his

Introduction to the New Arden edition of the play, which I have used for all quotations from the text.

3 Roy Walker, 'Unto Caesar: a Review of Recent Productions', *Shakespeare Survey*, 11; reproduced in part in Maurice Charney's edition of *Timon* (Signet Classics), p. 212.

4 R. P. Draper, '*Timon of Athens*', *Shakespeare Quarterly*, VIII, 2, Spring, 1957.

5 See Terence Spencer, 'Shakespeare learns the value of money', *Shakespeare Survey*, 6.

6 *The Crisis of the Aristocracy, 1558–1641*.

7 T. S. Eliot, Introduction to S. L. Bethell, *Shakespeare and the Popular Dramatic Tradition*.

8 See the New Arden notes at IV.iii. 279 and 394.

9 Geoffrey Bush, *Shakespeare and the Natural Condition*, p. 62.

10 Coleridge, *Shakespearean Criticism*, ed. T. M. Raysor (Everyman edition), Vol. I, p. 211.

XI. The Tempest

1 I. A. Richards, *Internal Colloquies: Poems and Plays* (Harcourt Brace Jovanovich, N.Y., 1971: Proem to 'Goodbye Earth and Other Poems', 1958), pp. 76–77.

2 For example, by Enid Welsford in *The Court Masque*, chapter 12, 'The Masque Transmuted', and by Frank Kermode in the Introduction to his New Arden edition of the play.

3 Especially in *The Shakespearean Tempest*.

4 The essay was first published in *Encounter*, December, 1957; it is in Auden's collection of critical essays, *The Dyer's Hand* and in the World's Classics volume, *Shakespeare Criticism, 1935–60*, ed. Anne Ridler.

5 F. R. Leavis, 'Shakespeare's Late Plays', *The Common Pursuit*, p. 79. See also Professor Kermode's Introduction to the New Arden edition; D. G. James, *The Dream of Prospero*; Philip Brockbank, '*The Tempest*: Conventions of Art and Empire', *Shakespeare Survey* 8; and the commentary of Henri Fluchère, *Poèmes de Shakespeare, Suivis d'Essais Critiques sur l'Oeuvre Dramatique* (Bibliothèque de la Pléiade), pp. 581ff.

6 Anne Barton, Introduction to the Penguin edition of *The Tempest*, p. 19.

7 Frank Kermode (ed.), *The Tempest*, p. 103.

8 Harold Goddard, *The Meaning of Shakespeare* (Chicago University Paperbacks), Vol. 11, p. 290.

9 *Op. cit.*, p. 284.

XII. Shakespeare: Four Histories

(i) *The Background*

1 E. K. Chambers, *A Short Life of Shakespeare* (1933), pp. 242–3.

2 *Middle-Class Culture in Elizabethan England* (Chapel Hill, N.C., 1935), Chap. IX, 'The Utility of History', p. 301.

3 *A Mirror for Magistrates*, ed. Lily B. Campbell, pp. 65–66. The motto on the title page of the early editions is, '*Felix quem faciunt aliena pericula cautum*'. On the conception of history as a mirror see Miss Campbell's Introduction, pp. 48–55. Compare *Gorboduc* (acted 1562), I.i. Chorus:

> And this great king, that doth divide his land,
> And change the course of his descending crown. . . .
> A mirror shall become to princes all,
> To learn to shun the cause of such a fall.

4 *Woodstock: a Moral History*, Preface, pp. 9–10 and *passim*. *Woodstock* itself 'is no "Chronicle-history-play". The chronicle materials are lifted from their time-sequence to operate in a timeless conflict of moral forces, in a strictly patterned plot' (p. 25).

5 *The Two Books of Homilies Appointed to be Read in Churches*, ed. John Griffiths (1859), pp. 104–5.

6 *op. cit.*, p. 568.

7 Winthrop S. Hudson, *John Ponet* (1516?–1556), *Advocate of Limited Monarchy*. See also J. W. Allen, *A History of Political Thought in the Sixteenth Century*, Part II, Chap. III, 'The Very and True Commonweal'; Ernst Cassirer, *The Myth of the State* (Yale University Press, 1946), Chap. viii.

(ii) *Richard III*

8 *Angel with Horns, and Other Shakespeare Lectures*, 3, 'Ambivalence: the Dialectic of the Histories', p. 59.

9 There is an excellent account of this soliloquy by D. A. Traversi in his essay, 'Shakespeare: the Young Dramatist', *The Pelican Guide to English Literature*, 2, *The Age of Shakespeare*, pp. 180–2.

10 See my essay, 'The Question of Character in Shakespeare', in *Further Explorations*.

11 See Grace Stuart, *Narcissus: a Psychological Study of Self Love* (1956), especially pp. 81, 221.

12 In the chapter on the play in his *Political Characters of Shakespeare*.

(iii) *King John*

13 See John F. Danby, *Shakespeare's Doctrine of Nature*, pp. 68–9.

(iv) *Richard II*

14 See Brents Stirling, *Unity in Shakespearian Tragedy*, Chap. III. As so often with Shakespeare's Histories, Marvell's 'An Horatian Ode' provides a useful gloss:

> Nature that hateth emptiness,
> Allows of penetration less. . . .

15 In *Shakespeare: from 'Richard II' to 'Henry V'*.

(v) *Henry V*

16 In *Some Shakespearean Themes*.

17 *Some Shakespearean Themes*, p. 128.

18 *op. cit.*, p. 177.

19 Harold C. Goddard, *The Meaning of Shakespeare*, Chicago (1951), Vol. I, pp. 29, 147.